June 12, 1987

Dear Eugene

I thought you might enjoy this
recent collection of works on
rationality.

Thanks once again for all
of your support!

Business Strategy
and Retailing

Business Strategy and Retailing

Edited by

Gerry Johnson

Manchester Business School

JOHN WILEY & SONS

Chichester · New York · Brisbane · Toronto · Singapore

Library of Congress Cataloging-in-Publication Data:

Business strategy and retailing.

  Bibliography: p.
  1. Retail trade—Great Britain. 2. Retail trade—
United States. 3. Corporate planning—Great Britain.
4. Corporate planning—United States. I. Johnson,
Gerry.
HF5429.6.G7B86 1987   658.8'7   86–23404
ISBN 0 471 91337 5

British Library Cataloguing in Publication Data:

Business strategy and retailing.
  1. Retail trade—Great Britain
  I. Johnson, Gerry
  658.8'7'00941   HF5429.6.G7

  ISBN 0 471 91337 5

Typeset by Input Typesetting Ltd.
Printed and bound in Great Britain.

Contents

PART 3   MANAGING RETAIL STRATEGY

PART 4   THE SOCIAL IMPACT OF RETAILING STRATEGY

Preface

In November 1985 a group of mainly UK academics, interested in and carrying out research in retailing, met to share their research in retailing strategy. Most of the chapters in this book have been developed from the draft papers and presentations at that workshop. In addition, there have been a number of other chapters, mainly from the USA, which have been specially commissioned for this book.

As editor, and on behalf of the participants in the workshop, I would like to express all our thanks to Arthur Young, who acted as sponsors and organizers for the workshop and have so much encouraged the research upon which the book is based.

GERRY JOHNSON
EDITOR
Manchester Business School
UK

Foreword

Retailing is widely accepted as one of the more dynamic and rapidly changing sectors of the British economy. Many of the pressures to innovate and adapt which British industry is experiencing manifest themselves first and most dramatically in the High Street. Some of our better retailers are obviously responding well and thriving, but many others appear to be losing their way. If the service industry is indeed going to provide employment levels which offset the job losses incurred as a result of the decline of the more traditional industries, a strong retail sector is important to our nation's future. British retailers will not only have to protect themselves from foreign incursion but should also look to export markets as the basis of future growth.

It is thus vital to understand what lies behind the successes and failures of our retailers. The major issues are clear, and include questions such as:

(1) How are retailers coping with their changing economic and social environment?
(2) How is strategy determined and implemented?
(3) What is the impact of public policy, at national and local level, on retailing strategy?

At the same time as the issues appear clear, however, the retail environment itself appears to be changing fundamentally. Major take-overs, Sunday trading, late opening, corner stores, the growth of DIY chains and garden centres, and many other such influences are rapidly changing the face of traditional retailing. Banks and building societies, and even some insurance companies, now see themselves, at least in part, as retailers.

However, research into the major issues has never seemed to excite much attention. For this reason, in November 1985, Arthur Young sponsored and organized, in conjunction with the Aston Management Centre, a Retailing Strategy Workshop. For the first time in the UK those known to be researching retail issues were brought together. The Workshop sought to reveal what lessons are to be learnt from a study of recent successes and failures and what themes need further research. It is hoped that the collection

of papers presented at that Workshop will prove useful to retailers and
stimulate further discussion as well as encouraging more work on some of
the issues raised.

J. LIDDANE
Director of Educational Services
ARTHUR YOUNG

Contributors

The following is a brief biography of each of the authors contributing to this volume.

Gerry Johnson is the editor of the book and co-author of one of the chapters. He is currently Senior Fellow in Strategic Management at Manchester Business School and was previously at Aston University Management Centre. His research and consultancy work has been concerned with the management of strategic change especially within retailing companies. He is also the co-author of *Exploring Corporate Strategy* (Prentice-Hall).

Joshua Bamfield is senior lecturer in Business Economics at the City of Birmingham Polytechnic. His previous experience in the retail sector includes several years in retail management education and he has also worked as a partner in a business consultancy specializing in retail needs. He is engaged in research on the use of microcomputers by smaller retailers and is the author of several articles and papers on retailing.

Julie A. Barnes is a graduate assistant to Dr Leonard Berry at Texas A&M University, where she is currently pursuing a Master's Degree in Business Administration. She is a 1975 graduate of the University of Texas at Austin in marketing management.

Leonard L. Berry is Foley's/Federated Professor of Retailing and Marketing Studies and Director of the Center for Retailing Studies in the College of Business Administration, Texas A&M University. Dr Berry's teaching and research interests include services marketing, financial services marketing, and retailing strategy. He is the author of many published articles and papers and is co-author or co-editor of eight books, including two published in 1985, *Marketing Financial Services: A Strategic Vision* (Dow Jones–Irwin) and *Bankers who Sell* (Bank Marketing Association and Dow Jones–Irwin). Dr Berry writes a marketing column for *American Banker*, serves as Editor of the *Journal of Retail Banking* and the *Zale Retailing Issues Letter*. He became president of the American Marketing Association in 1986.

Gary Davies is Professor of Retailing in the Business Studies Department at Manchester Polytechnic. He is Course Leader of BA (Hons) Retail Marketing, Britain's first undergraduate Retailing degree course. He is the author of books and monographs on distribution and is currently co-authoring a new text on Image Strategies in Retailing.

John Dawson is Fraser of Allander Professor of Distributive Studies at the University of Stirling, where he is also Director of the Institute for Retail Studies. Professor Dawson has held university posts at London and Wales and visiting research and teaching positions at several American and Australian universities. Current research is focusing on structural change in distribution, particularly in a comparative context, approaches to the introduction of new technology employment in retailing, and public policy approaches to the retail sector.

Bethamy Emme is a marketing representative for the R. R. Donnelley & Co. printing firm in the USA. She graduated from the University of Illinois at Urbana-Champaign in May 1985 with a degree in Business Administration. Her academic interests are in the area of organizational structure and strategy and she plans to continue for an advanced degree in the near future.

Colin Gilligan is a Principal Lecturer and the Subject Leader in Marketing at Sheffield City Polytechnic. He is the author of *Advertising Management* (Phillip Allan, 1979), *Business Decision Making* (Phillip Allan, 1983), and *International Marketing: Strategy and Management* (Croom Helm, 1986). The research project from which his chapter emerged was funded by the Economic and Social Research Council and focuses upon structural changes in British retailing and the implications for competition.

Rob Grant took up an appointment in 1986 as Assistant Professor at the University of British Columbia (Canada). At the time of contributing to this book he was a research fellow at the London Business School and was previously at City University, the UK Monopolies and Mergers Commission, and the University of St Andrews. His principal research interests are industrial regeneration and the impact of firm diversification upon performance.

Sebastian Green is Research Fellow at the London Business School. He was an Economic Adviser at the Price Commission and a researcher at the National Consumer Council. He is engaged in research on management buy-outs and on the relationship between corporate culture and strategic change. He is the joint-author of *Minorities in the Market Place* and a forthcoming book on Buy-outs.

Robert F. Lusch is at Arizona State University where he is Professor of Marketing. He has conducted work for such retail trade associations as the National Retail Hardware Association and the Retail Floorcovering Institute as well as for many retail companies. He is engaged in research on the profit impact of retail marketing strategies and is the author of two books, *Management of Retail Enterprises* and *Patronage Behaviour and Retail Management* (with William R. Darden).

John McGee is a Fellow in Corporate Strategy at Templeton College, Oxford. His special interests are in industry structure and corporate strategy and the competitiveness of British industry. His current research includes publications on the strategy–technology interface, the software industry, professional service organizations, retailing, and the analysis of complex industries. He is consultant to various business, professional, and government organizations. He was previously Foundation for Management Education Fellow at Stanford University and founding Director of the Centre for Business Strategy at the London Business School.

Martyn Pitt is a lecturer at the Management Centre, Aston University, where he is responsible for teaching and course development in the subject area of business policy and strategic management. He was previously employed as UK marketing planning manager for an internationally known clothing firm and has considerable practical experience of the retail trade in this capacity. His main research interest is the effective management of strategic change, which forms the topic of his research studies.

Joe Porac is Associate Professor of Business Administration at the University of Illinois at Urbana–Champaign. His doctorate was in social psychology and his interests are primarily in the cognitive bases of managerial decisions. He has published extensively in managerial behavioural journals, including *Organizational Behaviour and Human Performance* and the *Journal of Applied Psychology* as well as the *Academy of Management Journal*.

Ronald Savitt is the John L. Beckley Professor of American Business in the School of Business Administration at the University of Vermont. He has undertaken research on a variety of retailing topics, including issues of shopping centres, retail product management, economic development, and trade areas. He is the author of articles on retailing appearing in the *European Journal of Marketing* and *California Management Review* and is a co-author of *Modern Retail Management* (10th ed, Irwin, 1983).

Susan Segal-Horn is Principal Lecturer in Organizational Behaviour at the Business School, Brighton; where she has responsibility for the development of consultancy in the retail sector. Her research and publications include the implications of microtechnology for the structure of work, the management of professionals, and the careers of women managers. She is currently engaged in research on changes in retail management, in particular the take-up of information technology and its effect on organization structure and human resources.

Gareth Shaw is a lecturer in Geography at the University of Exeter. He has acted as consultant to a number of local authorities on the impact of super-stores and shopping centres. He is engaged in research on retail locational planning, retail change in West Germany, and shopping-centre development in the UK and Canada.

Leigh Sparks is a Lecturer at the Institute for Retail Studies, Department of Business Studies, University of Stirling. He has been engaged in research on issues concerning employment within retailing for several years and is the author of a number of papers on aspects of retail employment.

Clive Sutton is Assistant Principal at Sheffield City Polytechnic, where he is responsible for Personnel and Resource Policy. He is engaged in research on food distribution and is the author of *Industry and Competition* (Macmillan, 1976) and *Economics and Corporate Strategy* (Cambridge University Press, 1980). The research project from which his chapter emerged was funded by the Economic and Social Research Council and focuses upon structural changes in British retailing and the implications for competition.

Howard Thomas is Professor of Business Administration at the University of Illinois at Urbana–Champaign. He has held previous academic posts at the Australian Graduate School of Management and the London Business School. He is the author of numerous books and papers on decision analysis, risk analysis, and business strategy.

Robin Ward is a Principal Lecturer in the Department of Business and Management Studies at Trent Polytechnic where he teaches Business Policy. He was previously a Senior Research Fellow at Aston University Management Centre. He is engaged in research on ethnic entrepreneurship, including work on inner-city shopping centres for the Department of the Environment. He is the editor of *Ethnic Communities in Business* (Cambridge University Press).

CHAPTER 1
Introduction

GERRY JOHNSON
Manchester Business School

Each week from 1983 onwards on British television news reports were given of the gains and losses of jobs in the UK. Week after week, job losses were reported in the car industry, the steel industry, ship-building, textile industry, and most other sectors of manufacturing. Each week, job gains were reported in new-technology industries and the service sectors, notably retailing. At a time when British manufacturing industry was declining, British retailers were claiming to become some of the most professional, successful, and innovative in the world. These changes in the UK were mirrored in worldwide changes in retailing. At a time when the world was in economic recession, retailing was continuing to forge its own revolution. From robotized gallerias in Japan to forecourt-dispensing of financial services in gas stations, from the introduction of 'pubs' into New York stores, to the retailing of cars in out-of-town superstores, the 1980s became an era of change in retailing.

Despite such changes in retailing in the 1970s and 1980s there have been relatively few serious studies of business strategy and retailing. The purpose of this book is to bring together some examples of such research work and, hopefully, encourage further work from others. It is not meant to be a definitive text on retailing strategy but a book the contents of which illustrate aspects of the strategy of retailers and some of the impacts that strategic decisions by retailers have on us all.

STRATEGY AND STRATEGIC MANAGEMENT IN RETAILING

The theme of this book is strategic: this merits some explanation. We are not here so much concerned with the day-to-day administration and management of retail operations; these are aspects of management which are vitally important, of course, but they are dealt with elsewhere (e.g. Arnold *et al.*, 1983; Bolen, 1978; Marquardt *et al.*, 1979; Widgate and Friedlander, 1978). Rather we are concerned here with business strategy and retailing. Drawing

1

on previous work which discusses the characteristics of strategic decisions (Johnson and Scholes, 1984) it might be useful to begin by illustrating what is meant by business strategy in retailers.

Strategy is concerned with the scope of an organization's activities

In a radio broadcast on the BBC in 1986 Ralph Halpern, the Chairman of the Burton Group, said that the traditional boundaries of retailing were breaking down. He suggested that listeners might identify with traditional images of department stores, or banks, or insurance companies, but went on to point out that Burtons, traditionally a clothing retailer, were now offering financial services, that department stores were selling houses, and that the public could buy a washing machine by television. He was making the point that retailers who had in the past seen their businesses in commodity terms—in his company's case it had been men's suits—or in terms of a particular form of trading were beginning to define their businesses quite differently; that traditional boundaries of retailing were breaking down. So a fundamental strategic decision facing the retail executive is to decide just what the scope of business activities should be.

Strategy is about matching an organization's activities to its business environment

A tenet of both marketing and strategy texts is the significance of keeping a close eye upon changing business environments. A danger is that businesses become obsessively preoccupied with their own technologies and histories, and wedded to 'the business they are in', even if the market in which they are trading no longer values their services, and competitors offer different and better services, more attractive to customers. Such changing circumstances can be painful for those managing and staffing such businesses. With the advent of sophisticated computerized technology in the 1980s, the banks found themselves competing with quite different and new businesses for financial services. Department stores might offer cash-dispensing facilities, and if the clearing banks felt that they might provide such services for the department stores they found that in fact quite new companies, with their roots in computer technology, were able to offer such services and perhaps more competitively. The banking environment and the retail environment had changed at one and the same time, and the strategies of both had to adjust accordingly. Those banks which felt that they had some right to provide financial services had to learn to compete with new entrants into their traditional domain; and those retailers who were slow to seize the opportunity of adding financial services to their retail offering ran the risk of losing out competitively to those who did.

Strategy is also concerned with matching the activities of a business to its resource capability

It is one thing to say that strategy is concerned with adjusting to the opportunities and changes in the business environment; strategy is also to do with making such adjustments within the realistic constraints of the business's resources or such resources that can be obtained. In the 1980s in the UK, traditional department stores suffered. A combination of out-of-town shopping for furniture, furnishings, and household goods grew, together with a move by grocery retailers into hypermarket trading with an enlarged consumer durable product range and a rise in the popularity of specialist clothing stores, eroded the demand for traditional department store products. How were the department stores to respond? One chain of stores in the UK operated out of scores of city-centre stores of varying sizes, from a few thousand square feet in country towns to five storeys in a major conurbation. Not only were the sites inflexible but they were difficult to dispose of. For that retailer a major strategic problem was how to adjust strategy in the context of a changing environment, given the undoubted and significant resource constraints under which they had to operate.

Strategic decisions usually involve the major allocation or reallocation of resources

One of the key distinctions between operating and strategic decisions is the magnitude of the decision in terms of business resources. Strategic decisions typically involve the raising of funds, the disposal of sites or acquisition of sites, the demand for new skills in the business, perhaps the acquisition of whole new businesses and the disposal of those no longer competitive. So it was, for example, with Woolworth internationally. In various countries the name and operation was sold to local operators: in the UK a policy of diversification was followed by acquiring whole new businesses, entering electrical discounting and DIY whilst disposing of many High Street sites completely, allocating over £100 million to the redevelopment of remaining stores and recruiting many new senior managers.

The strategy of a business is concerned with its long-term direction

Strategic decisions are usually conceived of as long-term decisions, or at least as decisions which have long-term implications. To take an extreme example in manufacturing, ICI might have a strategic planning horizon of twenty years, as they consider and conceive of capital projects of billions of pounds' worth of investment. The comparison with retailing is interesting, and will be developed in some of the chapters in this book; it is argued that retailing

strategy may be thought of in terms of relatively short time-horizons. Products are tried and tested, succeed and are adopted, or fail and are dropped.
Retail sites are disposable, at least theoretically so. Yet as the traditional
boundaries of retailing become more blurred and the consumer becomes
more sophisticated, and as retailers diversify and add to the scope of their
business, so do the time-horizons for decisions lengthen. The retailer who
chooses to divest himself of one retail operation and diversify into others is
making a decision with a relatively long time-horizons. Retailers can no
longer regard their businesses as concerned mainly with merchandise
decisions: they must ask 'what business are we in', an altogether longer-term
question.

**Strategic decisions are therefore likely to have implications throughout the
organization and be complex in nature**

Strategic decisions in businesses are some of the most complex managers
have to face. They require managers to assimilate a changing and diverse
environment and, by adjusting a constrained resource base, ensure the
profitable survival of their organization. Moreover, managers must do this
whilst also managing the business on a day-to-day basis. They must also
ensure that the performance of their business satisfies stakeholders, both in
the current financial year and in years to come. How such complexity is
actually managed is a theme for analysis and debate in management literature, and is explored in some of the chapters in this book.

THE SCOPE AND STRUCTURE OF THE BOOK

The theme of the book is, then, strategy in retailing. It is, by the nature of
strategy, wide in its scope, and the chapters deal with varied subjects. There
is an economic analysis of the relationship between retailers and their
suppliers; a study of the psychology of retailers' perceptions of their competitive environment; surveys of retailing strategies in the UK and USA in terms
of generic business strategies; 'case studies' of retailers' attempts to change
strategies, and customers' perceptions of the affects of such attempts; studies
of strategic planning in retailers, and of how one Chief Executive perceived
the process of managing strategic change; and chapters on the impacts of the
strategies of retailers in terms of employment, public policy on the provision
of retail sites, and inner-city retailing.

Not only are the subjects covered broad but the approaches taken to those
subjects are diverse, as are the contributors to the book. They include
economists, psychologists, market researchers, and anthropologists; they also
include those with their roots in retail practice and researchers who simply
find the field of retailing fascinating. As editor, I welcome and have encour-

aged this diversity as a means of exploring the more fully the complexity of strategy in retailing.

Whilst the scope of this book is wide, it is thematically linked in two ways. First it is structured into four sections. The first comprises chapters concerned with the changing retail environment. The focus here is on those forces at work which affect retailers and have to be considered in the formulation of retail strategy. Second, there is a section on retail strategies and, in particular, 'positioning strategies' of retailers. This section comprises chapters which focus more on the strategies being followed by retailers, and the consequent patterns of strategy that have emerged in recent years in retailing. It has already been said that retailers are facing a changing environment and that retail strategies have shown accelerating degrees of change. The third section of the book includes chapters which examine how retail management has attempted to effect changes in strategy and some of the problems associated with this. Finally, the fourth section of the book includes chapters which look at the social effects of strategies being followed by retailing. Here, then, the focus switches away from the retailer as such and rather more to the wider society in which retailers operate.

The second means of assisting in the thematic development of the book is through section introductions. Each of the four sections has a brief introduction which both provides a general overview of the theme of that section and shows how the different chapters contribute to that theme.

REFERENCES

Arnold, D. R., Capella, L. M., and Smith, G. D. (1983). *Strategic Retail Management*, Reading, Mass.: Addison-Wesley.

Bolen, W. H. (1978). *Contemporary Retailing*, Englewood Cliffs, NJ: Prentice-Hall.

Johnson, G., and Scholes, K. (1984). *Exploring Corporate Strategy*, Englewood Cliffs, NJ: Prentice-Hall.

Marquardt, R. M., Makens, J. C., and Rue, R. G. (1979). *Retail Management*, Hinsdale, Ill.: Dryden Press.

Widgate, J. W., and Friedlander, J. S. (1978). *The Management of Retail Buying*, Englewood Cliffs, NJ: Prentice-Hall.

PART 1
The Changing Retail Environment

GERRY JOHNSON
Manchester Business School

Leonard Berry began a paper on retailing by stating:

> Slowing economic growth, the sharply spiralling costs of crucial resources, fierce competition and tougher, more demanding customers are turning retailers into all out, no holds barred competitors. It is becoming more and more clear that the growth of individual retailers in the 1980's will come at the direct expense of competitors rather than from the ebullient consumers and booming economies of an earlier era. Now everybody is getting into everybody else's business (Berry, 1982, p. 45).

The fact is that retailing is now a mature industry. It is characterized by increasing price competition, falling gross margins and returns within the industry, the closure of independent and medium-sized outlets, and acquisitions and mergers as the industry rationalizes and becomes more concentrated. The implications for retailing and retailers are significant. Certainly, competition in retailing is much tougher, and some of the chapters in this book show how retailers have attempted to cope with increasingly tighter conditions. However, there are also opportunities arising as the industry restructures and retailers rethink the bases of competition.

Within the UK economy in the last decade there has been relatively slow economic growth which, in turn, has depressed any real growth in expenditure on retailing. For example, food retailing has shown constant but only slow growth in volume. The major retailers in the sector, some of them pioneers of new modes of retailing in the 1960s, have therefore been faced with problems of growth. Their strategies in the past years have been characterized by increasing price competition, diversification away from a reliance on food, and the acquisition of more space through corporate acquisition and the opening up of increasingly larger stores. Food retailing is thus becoming a more concentrated industry. Such characteristics have also begun to show themselves in other sectors. For example, household goods retailing, an area in which there has been some growth (and within which consumer expenditure, linked to levels of disposable income, has shown rather more fluctuation), has also entered an era of growing concentration and corporate acquisition.

There are, however, grounds to say that the very industry maturity and increasing concentration which we see in retailing can give rise to opportunities strategically. Hand in hand with greater concentration has come the search for opportunities for specialization in different market niches; and, together with this, the ability of retailers to change at a much faster rate with market needs and opportunities. 'Next', the fashion retailer launched in the UK in 1981, seeks to appeal to the 25–40-year-old fashion-conscious woman. To do this, management plan very precise, if limited, merchandise ranges and change them virtually entirely three or four times a year.

Those retailers who are busily growing through acquisition are also looking for new areas to enter. The food retailer is no longer merely interested in food; he may look to sell household goods or clothing. More generally, retailers have sought to branch out into new services. For example, they have seen the growth in credit cards and are beginning to exploit retail credit facilities through their own financial service companies. Retailing can no longer be regarded as a fragmented industry run by 'traders'. Recent surveys (LBS/Zehnder, 1985; Liddane and Shelton, 1985) have shown that major retailers are increasingly concerned about the quality of their recruitment, the need for management to be more professional and more highly trained, and the requirement to think strategically about their future. Retailers are aware that in the business environment of the 1980s and 1990s in which competition will become more, not less, intense the need for the manager to understand the forces at work in the retail environment and to translate these into effective strategies is becoming increasingly pronounced.

The future of retailing?

The successful retail manager of the next decade will be sensitive to a changing retail environment. Expenditure in retail will be dependent on levels of real income certainly, and there are, of course, debates about the extent to which this can be expected to rise in the next decade. There are also differences of opinion about the extent to which disposable income will become more polarized between those in secure and higher-income positions and those with low-income jobs or no jobs at all. Certainly, in the UK there is likely to be little prospect until the 1990s of major reductions in what is already a high level of unemployment. Linked to these changes will be

fundamental changes in demographic profiles. In the 1970s retailers capitalized on the growing spending-power of a young population. Over the next
decade the emphasis may well switch to a more ageing population and
certainly one with an increasing proportion of families whose children will
have left them; retailers may find that the buying-power of the late 1980s
and 1990s rests with the employed middle-aged family. Other retailers may
well seek to capitalize on an even more ageing population sector: still others
may see an opportunity in the likelihood, at least in the USA, of a baby
boom in the later 1980s, giving rise to a demand for baby and children's
wear and nursery goods. Others again will see opportunities in the increasing
proportion of one-person dwellings as fewer people live within family units:
the demand for furnishings and household goods will be correspondingly
affected.

The working population itself will change in nature. There will be shorter
working hours with the opportunity of a developing market for leisure goods
and the demand that shopping itself should become a more pleasurable
leisure activity. Already there are signs that retailers and planners understand
this and are seeking to provide more attractive shopping environments. Such
changes will go hand in hand with a continuing rise in female employment
and an increasing mobility of households. The implication is likely to be that
shopping trips may be further afield, longer, less frequent, and increasingly
family occasions. With an increasing move, particularly of higher-income
households, from inner cities to suburbs, the need for retailers to consider
site-location will become more crucial.

Together with these demographic changes will come further changes in the
technology of retailing. Already electronic point-of-sale (EPOS) is common
in both the USA and the UK. As a system of data-capture it can provide
significant staff savings in the auditing of sales and stock movements, as
well as more efficient bases of stock control and handling. Less direct, but
nonetheless very significant benefits can include the ability of management
to monitor sales movements and variations more closely. The extent to which
such systems have been introduced has varied from country to country, being
much more rapid in the USA than in the UK (e.g. Loveridge, 1985). The
extent and speed at which more advanced technological systems in retailing
will be accepted must therefore be, at least, debatable. For example, Electronic Funds Transfer at Point of Sale (EFTPOS), which provides for direct
debiting of the customer's bank account through the retailer and thus a
cashless form of transaction at the point of purchase, is currently heralded
as a major innovation. Yet at the time of writing there are signs of quite
variable rates of installation of such systems. By 1983 it was France and
Japan which had shown the most rapid acceptance of such systems, with
some reluctance for its adoption in both the USA and the UK (Channon,
1986).

Sensitivity to change and the advent of life-style retailing

The most successful retailers will be those who can be the most sensitive to the changes taking place around them. The evidence is that many have, indeed, built their success on such sensitivity. Many of the chapters in this book give evidence of how this is occurring and the dangers of failing in such sensitivity.

One of the most significant changes in retail strategy in recent years has been the growth of 'life-style' retailing. Retailers have sought to base their strategy on a thorough and comprehensive understanding of the ways of life, expectations, values, habits, and product usages of groups of consumers. They see their task not as providing mass merchandise provision for relatively anonymous markets but the very clear provision of a precise retailing mix for the needs of a clearly identified group. The aim is to identify clear opportunities from the demographic changes that are occurring, understand these in terms of the ways of life of identified population sectors, and tailor the retail offering specifically to such groups. So the retailer becomes defined not in terms of products so much as in terms of the needs of the customers: the life-style fashion retailer would not see himself selling merely clothes, for example, but a more total range of products, accessories, and services in an environment designed to be in sympathy with the expectations of the potential customer. Moreover, the life-style retailer would expect that the expectations of his customer may well change quite rapidly and that, in consequence, the retail offering would need to change accordingly.

Such retailers see their strengths in management skills which build sensitivity to environmental change and changing customer expectations. It is a far distance from the era of mass merchandising: it is a style of management which has contributed to what authors of some of the chapters which follow have called a 'retail revolution'.

The chapters which follow . . .

The chapters which follow serve to set a background for the discussion of strategies being pursued by retailers.

Susan Segal-Horn (Chapter 2) traces the major environmental trends in retailing in the UK, shows how retail structures have also changed, and provides a background to a 'retailing revolution' that, she argues, is taking place. Her analysis examines the impact of economic and demographic changes and income and expenditure patterns on the changing retail structure, and seeks to explain the growth of new retail strategies in terms of such influences. The chapter goes on to discuss some specific retail responses, in terms of design management, organization design, technology, and control-system and distribution policies.

The brief chapter by Bob Lusch (Chapter 3) is a commentary on Susan Segal-Horn's contribution. Its purpose is to examine to what extent the key environmental influences on UK retailers are mirrored in the USA. Professor Lusch does this by identifying the central propositions advanced by Susan Segal-Horn and discussing these in a US context. The picture which emerges is one of a high degree of similarity in the influences on retailers in the two countries. It is a conclusion which is significant in relation to the other chapters in the book, since it indicates that some of the more detailed discussions of retail strategies included in them are likely to be of interest and have relevance wider than the national boundaries in which they are grounded.

Rob Grant (Chapter 4) addresses the relationship between retailers and manufacturers; as such he deals with the key aspect of supply in the retail environment. His approach is essentially that of an industrial economist, and he comes to what some might regard as unconventional conclusions. He argues that 'the ability of large retailers to obtain preferential discounts is a consequence of the market power of manufacturers rather than of retailers'. Building on this argument, he examines the structure of the retail industry and manufacturer–retailer relationships and identifies effects of the inter-relationship of both parties on each other, offering a framework by which to consider relative power in the manufacturer–retailer chain.

The chapter by Joe Porac, Howard Thomas, and Bethany Emme (Chapter 5) examines from a psychological point of view how retailers understand their competitive environment. Accepting the notion that there exist within the industry 'strategic groups', the authors postulate and show how the retailers in a region of the USA conceive of those strategic groups. Unlike other chapters which have examined similar issues, the authors therefore arrive at a description of industry structure not through economic analysis but through the perception of the managers involved in the industry (in this case, retailing) themselves. The chapter then goes on to suggest how such an understanding of industry structure, from the managers' point of view, can help in the analysis of the competitive environment in retailing and the formulation of competitive strategy in firms.

REFERENCES

Berry, L. L. (1982). 'Retail positioning strategies for the 1980s.' *Business Horizons*, Nov./Dec.

Channon, D. (1986). *Global Banking Strategy*, Chichester: John Wiley/IRM.

Liddane, J., and Skelton, L. (1985). 'Training in the retail sector.' *Retail and Distribution Management*, May/June.

LBS/Egon Zehnder (1984). *Management Resources; Present Problems and Future Trends*, London Business School, June.

Loveridge, R. (1985). 'Strategic innovation and new technology in retailing: a learning approach.' Presented at the Workshop on Retailing Strategy, November 1985.

CHAPTER 2
The Retail Environment in the UK

SUSAN SEGAL-HORN
Brighton Business School

INTRODUCTION

In order to appreciate the strategic issues currently facing the retail sector it is necessary to define the context from which they have emerged. This introductory chapter will review the recent market developments and changes in the UK which make up the distinctly different retailing environment of the 1980s. It will then outline the major changes in retailing behaviour which have occurred in response to these market changes. The discussion is developed around the idea of a 'retail revolution' which is market-led, technology-assisted, and has ushered in a new era of strategic change in retailing.

Retailing in the UK has been regarded as staid, traditional, and unexciting. The market has the hallmarks of 'maturity', where conventional retail shops are slowly and steadily losing a share of consumer expenditure. While 51% of all consumer spending went through retail shops in 1961, by 1982 the figure had declined to 41% (Mintel). Increasingly, consumers are spending any additional discretionary income on leisure activities or other services, e.g. housing and home-care and financial (United Kingdom National Accounts, CSO Blue Book, 1985).

However, this conventional impression is a caricature of the actual importance of retailing in the UK economy:

(1) The contribution of retail sales to GDP increased from 18.8% in 1980 to 36.5% in 1984;
(2) Retail employment is a job-growth area: in 1984 the distributive trades provided the first employment destination for 18.1% male and 26.3% female school-leavers;
(3) 25% of the UK's 100 richest people derive their wealth from retailing of some sort (*Sunday Times*, 7 October 1984);
(4) Turnover in retailing shares on the stock exchange is the highest of all

13

groups (for example, for de Zoete Bevan, coverage of 10% of all the market dealings in textiles is worth £14 million p.a., whereas coverage of 1% of retail dealings is worth £10 million);
(5) The leveraging effect of retailing on local economies (for example, the multiplier effect of the opening of a Tesco or Sainsbury superstore) is such that many local councils are looking again at planning regulations in the light of the impact of retailing investment on jobs and living standards.

The traditional view of retailing is now changing. It is increasingly seen as a dynamic, 'trendy' industry. This chapter examines some of the reasons why. It looks at changes in the general business environment and the resultant changes in markets. It then reviews the major changes within retailing which have occurred in response to these shifts in markets and have given rise to the idea of a 'retailing revolution'.

CHANGES IN THE BUSINESS ENVIRONMENT

The economic background

During the 1970s the long period of inflation tended to hide the fact that some retailers were running their operations very inefficiently. Inflation provided the illusion of growth without its reality. Retailers appeared to be surviving and prospering while becoming progressively out of touch with their markets. In addition, during the period 1974–9 high wage settlements combined with an incomes policy improved the position of lower-income groups and stimulated a growth environment for the mass merchandisers. However, from 1979 onwards the business climate changed dramatically back in favour of higher-income groups, so that it became more attractive to appeal to the higher-income markets with their more specialized demands. Mass merchandisers found themselves in difficulties as demand swung in favour of specialist retailers. Even in lower-income segments, price-competitiveness was a necessary but not a sufficient condition to retain market share. Mass merchandisers such as Tesco and Woolworth began refurbishment and 'quality' programmes.

As inflation declined throughout the 1980s, coupled with the recession and its effect on disposable incomes, inefficient operations found it difficult to survive in what had become a tough and highly competitive environment. The recession brought vividly to the attention of retailing management the importance, for survival, of good standard management practices. These have included: tighter stock controls; more centralized decision-making and budgetary controls; growth in strategic thinking; greater emphasis on design; and an appreciation of the importance of marketing.

In the changed competitive environment it is the target marketing techniques in particular which have come to the forefront. The big High Street variety chain stores found themselves increasingly under attack from either small specialist shops or, more often, specialist multiples. As has already happened in the USA, the UK retailing companies have been forced to seek out specialist market niches to confront the attack head-on. The current well-publicized battle for market share amongst the variety and specialist women's clothing retailers is a classic illustration of the process. However, it is equally visible in other retail sectors (for example, men's clothing, electrical, home-care, and home-furnishing).

The need to differentiate one's business from that of one's competitors is now one of the key challenges in retailing. It is being pursued by means of identification (or creation) and capture of narrowly defined market segments.

Demographic influences

One factor which dominates the way in which retail markets are changing is the shift in the age profile of the UK and indeed of all the advanced industrial economies. They are all ageing populations (Table 1).

Table 1.   Sex and age structure of the UK population (millions)

Age	0–14	15–29	30–44	45–59	60+	Total
Males						
1931	6.0	5.4	4.5	3.8	2.4	22.1
1961	6.3	5.2	5.2	5.1	3.6	25.5
1991 (proj.)	5.6	6.5	6.0	4.7	4.9	27.6
Females						
1931	5.9	5.7	5.2	4.2	3.0	24.0
1961	6.0	5.1	5.3	5.5	5.3	27.3
1991 (proj.)	5.3	6.2	6.0	4.8	6.8	29.1

Source: OPCS (1985) (adapted).

The 1980s are experiencing the opposite trend to the 1960s. In the 1960s retailing responded to the numerical and cultural dominance and high disposable income of the teenagers of the post-war baby boom. This same generation is still one of the most lucrative UK retail markets, but it is now in its middle to late 30s, with different tastes and needs. The teenagers of the 1980s do not constitute a very attractive market, since it is much smaller in size than its predecessor (*Social Trends*, 1985) and, even more importantly suffers from high unemployment and therefore low spending-power. Indeed, it is curious to note that the very word 'teenager' seems to have currently fallen into disuse.

Population projections for the 1990s (Table 2) show a relative decline in

Table 2.   Key UK age group projections to 2001 (millions)

Age	15–29	30–44	45–59	Total
Males				
1986	6.8	5.7	4.6	17.1
1991	6.5	6.0	4.7	17.2
2001	5.4	6.5	5.3	17.2
Females				
1986	6.6	5.7	4.6	16.9
1991	6.2	6.0	4.8	17.0
2001	5.1	6.4	5.5	17.0

Source: OPCS (1985) (adapted).

the 15–29 age group after its peak in 1986, whilst the 30–44 and 45–59 age groups increase within a static total.

Household structure

Apart from the age structure of the population the number and structure of households is changing. The trend is towards more but smaller households. One of the major contributory factors is the continually rising divorce rate, combined with buoyant rates of marriage and remarriage. The 'typical' nuclear household of two cohabiting adults and two children now represents only 25% of all UK households and is still declining. (The comparable figure for the USA is 7%.) 'Non-traditional' households are made up of increasing numbers of people who live alone, or as childless couples, or in single-parent households with children.

These changes in household structure affect patterns of consumption, since they constitute different market groupings. They therefore affect demand for existing and new types of products and services (for example, the 'family' versus small-car market or holiday packaging).

Changes in workforce

When the demographic changes described above are coupled with the high rates of male and teenage unemployment of the 1980s and the rise of the female breadwinner a picture of the main new profitable types of customer emerge:

(1) 30–40 year-old upwardly mobile couples and families; and
(2) 25–45 year-old working women.

Tables 3 and 4 show the changing male/female distribution of the UK workforce. It is particularly interesting to note the opposing trends (male

Table 3. UK civilian labour force (millions)

	Males	*Females*	*Total*
1971	15.6	9.3	24.9
1979	15.6	10.4	26.0
1983	15.5	10.7	26.2

Source: Department of Employment (adapted).

Table 4. UK economic activity rates by age and sex (%)

	16–19	*20–24*	*25–44*	*45–54/9*[a]	*55–9/ 60–64*[a]	*60/65+*[a]	*Total 16+*
Males							
1971	69.4	87.7	95.4	94.8	82.9	19.3	80.5
1979	71.4	86.5	95.8	93.8	73.0	10.3	77.3
1983	73.9	84.2	94.6	90.2	59.5	8.5	74.7
Females							
1971	65.0	60.2	52.4	62.0	50.9	12.4	43.9
1979	70.7	67.5	61.7	67.0	53.8	7.4	47.3
1983	70.2	68.6	62.5	68.3	50.8	8.1	47.6

[a] Female/male.
Source: Department of Employment (adapted).

downward/female upward) in the three central age groups of 20–24/25–44/ 45–54/9. Perhaps the most dramatic change is the drastic drop in male employment beyond 60, following vigorous implementation of 'early retirement' programmes, bringing male/female employment rates for this group within parity for the first time.

This increased female economic activity rate is the basis for so much retailing strategy targeting the working woman, most noticeable in the current segmentation in the women's clothing sector but spilling over into concepts for homewares and recognition of changed patterns of grocery purchasing.

Income and expenditure patterns

A further socio-economic factor underpinning current segmentation of retailing markets is not just the recent rise in disposable income since 1981 (see Figure 1) but the uneven distribution of that income across households.

Although Table 5 shows a decline in the number of husbands working, it also shows that working husbands are more likely to have working wives; similarly, husbands who are themselves unemployed are more likely to have unemployed or economically inactive wives. Thus the rise of the dual-income household.

Table 6 provides a breakdown for selected sectors of patterns of expenditure between 1973 and 1983. Concentrating particularly from 1981 onwards

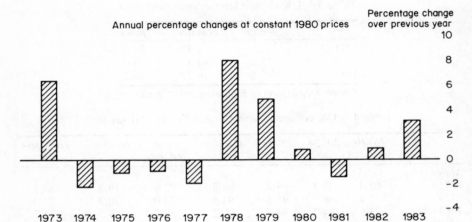

Figure 1.   Annual changes in United Kingdom real household disposable income per head (year-on-year percentage change in household income, after allowing for tax and inflation). (Source: Central Statistical Office)

Table 5.   UK economic activity of married couples (%)

	1973	1982	%+/−
Earned income			
Dual income	52	54	+2
Single income—husband	42	33	−9
—wife	2	4	+2
Nil income	3	9	+6

Source: Adapted from *General Household Survey*.

Table 6.   UK consumers' expenditure (indices at constant 1980 prices)

	1973	1977	1979	1981	1983	(1983 £m)
Food	98	96	100	99	100	27 148
Alcoholic drinks	93	95	104	97	98	13 372
Clothing and footwear	85	87	101	103	118	12 114
Household durables	97	88	105	98	110	6 664
Purchase of vehicles	101	75	106	101	125	9 142
Television, video, etc.	65	84	99	109	140	4 551
Books, newspapers, etc.	110	98	100	97	90	2 528
Other services	83	89	97	103	118	8 009
Total consumer expend.	93	91	100	100	105	182 427

Source: *Social Trends* (adapted).

(the start of the most recent upturn in consumer spending), expenditure on food stays constant in absolute terms but declines in relative terms, as would be expected in a period when incomes are rising (coupled in this case with a period of exceptional growth in consumer credit). The main growth sectors in absolute terms are clothing and footwear, household durables, vehicle purchase, and television and video entertainment and services. These are all products which would show higher income elasticities of demand.

Emerging opportunities

The significance of the shifts in economic and demographic trends, coupled with the changed distribution of income and employment described above, has been to create new product and market opportunities for retailers. More and different market segments have emerged. The spread of earlier retirement means a proportion of younger, healthier, active pensioners, creating a new segment in the leisure market which responsive service retailers have been quick to develop (for example, Saga's discounted off-peak and, more recently, 'adventure' holidays for the over-60s). Hotel chains offering a differentiated product to attract the small but growing female executive market; increased demand for disposable and convenience items, attractively and often individually, packaged; retailers identifying the higher margins available from trading up to cater for older, more sophisticated, higher-spending groups; these are a few examples of direct responses to reshaped workforce, household, and expenditure patterns. The successful retail strategies have identified such life-style trends and re-positioned accordingly.

DEVELOPMENTS IN RETAIL MARKETS

Market structure

The retailing sector contains six distinct groupings of stores:

(1) Department store groups: e.g. John Lewis, House of Fraser;
(2) General multiples (variety chain stores): e.g. Marks & Spencer, Woolworth;
(3) Specialist multiples (focused chain stores): e.g. Superdrug, Burton Group;
(4) Independents/small operators (from one shop to regional chains);
(5) Co-operatives;
(6) Mail order.

One of the most interesting trends in retailing over the last 10–15 years has been the increasing overlap between the first three major groupings. All have been changing their market positioning, so that the rationale for the differentiation into the traditional categories is becoming difficult to sustain. As these groupings have become more blurred, market shares have shifted.

Clearly, the feature which dominates Table 7 is the huge increase in market share of the multiples (mainly the specialists but increasingly the general multiples also), almost entirely at the expense of the independents. The multiples have in fact been quite dependent on market-share gains for volume growth in the last decade. Gains from market share have contributed over 40% to multiples' total sales growth, while volume growth in the overall market has contributed only 15%. Since the independent sector does have a long-term role and will therefore not shrink indefinitely, the rate of erosion of the independent sector must slow down. When combined with the relatively slow growth in the overall market, this points to slower overall growth for multiples and increasing pressure on margins.

Table 7.   Market share trends (%)

Market shares	1972	1977	1982
Independents	46	38	31
Multiples	38	46	55
Department stores	5	5	5
Co-ops	7	7	5.5
Mail order	4	4	3.5

Source: Phillips and Drew.

However, the relative position of multiples differs across major specialist sectors of the retail trade (Table 8). Multiples penetration is greatest in the grocery sector, with a market share of almost 80%. In household goods/clothing and footwear multiples have a dominant position of around 60%. In the CTNs (confectioners, newsagents, and tobacconists) and other non-food (including booksellers and jewellers) multiples market share is still at or below 40%, which provides room for major expansion in these sectors.

Table 8.   Multiples penetration of individual sectors (%)

	1977	1982
Grocers & food	71	79
Clothing and footwear	52	58
Household goods	52	59
CTNs	25	35
Other non-food	28	39

Source: Phillips and Drew.

The different rates of penetration may be explained by:

(1) The stage of evolution of the individual sector, with the grocery sector the first in the field and the furthest advanced; and

(2) The relative income elasticities of demand for, for example, food versus jewellery, affecting their respective cost and market structure.

Emphasis solely on trends in market share can be misleading. Wide divergences in volume trends are not necessarily reflected in sales value. The same point may be made for selected merchandise sectors, as illustrated by Table 9.

Table 9. Growth by volume and value in selected merchandise sectors

Merchandise sector (to 1983)	Volume growth (10yr)	Value growth (10yr)
Menswear	1	14
Womenswear	4	14
Electricals	7	17
Books, etc.	−1	15
Average	2	16

Source: Phillips and Drew.

Despite the striking differences in volume growth for menswear and womenswear, their growth in value terms has been identical. Electricals have shown only marginally above-average growth in value terms, despite the dramatic performance in volume terms. Books and newspapers have notably underperformed in volume terms, yet only marginally so in value terms.

The pressure-points of market change

The conventional attributes of market structure do not do justice to the underlying and fundamental changes in consumers and their buying habits. As in other examples of 'maturity', new bases of segmentation have become significant. In retailing, the rise of 'life-style' retailing ('target marketing', 'specialization'), is the new basis for segmentation. Distinctions are made between 'wants' and 'needs' (Sheth, 1983b), and therefore speciality markets are identified according to image, fashion, and customer profiles. Targeting is achieved through new outlet types such as shops-within-shops, 'galleria' treatments of department stores, specialist satellite stores launched by multiples, 'convenience' stores with extended opening hours, a broad sales mix and distinctive social ambience (for example, 7-Eleven), and franchising.

Although specialization is gathering pace, the boundaries between products and services are becoming increasingly blurred. Food outlets are selling increasing proportions of non-grocery products. Department stores are expanding into estate agency and financial services (for example, the Quilter-Goodison Money Centre which opened in a Debenhams store, in September

1985). Marks & Spencer at last launched its own credit card in 1985. The American Express card division runs a mail-order merchandise operation. Guinness has recently launched a high-quality designer goods catalogue.

If retailing is a service industry then anything in the service sector is a potential retail market. Retailers are beginning to compete with banks and insurance companies in the financial services market, and some of the recent building society mergers may be taken as part of a response to new entrants into their traditional markets. Products are offered with services; services are offered with products. This has become another means of both expanding the portfolio of businesses and of differentiation in the eyes of the customer via service add-ons.

Attitudes regarding hours of trading (extended opening hours, Sunday trading) are becoming more flexible. Although changed legislation to liberalize Sunday trading was recently defeated, it is still the case that 'do-it-yourself' (DIY) superstores and garden centres regularly trade on Sunday, attracting significant customer support. Existing legislation is muddled, rarely enforced, and unsympathetic to either consumer demand or market trends. Therefore legislative change affecting both retail and leisure trading (for example, licensing hours) can still be expected. Retailers' attitudes on this issue vary according to the elasticity of demand for their retail offering. Food retailers anticipate higher overheads with little increase in turnover. Nevertheless the workforce changes described earlier have produced changed shopping patterns and a climate conducive to further change.

The 'pile it high, sell it cheap' era of mass marketing is clearly over. Two of the best-known proponents of this style of retailing, Tesco and Woolworth, have both recently been making strenuous efforts to change their image and re-position themselves further up-market. These efforts have included refurbishment, redesign, some divestment, rethinking the product mix and the merchandising strategy, but, above all, staking a claim to 'quality'.

The demand for exclusivity creates real problems for the giant national retailers. One of the ways it is being tackled is by increasing use of 'designer'-label merchandise, often linked to 'shop-within-a-shop'/boutique purchasing and presentation. Indeed, a particular facet of the demand for quality is concern with product range design and store presentation. There are real commercial benefits to the retailer too. While the provision of colour-co-ordinated clothes and soft furnishings (both in range and presentation/layout) makes selection and taste easier for the shopper, it also has the added advantage of selling more goods to the same customer at the same time. It is therefore a way of locking in the customer.

In clothing, this marketing of co-ordinates itself reflects the life-style trend in dressing, away from more formal one-piece suits or dresses towards separates. In 1981, Hepworth's 'Next' chain grouped separates together in this way and scooped a new pool of high-spending 25–45-year-old working-women customers.

Shops are competing for the time and custom of relatively affluent sectors of the market. They are increasingly reluctant to endure conditions for shopping which are of a lower standard than those of their home or place of work. This is especially relevant for browsing, additional purchases, and repeat purchases.

Image and design have finally been recognized in the UK not only for products but for creating a total environment. An example of the dramatic difference that presentation and environment can make to sales is provided by the Richard Shops chain, extensively redesigned and refurbished by Conran Associates (Habitat–Mothercare) after the 1983 take-over. A 300% increase in turnover on the same merchandise was reported by refurbished branches. Complete refurbishing by multiples of the image and presentation of outlets is now normal every three years. This is in response to expected rates of change in customer tastes and expectations. A pleasant, comfortable, welcoming, and imaginative environment is expected to appeal to those shoppers to whom time is relatively more important than money. They cannot afford the time to compare offerings from shop to shop but are looking instead for a co-ordinated look in both clothes and home furnishings which fulfils their notions of style and is preferably available under one roof as one-stop shopping.

In fact the real issue underlying the concern with the environment is that shopping can no longer be viewed as an end in itself. It highlights the gradual shift of retailing to become part of the leisure industry. If so, for future planning purposes retailing may need to redefine both itself and its markets.

In four different scenarios developed by Martin and Mason (1982), ranging from 'Conventional Success' (high economic growth and individualist consumer values) to 'Self-restraint' (low economic growth and 'transformed' social values), there are significant differences in consumption patterns across main retailing sectors. For example, projections for UK leisure spending as a proportion of total consumer spending by 2001 varied from a low of 23% (similar to current levels) to a high of 32%. If leisure is a growth market and one providing enormous opportunities for retailers, the variation in these projections suggests the likelihood of continuous, deep-rooted market shifts over the remainder of this century.

SPECIFIC CHANGES IN RETAILING BEHAVIOUR

The recent social, economic, and demographic changes faced by UK retailing shows the centrality of change to understanding the new patterns of retailing.

These are not just changes in spending power but root-and-branch changes in the underlying social and psychographic patterns of retail markets. They have therefore called forth a wide variety of responses by retailers. External change, in the business environment and in markets, exerts pressure within companies for internal change, in structure, people, systems, and operations. It also changes the nature of competitive advantage within that business sector. Critical leverage in retailing is now derived from the factors discussed below.

The management of design

Retailing management techniques and organization structures are being critically reviewed throughout the sector, particularly by the large multiples and store groups. Trends in market requirements are having spin-off effects on both organization and management structure. One major area where this process is highly visible is design, whose contribution to competitive advantage in retailing has only recently been fully recognized.

Design is the vehicle of formula retailing and the means by which product differentiation is achieved. The major High Street retailers have become the public's purchasing agency rather than the manufacturer's selling agency. They assess what their customers want and then pass on those demands to manufacturers and suppliers. Retailers now also act as market interpreters for the manufacturers, which is one of the main reasons design is so important, since it acts as a briefing for manufacturers.

Successful retailers are targeting a specific customer market segment. In order to meet the needs of the target segment: retailers require a total image or look. To achieve this, they more often now employ their own designers rather than just choosing from a manufacturer's range. For example, Habitat created its own market based on Conran's own design concept. Co-ordinated clothes and homewares did the same thing for Next. It is retailer design teams which provide the link with the manufacturer, working together to understand and develop ranges to meet the retailer's concept. These teams represent a change in management skill requirements in two ways. The buying function must become multi-product and the design staff must be vertically integrated into the organization. An example of this process is colour-co-ordination marketing ('Paletting'), which creates a new logic for management responsibilities. Agreement on a range of clothes or homewares may have to be made across several individual merchandise buyers or departments, each of which may be treated as a separate profit centre. At the very least, buying departments and responsibilities have to be regrouped. Both Marks & Spencer and British Home Stores are currently redesignating responsibilities along these lines. The traditional organization structures of retailing may well therefore need to be redrawn.

Centralization and decentralization

Many retailers are now running a portfolio of related businesses, outlets, and approaches. They have multiple target markets, geared to many different life-style consumer segments. A variety of price and merchandise formats, product lines, and services are offered. The ability continually to refocus is required. To achieve this, retailers must have flexibility, which requires decentralization.

At the same time, this flexibility must be supported by extremely tight cost management and financial controls, through computerization and sophisti-cated management information systems covering each merchandising group and store. Group warehousing and distribution networks must be reorgan-ized. Sales growth and increased market share have an impact on inventory levels, working capital needs, and financing costs. An integrated approach is needed to logistics, consumer research, personnel and training needs, warehousing and merchandising policies. These financial, information, and control systems to ensure the most effective use of assets require centraliz-ation of policy, planning, and investment.

Above all, they need central strategic direction in the 'reconceptualization' (Naisbitt, 1982) of the business. There is therefore a push towards centraliz-ation. Yet centralization is associated with inflexibility. So retailers are experiencing the organizational paradox associated with managing in complex environments. To compete effectively, they need to sustain both high control and high flexibility—'simultaneous loose–tight properties' (Peters and Waterman, 1982). Usually this is provided by autonomous divisional manage-ment linked to central strategic planning. Nevertheless, the relationship between centre and periphery is a difficult one for the multiples to manage. It is exacerbated by two other factors. Re-positioning up-market places emphasis on customer service, with contingent demands for staff quality at the lower levels. Also, increasing proportions of technically qualified, professional managers must somehow be provided with an appropriate range of experience within the narrower bands available.

Human resources and the management of change

Retailing is labour-intensive. A dominant concern for retailing senior management (LBS/Egon Zehnder, 1984), beyond changes in markets or technology, was the impact of these changes on retailing management and staff. The requirements of decentralization and flexibility create a need for a retail manager able to exercise personal and professional freedom of judge-ment. At the same time these same people are likely to respond least well to the constraint of highly centralized systems of planning, control, and decision-making. Some retail groups are currently investigating ways of redesigning the job of the branch manager to address the de-skilling and motivational problems which have emerged with tighter central control. However, at the same time, technology and systems are making retailing tasks more sophisticated. This may make retailing a more attractive, interesting career for well-qualified staff but it also requires a change in management style, as well as an active retraining programme.

Technological change in warehousing, inventory control, and even in customer sales methods are generating productivity gains and considerable cost-savings. Much of the cost-saving has been on staff costs (which can account for up to 50% of overheads), especially from employment of a greater proportion of part-time to full-time employees (NEDO, 1985).

Retail markets have been gradually adapting and evolving, but the retailing industry in general has been slow to respond, especially in the UK. There has been a rapid evolution of specialist markets but the corresponding 'revolution' amongst retailers has been patchy. Retailing is changing faster than most retailers. Whilst market segments have changed, traditional retailers have not been well positioned to respond. They continued to focus on their traditional markets even where these were obviously declining. The longer the response is delayed, the more drastic it must eventually be. For some, it is already too late (for example, the comment in Greenwell's retail sector newsletter (11 November 1985): 'In terms of potential worth, Littlewoods no longer ranks among the retail giants'). They watch their market share disappear, poached by more competitive, more responsive rivals.

Innovation and the ability to respond to change are critical to success in today's changing markets. Corporate success can only be maintained in the long run if innovation is acknowledged as an activity demanding close top-management support and involvement (Johne, 1983). Some retailers (for example, the Burton Group) have already recognized this need for the institutionalization of change and have built it into both their corporate philosophy and management structure. Appropriate management style is essential in building and reinforcing a corporate culture supportive of change. A change to a more appropriate management style may involve a shift to more formal techniques and procedures (for example, in information and control systems), but simultaneously also to greater risk-taking attitudes.

The most important retailing management shortages that emerged from the LBS/Zehnder study (1984) were:

(1) Store managers to manage the expansion; and
(2) Commercially astute senior managers with Board potential.

Retailing has not been a popular area for graduate entry, but with the increased excitement and skill requirements in the sector and reduced opportunities in more traditional fields this may now be changing. Traditionally retailing exhibits the highest level of self-recruitment to all management levels of any industry sector (LBS/Zehnder, 1984). The rates of promotion from within retailing to each of three levels of management, are given below (the industry mean for each category is given in brackets):

First line: 96.87%   (88.49%)
Middle: 92.14%   (84.84%)
Top: 91.14%   (81.61%)

For the top management group, those who would have to initiate change, the figure is 10% above the industrial mean.

What these figures reveal is a very closed industry, with a culture emphasizing intuition rather than systematic analysis. This may be responsible for a preoccupation with retailing as an industry at the expense of a wider business perspective. This would leave companies poorly positioned for change.

Technology and control

Computer technology has a critical role throughout retailing not just for monitoring and control purposes but also as a direct input for enhanced profitability. The recovery in the mail-order market is not just due to recovery in consumer expenditure but to installation of new technology which speeds up response times to give faster and more efficient service (for example, Grattans). Both the high costs of such systems and the learning-curve effects for early users change the scale of entry costs to retailing.

Many aspects of retailing management are now dependent on computer technology. Although installation of EPOS (electronic point-of-sale) equipment for inventory control and sales monitoring has been notoriously slow in the UK, as in most of Europe, there are now signs that take-up is starting to expand rapidly. Major retailers such as John Lewis, Dixons/Curry's, and British Home Stores have well-established systems. The report 'Retailing tomorrow' (*Computing*, 18 July 1985) found better stock control, improved store-level information, and more effective exercise of central management control to be the most important benefits mentioned by retailers in connection with investment in EPOS systems. (Reports by *Euromonitor* and the European Foundation, however, still focus on caution and difficulties for computerized retailing.)

Despite a well-publicized regional experiment in Northampton by a consortium of local retailers, ICL and the Anglia Building Society, EFT-POS (electronic funds transfer at point-of-sale) is also still struggling to become established. Plans for a single national network between banks and retail outlets have been delayed (*Computer News*, 12 September 1985), in spite of a total UK market potential of 250 000 terminals (RMDP—Retail Management

Development Programme/DP research group). However, other national EFT-POS initiatives are being launched for particular markets (for example, the 1986 launch by British Petroleum of its network enabling customers at more than 2000 BP filling stations to buy petrol, other goods, and also to withdraw cash from the till via an ordinary bank cash card). This type of development would further enhance opportunities for retailers in the financial services market, for interactive electronic selling, and for wholly new forms of credit arrangements.

Use of computerized databases is less problematic and better established, particularly for customer servicing (for example, Debenhams' Viewbase system: DTI, 1985). In-store credit cards provide a detailed customer database. Systems such as the direct product profitability (DPP) system have been developed by Procter and Gamble in the USA (*Financial Times*, 13 June 1984). It is used as a management tool in co-operation with the retail trade, enabling the retailer to assess costs incurred on each product item. Not only does it give an accurate indication of net profitability of each item but it also offers scope to identify where cost savings might be achieved.

Management of margins is critical, as is more intensive use of space. As market-share battles continue between the multiples, the importance of productivity is highlighted by this comparison (1983 figures) of sales per square foot of three well-known High Street competitors:

Marks & Spencer　　340
British Home Stores　138
Woolworth　　　　　　82

Technology offers competitive advantage via more efficient cost control and product advantage and via speed and quality of market information on range, variety, and availability of goods. The core technological requirement here is for centralized data on inventory, sales, re-ordering, distribution, and costs.

Technology also makes possible new forms of retailing (for example, interactive systems for teleshopping, electronic display systems) and new types of delivery systems. For example, the lower cost base of automated teller machines (ATMs) has transformed retail banking and the retailing of financial services (Channon, 1986). In the USA the majority of ATMs are located in retail stores, not in banks. Remote-access delivery systems remove the need for a direct link between a customer in a given catchment area and a particular physical location for provision of goods or services. New ways of clustering offerings become possible.

Control is more important now than previously, because the degree of uncertainty, volatility, innovation, experimentation, and fast feedback required is so much higher than in the 1960s or early 1970s. This is in turn a response to the changed competitive climate for retailing.

Property: location and sites

Property has always been a key strategic variable in retailing, but the stakes are now even greater. The shortage of High Street sites and the planning constraints on out-of-town development have forced up property prices and provoked a UK form of land-rush. The movement of population away from traditional industrial areas and the decline of the inner cities have made an impact on location strategy. Future superstore developments are likely to be concentrated in more rural, less densely populated areas, such as the South-west.

In the thrust towards edge-of-town and out-of-town developments it is scarcity of suitable sites for development that is the main competitive issue. There is a scarcity of sites in appropriate catchment areas large enough for both the expected range of customer services (for example, car parking) and the necessary operational economies of scale. Problems with local authority planning permission also affect site-availability.

The retailing industry has become preoccupied with site-identification and acquisition as the saturation-point for superstores gets closer. A national market potential for 800 units is now considered a maximum; 450 superstores are already in operation. The importance of this variable was highlighted by the merger in April 1985 of Asda with MFI. Both merchandising strategies were geared towards out-of-town shopping. Both need store space of at least 50 000 ft^2. Their joint purchasing strength can now be aimed at buying the best sites before their rivals.

Major retailing multiples are using cash flow from existing operations to pre-empt the competition by securing sites well in advance of building. This has the effect of driving up the price of key sites (Greenwell, 11 June 1985).

Out-of-town superstores are very cost-effective for retailers, not just from economies of scale but also because they are more capital-intensive than labour-intensive. This is one of the contributory reasons to the long-term decline in retail employment (NEDO, 1985).

In High Street versus out-of-town locations different things are being offered to the consumer. The High Street strength is for 'comparison' shopping (for example, clothing remains a strength); out-of-town strength is 'convenience' shopping. There are certain types of merchandise sectors whose bulk, size, weight, and display requirements lend themselves to super-store selling. These include food (including ex-High Street stalwarts like Tesco and Sainsbury); furniture (MFI/Queensway); DIY (B&Q/Home-charm); carpets (Allied/Harris); motor accessories (Halfords); and electricals

(Comet/Dixons). These are now most frequently to be found in trading 'clusters' on the same sites.

Since land is a scarce resource in the UK and sites for development are being appropriated by existing dominant companies, a new and expensive barrier to entry may be emerging.

Retailer buying power

In the past the manufacturers owned or controlled the wholesalers and retailers through forward-integration and control of the product. The retailers have now largely taken over this power from the manufacturers. Backward-integration from the retailer is now changing the relationship in the supply chain.

Retailer buying power offers one of the biggest advantages of centralization and economies of scale (see also Chapter 4). The most extensive development and refinement was by the food mass merchandisers in the search for ever-tighter margins. The British Shoe Corporation now exercises its virtual monopoly buying-power ruthlessly and Marks & Spencer a little more benignly with longer runs but just as tightly controlled.

The development of 'own-labelling' is another method increasingly used by retailers to block supplier-power as well as to improve profit margins. 'Own-label' goods are no longer automatically the poor relation of the premium brands. Retailers are using 'own-label' to establish house brands at the quality end of the market.

With so many large, efficient multiples in monopoly buying positions for their markets the strategic initiative has shifted to the retailer.

Distribution

The major influence on changed UK distribution patterns was the powerful grocery multiples such as Sainsbury and Tesco. Other multiples stores groups followed. Their determination to get deliveries to High Street outlets via central warehouses critically undermined the economic viability of the long-established depot networks and transport operations of many manufacturers.

In the 1970s 70% of UK distribution was handled by manufacturers. In 1980 the figure was still around 40%. The need to cut costs during the recession encouraged the large retailers to use their massive purchasing power in distribution as in other areas, to reduce stockholding on their own premises. They began to centralize stocks in large warehouses.

If storage space at retail outlets can be reduced to a minimum, floor space can be freed for sales use. So the need to keep supermarkets and superstores well supplied without maintaining large stocks on site has led to the development of large-scale centralized warehousing operations, which allow stock-replenishment at High Street outlets to be consolidated into one large delivery per day.

Management of such central warehouses is now either directly in the hands of the retailers or contract distribution companies working on their behalf.

CONCLUSION: THE NEW POWER-BASES

The 'retailing revolution' is the combination of market changes together with new ways of organizing and conducting retailing business. The areas reviewed in this chapter represent major changes and challenges to retailers. Some of them, such as retailer buying-power, have been in evidence for some time. Others have also been evident but have acquired enhanced significance and new urgency. New systems (courtesy of information technology) offer radically new ways of controlling the company and of conceiving of the nature of the business. The long-running debate between centralization and decentralization has acquired new impetus as a result of new technology. However, fundamental to all of these changes is the proposition that the nature and style of management in retailing is undergoing radical change. The traditional theme in retailing is 'retail is detail'. Instead, it must now be argued that strategic thinking has to be placed alongside the traditional preoccupation with operational detail.

Although this chapter has discussed the constituent elements of a retailing 'revolution' the industry is not moving from there towards a new state of equilibrium but to one of continued change within a continually changing competitive environment. Boundaries have become more permeable between businesses, sectors, products, and services. Anything in the service sector is a potential retail market. Retailing will form part of the leisure environment, as well as providing goods and services for it (Martin and Mason, 1982). Sheth's (1983a and b) analysis of emerging trends impacting on the retail industry provide general support for these conclusions. Fluidity characterizes the environment, the markets, and therefore the industry.

The anodyne way of discussing the sector (product, people, location), will no longer do. The retailing revolution has clearly led to the emergence of new power-bases, as well as many new ways of exploiting them.

Markets have changed due to changes in the general retailing environment. As a result, the basis of competition in the industry has changed. Competitive advantage is now primarily derived from:

(1) Property: limited sites giving rise to monopoly rents;
(2) Technology: information and control systems to monitor consumer demand; speed and accuracy of response; control costs; and
(3) Specialization: based on concepts aimed at target markets.

Although increasing concentration in retailing is a well-established trend it has not so far affected the traditionally low barriers to entry in the industry (Baden Fuller, 1984). However, the first two of the three factors listed above offer considerable advantage to larger firms already in the industry and effectively raise the barriers for later entrants.

Property and technology should be regarded as two major strategic issues for retailers. Technology is included because of its high cost, scale, the commitment required, and the extent of its impact on the total organization and the industry. Property is included for its long lead time, exclusivity, cost, economies of scale, and influence on formula.

Alongside property and technology is another potential leverage point for future change, arising from specialization and target marketing. If life-style retailing is about responding to changing markets, then they are markets which are similar throughout the developed economies. International common denominators in market segmentation form the basis for potential globalization of retailing (see also Chapter 6). This would also provide a route to expanding market share out of mature domestic markets once expansion via merger and acquisition had been exhausted.

Strategic management in retailing is still evolving. Retailing focus is still too often operational rather than strategic, but decisions must be taken at the strategic, not just the operational, level. Strategy is an essential part of the retailing revolution.

(Grateful acknowledgement is made to the extensive discussions with John McGee of Templeton College, Oxford, from which this chapter has benefited.)

REFERENCES

Baden Fuller, C. W. F. (1984). 'Rising concentration in the UK grocery trade 1970–82.' In Tucker, K. (ed.), *Firms and Markets*, London: Croom Helm.

Blackwell, R. D., and Talarzyk, W. W. (1983). 'Lifestyle retailing: competitive strategies for the 1980's.' *Journal of Retailing*, **59**, 4, Winter, 7–27.

Central Statistical Office (1985). *Social Trends*, London: HMSO.

Central Statistical Office (1985). *United Kingdom National Accounts 'Blue Book'*, London: HMSO.

Channon, D. F. (1986). *Global Banking Strategy*, Chichester: John Wiley/IRM.

Department of Trade and Industry (1985). *Viewdata in Retail and Distribution*, 24 June.

Economist Intelligence Unit (1985). *Retail Trade Review*, February.

Financial Times Report (1985). 'Retail property.' 15 March.

Financial Times Survey (1985). 'Superstores and shopping centres.' 23 July.

Johne, F. A. (1983). 'How to lead by innovation.' *Management Today*, September, 90–95.

Knee, D., and Walters, D. (1985). *Strategy in Retailing: theory and practice*, Oxford: Philip Allen.

Lev, B. (1983). 'Observations on the merger phenomenon and a review of the evidence.' *Midland Corporate Finance Journal*, **1**, 4, Winter, 6–16.

London Business School/Egon Zehnder International (1984). *Management Resources—Present Problems and Future Trends*, June.

Marketing Week (1984). 'Burton tries on some new ideas for growth.' 20 April.

Martin, W. H., and Mason, S. (1982). *Leisure and Work: the Choices for 1991 and 2001*, Sudbury: Leisure Consultants.

Naisbitt, J. (1982). *Megatrends*, New York: Warner Books.

National Economic Development Office (1985). Distributive Trades Economic Development Committee, *Employment Perspectives and the Distributive Trades*, March.

Office of Population, Censuses, and Surveys (1984). *General Household Survey*, London: HMSO.

Peters, T., and Waterman, R. (1982). *In Search of Excellence*, New York: Harper and Row.

Phillips & Drew (1985). *Retailing Review*, June.

Retail Consortium Bulletin (1985). No. 14, January.

Sheth, J. N. (1983a). 'Marketing megatrends'. *Journal of Consumer Marketing*, No. 1, Summer, 5–13.

Sheth, J. N. (1983b). 'Emerging trends for the retailing industry.' *Journal of Retailing*, **59**, No. 3, Fall, 6–18.

Time (1984). 'Sears' sizzling new vitality.' 20 August, 48–56.

Tichy, N. M. (1982). 'Managing change strategically: the technical, political and cultural keys'. *Organizational Dynamics*, Autumn, 59–80.

CHAPTER 3
A Commentary on the US Retail Environment

ROBERT F. LUSCH
Arizona State University

INTRODUCTION

Retailing is an inherently local phenomenon in which the demographics at the trade-area level determine retail structure and thus competitive strategy. As the demographics at this level change and as these changes occur in many trade areas, so the composition and character of the total population alters. Consequently the entire structure of retailing at the national level will change; not in a revolutionary but in an evolutionary way. Without doubt this is what has happened in the UK and is evidenced by the fact that the nature and scope of retailing in the UK in the late 1980s is different from that of the late 1960s.

A central question becomes whether these changes in retail structure and strategy are unique to the UK or whether they are also occurring in other industrialized countries such as the USA. One might expect that if the demographics of the USA were changing in a direction and fashion similar to that of the UK then retailing would be similarly changing. This chapter will explore the extent of parallelism in these changes. The frame of reference that will be used is that provided by Susan Segal-Horn in Chapter 2.

THE RETAIL ENVIRONMENT

Segal-Horn profiles many important trends in the UK retail environment, and, in large measure, these trends are being mirrored in the US retail environment. Without promising to be all-inclusive let us examine the more important trends that Segal-Horn identifies.

(1) High inflation in the 1970s provided an illusion of growth but fundamental financial performance was weak.

Comment. This was precisely the case for US retailers. In 1970 food chains had sales of $234 per square foot of selling area, but by 1980 this productivity measure was $221 after adjusting for the ravages of inflation. In 1970 sales per square foot of selling area at conventional department stores was $87 but by 1980 this had fallen to $64 after adjusting for inflation. The same type of dismal financial performance occurred for discount department stores, hardware stores, and home-improvement centres (Lusch and Serpkenci, 1983). In fact from the early 1950s to the mid-1970s retailers in the US experienced a declining return on capital (Ingene and Lusch, 1981). Although inflation during the 1950s and 1960s was relatively low, an increasing level of competition put downward pressure on return on capital.

(2) In the 1980s as inflation receded competition intensified and inefficient operators found it difficult to survive.

Comment. This same trend has occurred in the USA. As McCammon (1984) has observed, 'the American economy in the 1980s will be characterized by moderate growth . . . and thus competition for market share will intensify'. Unfortunately this struggle for market share leads to increased price-competition. This price-competition has a dramatic effect on the ability of retailers to reach breakeven and thus firms with weak liquidity are vulnerable to attack by retailers with deeper pockets.

(3) The population is aging.

Comment. The USA is experiencing a similar trend and the largest and most attractive age segment throughout the year 2000 will be 25–44-year-olds. These are the 'baby-boomers' of post-World War II. Predictably, this suggests that in the early twenty-first century the largest-growing age group will.be over 50 years old. Consequently retailers appealing to these age groups will be able to experience above-average growth (Bivins, 1985).

(4) The workforce is becoming more dominated by females.

Comment. The trend is very similar in the USA (Steinberg, 1983). In 1984 an estimated 69% of married US households had both husband and wife employed in the labour force (US Bureau of the Census, 1984). As more women enter the workforce the household will change because of their increased purchasing power. Also because of increased time constraints shopping patterns will change. Importantly, the female shopper will increasingly want convenience, value, and fashion orientation (because she will be in the public eye more often).

(5) Households are becoming smaller.

Comment. A similar trend is occurring in the USA (Michman, 1983). There is an increasing number of single households, childless couples, single-parent households, and two-person unrelated households. These smaller households will have different shopping and purchasing patterns than larger ones. Also 'smaller households' translates into more households and thus there will be a rapid growth in new household information.

(6) High-income households are rising in number.

Comment. With more households having two wage-earners this trend is also occurring in the USA. Especially important is the growth of two-income households, where both wage-earners are professionals or high-paid technical workers. These households represent a large and growing market for luxury goods and services (landscaping, travel, insurance, etc.).

(7) The independent retailer is declining.

Comment. The independent retailer in the USA has been a vanishing species since the 1920s. Chain-store organizations as well as a phenomenal growth in franchising since the early 1960s has accounted for the demise of the independent retailer. Importantly, the franchising trend is now moving to the services arena in the USA. Dental services, temporary help services, realty services, and a host of other service industries are being franchised.

(8) Good retail locations are becoming increasingly difficult to isolate.

Comment. This is also true in the USA, largely because the country has become overstored (Lusch, 1986). This overstoring increases competitive intensity and results in lower resource productivity. A retailer who enters an overstored market must confront this bleak financial outlook and also must find a store location in a market where the prime real estate has usually been acquired by competitors many years prior.

THE RETAIL RESPONSE

The unfolding of a dramatically different retail environment has created a retail response. Segal-Horn highlights the following responses.

(1) A rise in life-style retailing.

Comment. Life-style retailing is also experiencing explosive growth in the

USA. In an increasingly competitive environment characterized by overstoring and a growth in consumer sophistication life-style retailing becomes a
valuable marketing tool. A good example of such retailing is The Limited
Stores. These specialize in the sale of medium-priced fashion apparel tailored
to the tastes and life-styles of fashion-conscious, contemporary women. The
Limited Stores is the flagship division of The Limited, Inc., which has grown
from $78 million in annual sales in 1975 to $1343 million in 1984. Importantly,
it has a return on average shareholders' equity of 40%.

(2) The 'pile it high, sell it cheap' era of mass merchandising is clearly over.

Comment. This era of retailing in the USA is not over. In fact a new breed
of the 'pile it high, sell it cheap' retailer has evolved. These practise the
concept of warehouse retailing, which involves using relatively low-cost
physical facilities, having a large inventory investment per square foot of
space, use of self-service, self-selection displays and generating relatively
large average transaction sizes due to multiple purchases at a single time,
and finally utilization of thin markups. Examples include the Price Company,
with sales per square foot of selling area of over $800; Cub Warehouse Stores
(sales per square foot of over $700); Home Depot (sales per square foot of
over $270); and Toys 'R' Us (sales per square foot of over $230). These four
large retailers also have net profits of above $20 per square foot (McCammon,
1986).

(3) The boundaries between products and services is becoming blurred.

Comment. An increasing number of conventional retailers in the USA are
jumping on the services bandwagon. Sears has been in the insurance business
(Allstate) and car-rental (Budget) business for a number of years. However,
it is now a more diversified services retailer. Dean Witter Reynolds is Sears'
brokerage firm and Coldwell Banker is its real estate company, and in 1985
it launched the Discover credit card which is intended to compete with Visa
and Mastercard. It also has dental clinics and optometrists in some stores.
The fastest-growing economic sector in the USA is services, and it will not
be surprising to see other large retailers begin to offer services in their
product mix.

(4) Design of space is becoming a way of differentiating a retailer's merchan-
    dise mix. Retailers are beginning to refurbish and upgrade the quality of
    their stores.

Comment. This trend is very evident in the USA. Sears, J. C. Penney, K
mart, as well as a host of other retail chains are in the process of a major

rennovation of their physical facilities (Brauer, 1984; *Chain Store Age Executive*, 1984). Store atmosphere and interior design are being seen as keys to high-performance retailing (Lusch, 1982). Many retailers have experienced dramatic increases in space productivity as measured by sales or net profits per square foot of space upon completion of major renovations. Most store redesigns involve five elements: (1) redesign of store layout usually from a grid to a race-track layout; (2) bold use of colour and graphics; (3) strong point-of-sale signing; (4) heavy use of power end-caps; and (5) plannogrammed displays.

(5) Many retailers are now running a portfolio of businesses.

Comment. This trend appears to be occurring in the USA. The principal advantage it offers is diversification of risk. However, as Segal-Horn mentions, it does create major control problems in terms of costs and strategic planning. Diversified retailing has been practised by Dayton-Hudson, Melville Corporation, and Edison Brothers Stores Inc. with a good degree of success. Recently K mart has pursued this strategy; it has entered the cafeteria business via its acquisition of Furr's Cafeterias and Bishop Buffets; the home-improvement centre business, with its acquisition of Home Centers of America; super-drugstores via its acquisition of Pay Less Drug Stores; bookstores via acquisition of Waldenbooks; and off-price family apparel with its launching of Designer Depot. Despite these examples, the challenges of profitably managing multiple lines of retail trade cannot be underestimated (Lusch and Kenderdine, 1977).

(6) Increased use of computers and management information systems in retailing.

Comment. There is no doubt that this is a major trend in the USA. Computerization, especially via the micro- and minicomputer revolution, is allowing for the continuous evaluation of merchandising performance. This is especially prevalent in the retail grocery industry because of the rapid growth of the universal product code and electronic point-of-sale scanning. Retail managers regularly receive sku fine-line reports and use these to manage inventories and make buying decisions. In short, profit-engineering is becoming more of a reality due to rapid growth in computerization.

(7) An increased number of part-time employees are being utilized and college graduates are increasingly taking a closer look at retailing as a career option.

Comment. Retailers in the USA have found that one of the keys to labour productivity is to match the supply of labour with the level of store traffic. One of the most effective ways of doing this is the hiring of employees in four-hour increments. If employees are hired out in eight-hour increments and the store desires to stay open 12 hours then the result is often an oversupply of labour at certain points, which results in lower labour productivity. Unfortunately, part-time employees are often not as well trained, and if this is the case the use of part-time employees can be detrimental. In the USA college graduates are also taking a closer look at opportunities in retailing. There are two primary reasons for this. First, there is a decline or levelling off of job-opportunities in manufacturing industries. Second, several retail firms such as The May Company and Macys are offering very competitive starting-salaries to college graduates. Importantly, these firms are also demanding that the college graduates they hire are at the top of their graduating class. In short, they are willing to pay premium prices but are demanding high-quality merchandise.

(8) Retailers are gaining more control of the marketing channel.

Comment. This trend is also present in the USA. Evidence of this is the increasing amount of opportunistic buying that retail firms are doing, their increasing use of store brands, and their demands for more deal merchandise. Also the growth of off-price retailing in the USA has placed increased power in the hands of large off-price retail chains such as Burlington Coat, ClothesTime, Dress Barn, Marshalls, T. J. Maxx, Hitt or Miss, and Syms.

CONCLUSION

The evolution of retailing in the UK that Segal-Horn discusses is largely being mirrored in the USA. This suggests that many retail concepts and formats from the UK would fit in the USA and vice versa. Unfortunately, the US retail environment is overstored and any new entrants should expect to find it extremely difficult to obtain good financial returns. To obtain good returns in the USA a new retail entrant would need (1) state-of-the-art retail technology, including a high-impact merchandising information system; (2) store locations that are in trade areas that match the firm's target market; and (3) a store design and merchandising and marketing programme targeted at a well-defined market segment, preferably using the principles of life-style retailing. With this trinity of requirements met, the retailer has the potential to achieve high-performance financial results in the highly competitive US retail marketplace.

REFERENCES

Bivins, J. (1985). 'Adult boom: the aging of the wundergeneration,' *Chain Store Age Executive*, May, 27–30.

Brauer, M. (1984). 'K mart assumes new posture,' *Chain Store Age Executive*, August, 25–9.

Chain Store Executive (1984). 'Redesign programs bent on boosting sales,' *Chain Store Age Executive*, August, 51–3.

Ingene, C. A., and Lusch, R. F. (1981). 'The declining rate of return on capital in US retailing.' *International Journal of Physical Distribution and Materials Management*, **11**, 25–38.

Lusch, R. F., and Kenderdine, J. M. (1977). 'Financial and strategic trends of chain store retailers: 1974–1975.' *Regional Economics and Business*, **2**, 11–17.

Lusch, R. F. (1982). *Management of Retail Enterprises*, Boston, Mass.: Kent Publishing Company.

Lusch, R. F. (1986). 'Two critical determinants of retail profitability and productivity.' *Zale Retailing Issues Letter*, **2**, 1–3.

Lusch, R. F., and Serpkenci, R. R. (1983). 'Improving your financial performance in retailing.' *Business*, **33**, 9–18.

McCammon, B. C. (1984). 'The new strategic era in retailing.' Presented at the 1984 Annual Convention, National Retail Merchants Association.

McCammon, B. C. (1986). 'Distribution management in the 1980's: the new strategic frontier.' Presented at the 12th Paul D. Converse Symposium, American Marketing Association, University of Illinois at Champaign-Urbana.

Michman, R. D. (1983). *Marketing to Changing Consumer Markets*, New York: Praeger.

Steinberg, B. (1983). 'The mass market is splitting apart.' *Fortune*, 28 November, 76–82.

US Bureau of the Census (1984). *Statistical Abstract of the United States: 1985*, Washington, DC, 399.

CHAPTER 4
Manufacturer–Retailer Relations: the Shifting Balance of Power

ROBERT M. GRANT
University of British Columbia and
London Business School

INTRODUCTION

Since the ending in the UK of resale price maintenance in 1964 a fundamental shift in the balance of power in consumer goods distribution channels has taken place. Until the mid-1960s manufacturers held a pre-eminent position in distribution channels. They were the source of almost all product innovations and new-product developments, they controlled physical distribution to wholesalers and retailers, they were responsible for virtually all product advertising, they exerted a powerful influence on retailers' stocking and display of their products, and they controlled retailers' margins by setting retail selling prices.

A major feature of the 'retailing revolution' in the UK of the past two decades has been the replacement of manufacturers' dominance of distribution channels by that of the retail chains. This shift in power is apparent at three levels. In terms of structural change it is seen in the changing relative sizes of manufacturers and retailers—rapid growth and mergers of national retail chains has resulted in the largest retailing groups exceeding the sizes of their suppliers in terms of sales, assets, and stock-market capitalization (see Table 1). In terms of conduct, retailers have increasingly assumed control over a range of functions traditionally performed by manufacturers—these include physical distribution, advertising, packaging, product design, and product development. This increase in the span of activities undertaken by retailers is most clearly indicated by the growth of retailers' own brands. In the ten years to 1975 the share of retailers' brands of total packaged grocery sales rose from about 10% to over 22% (Baden Fuller, 1984). In terms of performance, the shift of power is reflected in the growth in the profitability of retailing companies relative to consumer-goods manufacturers.

A consequence of the growing economic strength of the large multiple

43

Table 1.   The market capitalization of leading manufacturing and retailing
companies, 25 October 1985

Manufacturers	£m	Retailers	£m
Food			
Unilever	1 922	Sainsbury	2 452
Cadbury Schweppes	766	Tesco	1 145
RHM	475	Kwik-Save	347
Electricals			
Thorn EMI	788	Dixons Group	823
Clothing/Textiles			
Vantona Viyella	437	Marks & Spencer	4 495
Dawson Int.	272	Burton	1 463
Tootal	76	Hepworth	295
S. R. Gent	24	Etam	113
Newspapers and Publishing			
Associated Newspaper	318	W. H. Smith	389
Fleet Holdings	311	Menzies	177
Furniture			
Silentnight	14	Habitat Mothercare	567
Gomme	6	Harris Queensway	382
Stag Furniture	6	Courts	23

retailers is the demand for government intervention to curb the growth
and exercise of retailer buying-power. Traditionally, it has been the smaller
retailers, pressured by the favourable discounts negotiated by the large
multiples, which have been the principal source of pressure for government
action. However, in recent years they have been joined by several manufacturers' associations. Over the past decade the food and drink manufacturers
have shifted their position from opposition to restrictions on the freedom of
suppliers and buyers to negotiate terms of business to strong support for a
code of conduct governing manufacturer–retailer relations.

Despite the finding by the Monopolies and Mergers Commission in its
Discounts to Retailers report (1981) that the power of large retailers has, on
balance, been favourable to consumers' interests, continuing disquiet over
the growing power of the large retailers resulted in the Office of Fair Trading
(OFT) initiating a fact-finding exercise to investigate the exercise of power
by large retail organizations. The Office's report, *Competition and Retailing*
(1985), has provided up-to-date evidence on trends in retailing and the extent
of preferential discounts to large retailers. However, it has done little to
clarify the key issues with regard to the welfare consequences of retailer
buying-power or the desirability of government intervention to curb or regulate discriminatory discounts.

In this chapter we seek to shed light on some of the issues that underlie manufacturer–retailer relationships. The key questions addressed are:

(1) What is retailer buying-power?
(2) What structural factors determine the power of retailers to obtain preferential terms of supply and what empirical evidence on preferential discounts exists?
(3) What are the effects of retailer buying-power on competition and economic efficiency?
(4) What are the prospects for government measures to curb retailer buying-power?

THE NATURE OF RETAILER BUYING-POWER

Critics of retailer buying-power have viewed it as monopoly power on the buyer side of the market. Where there is a single buyer in a market (for example, the government in certain defence industries) then it is true to view *monopsony* as the mirror-image of monopoly. However, where markets are dominated by a limited number of large buyers (*oligopsony*), can their influence be equated with the market-power of collusive oligopolists? Most analyses of buyer-concentration have presumed so: 'Oligopsony, analogous to oligopoly, would make buyers conscious of the potential impact of their own bids to purchase on the bids of other buyers. This interdependency might be expected to produce some collusion among buyers' (Lustgarten, 1975, p. 126).

However, this assumption that the influence of large buyers on price is based upon their propensity to collude is unsatisfactory as an explanation of retailer buying-power. The ability of large retailers to co-ordinate their purchasing behaviour is constrained by two main factors:

(1) Buyer-concentration ratios in the markets for most manufactured consumer goods are generally substantially below the corresponding seller-concentration ratios. Across a selection of non-durable consumer products the OFT found that sales to the top-ten largest customers varied between 15% and 70%. Yet in all these products five-firm seller-concentration ratios exceeded 60% (OFT, 1985).
(2) The prices for manufactured goods are normally announced by manufacturers, usually through price lists. Such arrangements are conducive to price-leadership among suppliers but render collusion or co-ordination between buyers difficult. Only where buyers directly participate in the price-setting process (in auction markets, for instance) is collusive behaviour readily feasible.

These constraints upon buyer co-ordination mean that the impact of large buyers on price is not typically upon the 'market price' as predicted by the theories of monopsony and collusive oligopsony but is exercised through bilateral arrangements between individual buyers and sellers. The principal effect of buying-power is not to depress price across the market but to induce price-discrimination in favour of large buyers, typically through specially negotiated discounts.

If retailers do not possess market-power in the form of a monopsonistic influence over wholesale markets, what, then, is the basis of the power of large UK retail groups to negotiate preferential terms of supply? The literature suggests three sources of retailers' influence over prices:

(1) Adelman's (1959) observations of the US grocery giant, A&P, suggested that large buyers can purchase at preferential prices simply through their capacity to exploit disequilibrium in the marketplace. Thus fixed information costs make it more profitable for the large buyer to seek out bargains, while larger warehousing capacity allows the fuller exploitation of such opportunities.
(2) Galbraith's (1980) countervailing power thesis, although essentially a theory of the structural development of markets, clearly recognized the distinction between monopsony power and buying-power: 'The opportunity to exercise such [buying] power exists only when suppliers are enjoying something that can be taken away, i.e. when they are enjoying the fruits of market power from which they can be separated' (p. 118).
(3) Porter (1974) views retailer buying-power as based upon retailers' contribution to the effective differentiation of the manufacturer's products. This is particularly significant in non-convenience goods where the retailer's reputation and his provision of information and after-sales service are important elements in consumer choice.

The author's approach to the analysis of retailers' influence on their buying prices rests upon the simple observation that in some products, principally manufactured goods supplied by concentrated industries, large retailers are able to negotiate substantial discounts, while in others, principally primary produce supplied through competitive markets, large retailers typically purchase at the going-market prices. Hence the key to understanding discriminatory retail discounts is not the *market-power of the buyers* but *that of the sellers*. The role of retailer-power is in counteracting that market-power. Hence a retailer's buying-power is his bargaining-power based simply upon his ability of the retailer to purchase from supplier A in preference to supplier B, and so inducing retailers to compete for the retailer's custom. The next section of this chapter outlines the analysis more precisely.

THE DETERMINANTS OF PREFERENTIAL DISCOUNTS TO LARGE RETAILERS

If the buying-power of large retailers acts simply to counteract the market-power of suppliers then it should be possible to examine the role of large buyers within the framework of elementary economic analysis. The level of price in a market (relative to the perfectly competitive level) may be seen as depending, most importantly, upon competition among existing suppliers and the threat of competition from new suppliers. Industrial economics predicts that within any market the intensity of both these competitive forces may be related to certain key structural features of the market.

The impact of large retailers on entry conditions

We start from the assumption that most consumer-goods industries are oligopolies where manufacturers have some discretion in setting prices. If this is the case, at what level do manufacturers seek to set prices? A major factor which retailers will have regard to is the level of entry barriers into their industry. The 'limit-price' principle suggests that firms will set the highest price that does not attract entry. However, entry barriers are not uniform across an industry. One dimension of market segmentation is by size of buyer. Marketing and distribution conditions vary considerably between supplying national retail chains and small retail outlets.

Lower entry barriers into supplying large rather than small retailers are likely to result from four principal factors:

(1) Fixed costs in distribution and sales functions. Since these form a major part of the cost of sales and distribution to each retailer this implies, first, that the average cost schedule for the small-retailer segment of a market is above that for the large-retailer one and, second, that the capital costs are higher for a firm seeking to supply small retailers than large ones.[1]

(2) The cost of advertising and brand promotion impose a substantial entry barrier into consumer-goods industries. The opportunities for supplying large retailers under their own brand names results in lower barriers to entry in supplying large rather than small retailers.

(3) Large retailers tend to be more price-sensitive than small ones in their purchasing. This is a reflection of the fact that larger retailers tend to compete on price, while small retailers' very survival is dependent upon their differentiating their products and services (through exploiting locational factors and market niches). As a consequence, entry into supplying large retailers tends to be easier than to small ones since, by supplying larger retailers, the new entrant can expect to gain sizeable sales by undercutting the established producers by only a small margin.

(4) Finally, entry barriers into supplying large retailers tend to be low because they are themselves a source of new entry. Such new entry may take the form of backward-integration in manufacturing (for example, Boots manufactures a significant proportion of its retail sales) or by inviting entry by a new or overseas supplier. (The major electrical chains have played a key role in inviting the entry of Spanish and Eastern European manufacturers of domestic electrical appliances into the UK.)

The inducement of large retailers to the breakdown of oligopoly co-ordination

Lower entry barriers is one reason for a differential to emerge in manufacturers' prices to large and small retailers. A second factor is differences in the strength of competition between established manufacturers in supplying large and small retailers. The level of price in a concentrated market depends crucially upon the ability of suppliers to effectively co-ordinate their price/output decisions so as to avoid price competition. The greater the homogeneity of transactions in a market, the easier it is for suppliers to achieve co-ordination—notably through parallelism of list prices. The presence of large buyers in a market increases the heterogeneity of transactions. Thus, large retailers' requirements for central warehouse delivery, their participation in joint promotional arrangements, and their specific requirements with regard to packaging, merchandising, etc. mean that prices and other terms of supply tend to be negotiated individually, making co-ordination much more difficult than with small buyers, where uniform prices and discount scales are simply announced.

The tendency for oligopoly co-ordination to break down in the presence of large retailers is all the greater when other market conditions are present. Three factors are likely to be of key importance here:

(1) *The level of seller-concentration.* The higher the level of seller-concentration, the more effective is co-ordination between manufacturers likely to be. Where a market is dominated by one or two suppliers it may be possible to maintain prices against both large and small retailers.
(2) *Excess capacity.* The presence of excess capacity makes manufacturers particularly prone to aggressive price initiatives with the objective of achieving better capacity-utilization. Manufacturers may be willing to accept any price that will cover their variable costs rather than lose an important customer. The size of the price concession manufacturers are willing to make is dependent upon the relative proportions of fixed and variable costs.

(3) *Product differentiation*. The closer are competing firms' products viewed as substitutes by buyers, the greater the propensity for price competition in seeking to attract the business of large retailers.

EMPIRICAL EVIDENCE

Empirical evidence on the impact of these various structural influences on the ability of large retailers to purchase at favourable prices compared with small retailers is available from a variety of sources. A cross-sectional regression analysis of preferential discounts to multiple retailers for seventeen products showed preferential discounts as a proportion of sales revenue to be

(1) *Positively* related to the proportion of sales to national retail multiples;
(2) *Negatively* related to industry's rate of output growth (a proxy for capacity-utilization);
(3) *Negatively* related to seller-concentration in the industry.

These three variables explained about 50% of total variance (see Grant, 1985a).

In addition, fragmentary evidence for different products provides useful supporting evidence. Where a combination of conditions favourable to price-differentials between large and small retailers have been present, competition has frequently degenerated into intense discount wars. During the late 1970s the UK bread-baking industry suffered substantial excess capacity in an industry characterized by an undifferentiated basic product and capital-intensive production. The 'big three' bakers paid discounts to the major supermarket chains exceeding 20% of wholesale price. By contrast, in products where seller-concentration is very high, brand loyalty strong, and excess capacity is low (such as canned pet foods and cigarettes) discounts to large retailers have been modest.

The relationship between seller-concentration and the level of preferential discounts is interesting. At low levels of seller-concentration prices are close to their competitive levels and there is little or no margin available for discriminatory discounts. At very high levels of seller-concentration, co-ordination tends to be effective against larger as well as small retailers. It is in the moderately concentrated oligopolies where prices are above their competitive levels, but large retailers are able to extract concessions, that discounts are at their highest.

Recent evidence collected by the OFT on discounts to large retailers for a range of consumer goods is presented in Table 2.

Table 2. The value of special terms negotiated with retailers, 1983, as a
percentage of total sales

Product	Sales to top 10 customers %	Own-label sales %	Special terms	
			To all customers %	To top 10 customers %
Baked beans	40–65	21	6.8	7.5
Biscuits	45	17	10.6	12.4
Bread	45	20	Not disclosed	
Flour confectionary	50	21	6.7	8.0
Canned beer	c.34	2	9.4	12.8
Cigarettes	15	Very small	1.8	3.7
Paint	25	10	Not disclosed	
Toothpaste	50	5	8.1	9.1
Paper handkerchiefs	70	23	11.2	n.d.

Source: OFT (1985, pp. 44–54).

THE EFFECTS OF RETAILER BUYING-POWER

The effects of the growing power of large retailers to negotiate preferential
discounts has had important effects upon:

(1) Competition in wholesale and in retail markets;
(2) The strategies pursued by manufacturers and retailers;
(3) The industrial structure of manufacturing and retailing;
(4) The profitability of the manufacturing and retail sectors;
(5) The public interest.

We examine these effects, first, upon manufacturers and second, upon
retailers.

The effects upon manufacturers

The implication of the above analysis is that powerful retailers are a particularly potent force for promoting strong price-competition among oligopoly
manufacturers. As a witness to the US Domestic Council Review Group on
Regulatory Reform explained:

> When a seller hungry for business decides to make a price concession, to whom
> will he make a concession? Almost inevitably to effect a larger sale. There is
> more payoff in it and therefore it is more likely than not that the first beneficiary
> of a break from the prevailing prices will be a large buyer.
>   Assuming that Seller No. 1 has gained a large buyer, someone else has lost a
> good customer, and in that sense now has excess capacity and has to go looking
> for some other buyer. So, the pressures are magnified for another price
> concession (US Department of Justice, 1977, p. 157).

How far such competition for the business of large retailers, extends into more general competition depends very much upon individual circumstances. In the UK petrol market, special discounts offered in 1974–5 to large retailers and in selected areas had by 1977 extended into general price-competition (Grant, 1982). Alternatively, manufacturers may seek to recoup lost margin due to discounts to large retailers by raising list prices to small retailers. The Monopolies and Mergers Commission (MMC) concluded that manufacturers' scope for such action was severely constrained (MMC, 1981, pp. 35–6).

The major consequence for manufacturers of the increased discount competition that has accompanied the growth of retailer-concentration has been pressure on profitability. Food-manufacturing has been particularly affected. Figure 1 shows that return on capital in food manufacturing has declined both in absolute terms and relative to both industry in general and food retailing. How far these trends can be attributed to the influence of growing retail buying-power is unclear. It is notable that in the USA, where the leading retailers account for a much smaller proportion of trade than in the UK and where their exercise of bargaining-power is restricted by the Robinson Patman Act, food manufacturers still earn a higher return on capital than the retailers (*Financial Times*, 11 October 1985).

Counteracting the power of the retailers has emerged as a key consideration in manufacturers' strategy formulation. Direct attempts at confrontation such as refusal to supply discount chains are now illegal. However, in both 'brown goods' (audiovisual products) and 'white goods' (major domestic electrical appliances) several leading manufacturers have used their selective

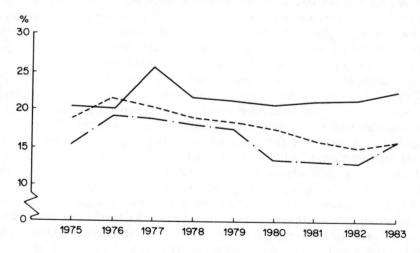

Figure 1. Return on capital employed (historic cost), 1975–83. ───── Food-retailing; – – – – food-manufacturing; ─── · ─── all sectors (excluding oil). (Source: OFT, 1985, p. 31)

distribution systems as a means of indirectly imposing some form of resale price maintenance (see Grant, 1984).

In the food and drink sector efforts to counteract the imbalance of bargaining power between manufacturers and retailers have focused chiefly upon investments by manufacturers in increased product differentiation. This is most apparent in increased brand promotion. Heinz's advertising has been directed at justifying the value for money of its products over cheaper rivals. Other manufacturers have similarly increased advertising to build brand loyalty and emphasize quality. Table 3 shows the increase in advertising expenditure for food and drink products.

Table 3. Media advertising expenditure as a percentage of sales revenue, 1976–82

Product group	1976	1977	1978	1979	1980	1981	1982
Food	0.79	0.90	0.92	0.82	0.99	1.06	1.08
Clothing and footwear	0.26	0.28	0.27	0.25	0.32	0.31	0.33
Drink and tobacco	1.08	1.08	1.06	1.13	1.34	1.20	1.24
Toiletries and medical	4.9	5.0	5.0	4.7	4.4	4.3	4.3
Household and leisure	1.47	1.71	1.95	1.83	1.95	2.01	N/A
Retail trade	0.63	0.68	0.70	0.69	0.74	0.76	N/A
Total manufacturing	0.99	1.06	1.13	1.08	1.21	1.23	N/A

Source: OFT (1985, p. 39).

The desire by manufacturers to escape from pressure on margins through establishing differentiation advantages has also encouraged increased emphasis on product development. In the grocery market the rate of new-product introductions has increased steadily over the past decade, the primary emphasis being higher value-added convenience foods and ethnic dishes. This trend is clearly revealed in the changing product range of the two leading frozen-food processors, Bird's Eye and Findus (see Grant, 1985b).

Manufacturers' objections at the retailers' exercise of bargaining-power has focused upon the threat of lower profitability to capital investment and innovation. Table 4 compares investment in capital and R&D in food manu-facturing with that in retailing and manufacturing in general. There is no evidence that growth of retailer buying-power depressed capital investment in food manufacturing, although R&D spending in this area has fallen both in absolute terms and relative to manufacturing as a whole. There is some evidence that, rather than harming investment, the bargaining pressure of retailers has increased manufacturers' quest for efficiency and in doing so has encouraged cost-reducing capital investment. At Bird's Eye Walls Ltd concern at shrinking margins promoted a £60m programme of investment in manufacturing and distribution between 1983 and 1987. In other cases pressure for increased cost efficiency has encouraged changes in ownership and management. Hillsdown Holdings has grown to be one of Britain's

Table 4.   Investment in capital and R&D

	1976	1978	1981	1983	1984
Fixed capital expenditure (constant prices, 1980 = 100)					
Manufacturing	100	112	75	71	81
Food manufacturing	89	112	89	89	103
Retail distribution	78	99	94	108	123
Fixed capital expenditure (percentage of gross capital stock)					
Manufacturing	3.6	4.0	2.5	2.4	2.7
Food manufacturing	3.9	4.7	3.5	3.4	3.9
Retail distribution	5.3	6.2	5.1	5.5	6.1
R&D expenditure by private industry (£m at 1975 prices)					
Manufacturing	1 172[a]	1 373	1 420	1 330	–
Food, drink & tobacco	50[a]	55	40	30	–

[a] 1975 data.
Source: OFT (1985, pp. 36–7).

largest and most profitable food-manufacturing companies as a result of acquiring unprofitable firms and brands and imposing vigorous cost control.

Effects on retailing

At the retail level the most important consequence of the quest for preferential terms of supply has been the propensity for retailers to grow—both by acquisition and internal expansion. Between 1980 and 1984 the multiples' share of sales of packaged groceries rose from 59.4% to 66.5%. This was almost entirely due to internal expansion among the 'top four' multiples (Tesco, Sainsbury, Asda, and Kwik-Save), whose share grew from 34.2% to 40.7% of total packaged grocery sales.

While in grocery retailing mergers have principally been among the 'second division' supermarket chains (for example, Dee Corp. of International Stores) in other retail sectors acquisitions have involved some of the leading firms. Most notable are Dixons' take-over of Currys, Associated Dairies' of MFI, Woolworth's of Comet, Habitat's of Mothercare and subsequently of British Home Stores, and the Burton Group's of Debenham's. The overall effect of these recent mergers has been to increase the concentration of buying-power, particularly in electrical goods, clothing, and furnishings.

Two important issues arise in relation to the public interests from growing retailer-concentration. The first is the effect on price-competition at the retail level, the second is the potential for an inefficient allocation of resources within retailing.

While increased retail-concentration tends to lower wholesale prices by increasing retailer buying-power it may simultaneously have the effect of raising retail prices by increasing retailers' market-power. Hence the proposition that increased retail-concentration is beneficial to consumers is based upon the assumption of assymetry in the effects of such concentration upon prices: i.e. at moderate levels of retail concentration, retailers are capable of exercising considerable influence on their buying prices but possess insufficient market-power to seriously limit competition between them.

The OFT's data largely support this proposition. Evidence of the exercise of market-power by large multiple retailers would be a failure by the multiples to pass on preferential discounts in lower seller-prices. A survey of gross margins by category of retailer gave the following result:

Major multiples	15.0%
Other multiples	14.6%
Co-operatives	11.3%
Independents	13.7%

The differences in these averages were not significantly different, leading to the conclusion that: 'These results are not inconsistent with the proposition that the benefits of lower buying prices are in general passed on in lower selling prices' (OFT, 1985, p. 60).[2]

A more serious potential detriment to the performance of the retail trades is posed by the likelihood that the quest for size in order to exploit opportunities for preferential buying terms causes a misallocation of resources in retailing. Not only may retailers seek to grow (particularly through acquisition) to beyond their most efficient size in order to exploit increased buying-power, but discriminatory discounts may allow inefficient large retailers to displace efficient small retailers. The MMC was doubtful if any of these inefficiencies had in fact emerged:

> We do not detect any indication that this is happening at present. We think that in general the large multiple retailers who have emerged so strongly in recent years represent an efficient response to changing market conditions. Also, the practice appears to have had some favourable effects on efficiency in retailing and wholesaling in that it has tended to break down traditional margins, to stimulate the search for reductions in cost and improvements in service and to encourage more competitive behaviour (MMC, 1981, p. 67).

However, this view is based upon sparse evidence. The most that can be said is that competition between the largest multiple retailers acts as a powerful constraint upon inefficiency. A second constraint is threat of take-over. However, the more concentrated retailing becomes, the weaker is the threat from both these sources.

THE PROSPECTS FOR GOVERNMENT INTERVENTION

The reluctance of the main competition authorities, the MMC and the OFT, to take action to regulate discriminatory discounts to large retailers on any general basis reflects three factors: the limits of the legislation, the absence of evidence of detriment to the public interest, and fears over the effectiveness of any intervention.[3]

As regards legislation, the key problem of applying monopoly provisions to discriminatory discounts arising from the exercise of large retailers' buying-power is that such discounts, as we have argued, are not a consequence of any market-power possessed by the retailers. Hence any application of monopoly legislation should be applied to the suppliers who offer the discounts, even though these may be the victims rather than the beneficiaries. Even this approach may be ineffective, however, since the most substantial discrimination in favour of large retailers occurs in competitive oligopolies rather than highly concentrated, collusive oligopolies.

Although the 1980 Competition Act greatly extended the OFT's powers to investigate and refer to the MMC issues of retail buying-power and discriminatory discounts the OFT has been notably reluctant to initiate such actions. An additional factor which has been influential in deterring the competition authorities from tackling price discrimination and the abuse of buying-power has been overseas experience. On the basis of a study of experience with anti-price discrimination measures in Australia, France, Ireland, and West Germany (Grant, 1981) and more recent evidence contained in the recent OFT report (1985, pp. 68–79), it can be concluded that in none of these four countries do price-discrimination controls operate satisfactorily: either the law is not enforced and is largely ineffective or it is enforced and the consequences are more harmful than the abuses it was designed to cure. Four general problems can be identified:

(1) It is extremely difficult to formulate laws against price-discrimination which permit *flexibility* in the negotiation of prices between buyers and sellers but which do not result in *ambiguity and confusion*. Both in Australia (Section 49 of the Trade Disputes Act) and in Ireland (the Groceries Orders of 1973, 1978, and 1981) differing interpretation of the prohibitions of price discrimination resulted in an unwillingness of the competition authorities to enforce the measures.
(2) Price-discrimination measures are notoriously difficult to enforce—not only can preferential discounts be concealed within the complexities of terms of supply between supplier and buyer (particularly through advertising and promotional allowances, credit terms, and provision of merchandising services), but determining whether or not a discount is cost-justified gives rise to horrendous problems of cost measurement. A

half-century of US experience with the Robinson Patman Act provides ample evidence of these difficulties.
(3) Price-discrimination controls provide an excellent framework for encouraging 'conscious parallelism' between oligopoly suppliers.
(4) Circumvention of price-discrimination legislation, particularly by manufacturers' differentiating their products between different retailers, can add substantially to cost. In the USA the Robinson Patman Act has led to a proliferation of private brands and the production of special models and formulations for individual large retailers.

CONCLUSIONS

The principal findings of this chapter may be summarized as follows:

(1) The ability of large retailers to obtain preferential discounts is a consequence of the market-power of manufacturers rather than of retailers; the source of retailers' buying power is the ability to encourage competitive pricing between manufacturers.
(2) The size of preferential discounts to large retailers depends upon market structure, in particular: retailer-concentration, supplier-concentration, excess capacity in the supplying industry, and product differentiation among suppliers.
(3) The effects of retailer buying-power upon the manufacturers of consumer goods has been to increase price-competition, to reduce profitability, to increase product differentiation (particularly through advertising and new-product introductions), and to increase the quest for cost efficiency.
(4) The potential for retailers to increase discounts through increasing their relative force has been a strong motivating force for growth (particularly by acquisition). At the same time there is no evidence that increasing retail-concentration is limiting price-concentration among retailers. There is, however, a risk that the quest for preferential discounts through growth of firm-size can distort retail competition, resulting in a misallocation of resources in the retail sector.
(5) The reluctance of competition authorities or government to intervene in the free negotiation of retail discounts has been due primarily to the absence of evidence of clear detriment to the public interest arising from discriminatory discounts. Even if such evidence does emerge, the difficulties and costs of enforcing price-discrimination regulations in other countries will provide a powerful deterrent to similar measures being introduced in the UK.

NOTES

1. The growth of the larger supermarket chains has greatly facilitated the ability of smaller companies to distribute on a national basis. In the frozen-foods industry Bird's Eye held a dominant position principally as a result of the entry barrier imposed by its distribution system (see Grant, 1985b).
2. These findings confirm those of the MMC, which were based upon data for 1979. For a range of products, regressions of retailers' selling prices upon their buying prices produced regression coefficients which for most products were close to unity, indicating that lower buying-prices tended to be reflected in lower selling-prices. Separate regressions for independent retailers and multiples showed a higher regression coefficient for multiples, indicating that multiples' pricing was more closely related to costs than that of independents.
3. The MMC has, however, criticized discrimination in favour of large customers in a number of monopoly reports, mainly cases where it was practised by a dominant supplier and where it resulted in raising barriers to entry (see, for example, the reports on Frozen Foods, plain paper copiers, contraceptive sheaths, and metal containers).

REFERENCES

Adelman, M. A. (1959). *A&P: a Study in Price-Cost Behaviour and Public Policy*, Cambridge, Mass.: Harvard University Press.

Baden Fuller, C. W. F. (1984). 'The changing market share of retail brands in the UK grocery trade 1960–1980.' In Angeli, F. (ed.), *The Economics of Distribution*, Milan: CESCOM, Universita L. Bocconi and IRM, New York University.

Galbraith, J. K. (1980). *American Capitalism. The Concept of Countervailing Power*, revised edition, Oxford: Blackwell.

Grant, R. M. (1981). 'Recent developments in the control of price discrimination in countries outside North America.' *Antitrust Bulletin*, **26**, Fall, 593–632.

Grant, R. M. (1982). 'Pricing behaviour in the UK wholesale market for petrol 1970–80: a "structure-conduct analysis".' *Journal of Industrial Economics*, **XXX**, March, 271–92.

Grant, R. M. (1984). 'A report of a study into the selective distribution of consumer electronics products in the United Kingdom.' Unpublished paper, London Business School.

Grant, R. M. (1985a). 'An analysis of retailer buying power.' Working Paper, Centre for Business Strategy, London Business School, March.

Grant, R. M. (1985b). 'Bird's Eye and the UK frozen foods industry.' Working Paper, Centre for Business Strategy, London Business School.

Lustgarten, S. H. (1975). 'The impact of buyer concentration in manufacturing industries.' *Review of Economics and Statistics*, **57**, 125–32.

Monopolies and Mergers Commission (1971). *Discounts to Retailers*, HC 311, London: HMSO.

OECD (1981). *Buying Power: The Exercise of Market Power by Dominant Buyers*, Paris: OECD.

Office of Fair Trading (1985). *Competition and Retailing*, London: OFT.

Porter, M. E. (1974). 'Consumer behaviour, retailer power and market performance in consumer goods industries.' *Review of Economics and Statistics*, **56**, 419–36.

Scherer, F. M. (1980). *Industrial Market Structure and Economic Performance*, 2nd edn, Chicago: Rand McNally.

Stigler, G. J. (1964). 'A theory of oligopoly.' *Journal of Political Economy*, **55**, 444–64.

US Department of Justice (1977). *Report on the Robinson Patman Act*, Washington, DC.

CHAPTER 5
Knowing the Competition: the Mental Models of Retailing Strategists

JOSEPH F. PORAC and HOWARD THOMAS
University of Illinois at Urbana–Champaign
and
BETHANY EMME
R. R. Donnelley & Co.

Competitive strategy in retailing can be roughly defined as the placement of a firm in relation to other retailers in such a way as to exploit a profitable niche in the marketplace (e.g. Duncan *et al.*, 1983). However, the relation between one firm and another is not given to the decision-maker as an objective fact. Rather, it is discovered, defined, and labelled by the retailer who uses an implicit understanding of the environment to make sense out of business opportunities. We assert that a central component in this 'implicit understanding' is a mental scheme that categorizes and classifies the varied assortment of retailing businesses existing in the marketplace. The use of such a scheme permits the decision-maker to distinguish between those businesses that are potential 'competitors' from those that are not. In this way it becomes possible for the strategist to devise co-ordinated business plans which minimize competitive threats.

The purpose of this chapter is to explore some of the psychological principles determining how retailers make sense out of their competitive environments. Current research in cognitive psychology and anthropology is drawn upon to address two fundamental questions regarding the sense-making process. First, what are the essential features of the mental categorization schemes used by decision-makers when interpreting the structure of the retailing environment? Second, how do such schemes influence and/or constrain the decision-maker's implicit competitive strategies? While examining these questions it will be argued that retail managers partition the environment into commonly accepted categories of business such as 'grocery stores', 'discount clothing shops', etc. It is suggested that such categories are 'fuzzy sets' with indefinite boundaries that are organized hierarchically into

59

'cognitive taxonomies'. We propose that it is from a retailer's cognitive taxonomy that the elements of a competitive strategy are derived. That is, we posit that a retailer's understanding of competitive conditions stems from a mental model of the structure of the retailing environment.

At the outset it is important to note two important differences between our treatment of competitive analysis and the dominant theoretical tradition in the strategic management literature. First, currently popular treatments of strategic choice (e.g. Porter, 1980; Day, 1984) are motivated largely by a fruitful union of marketing and economic theory. The orientation is focused upon the structure of the macro-industrial environment as an explanation for the actions of individual firms. Firm competition is analytically defined on the basis of theoretical criteria such as product line, manufacturing processes, degrees of vertical integration, size, etc. (e.g. Hofer, 1975; Porter, 1980; McGee and Thomas, 1986). Individual decision-makers are of concern only insofar as they are responsible for implementing actions dictated by the competitive structures so defined. In contrast, the focus in this chapter is upon the individual decision-maker looking out onto a complex industrial scene and using intuitively derived conceptual schemes to make sense of it all. Thus, rather than focusing upon the environment we examine the psychological principles which are involved in coming to *understand* the environment.

Second, our emphasis is descriptive rather than normative. One dominant trend in strategic management theory is toward building models which prescribe how industries and more restricted competitive groups *should* be defined on the basis of scientifically sensible criteria. Once such models are constructed, decision-makers are then advised regarding the appropriate strategic moves for their business to take. In contrast, in this chapter we suspend judgement regarding the normative desirability of analytic models of competitive strategy and instead focus upon how decision-makers *actually* go about competitive analysis. We try to describe the psychological bases of decision-maker perceptions rather than to impose a normative framework. Given the fact that many of the normative models of strategy are offered by scholars as an aid to making sense out of a world of complexity, this goal seems appropriate. Rather than focusing upon the mind of the academic, however, we focus upon the mental models of the retailing practitioner.

Our analysis begins with a discussion of the problems faced by a retailer when interpreting the business environment and deciphering its underlying organization. Our goal will be to advance a psychological model of 'attribute contrasts' as a basis for explaining how retailers scan the environment and differentiate one business from another. We will argue also that the attribute contrast model while valuable as a simple framework, cannot fully explain the details of intuitive competitive analysis. Slightly more complex cognitive principles are thus proposed—specifically the notion of 'cognitive taxonomy'—to explain perceptual competitive groupings in retailing. Finally, the approach is used to examine how retailers might use mental classification schemes to identify and monitor their most salient competition.

THE RETAIL DECISION-MAKER IN A COMPLEX ENVIRONMENT: FIRM-ATTRIBUTE CONTRASTS AND THE NEED FOR CLASSIFICATION

The retailing environment presents a double-sided problem to the manager attempting to chart a competitive strategy. On the one hand, the size of the industry (in terms of both industry sales and the number of firms) ensures considerable diversity. Retail businesses vary along any number of relevant dimensions, such as the type and selection of merchandise offered, product positioning, the amount and kind of customer service, pricing, location, geographic scope, organizational structure, form of ownership, attitudes of sales staff, ambience of display areas, etc. On the other hand, the low cost of change on many of these dimensions implies that, despite this diversity, a great deal of imitation will probably occur among firms—ensuring a certain degree of interfirm homogeneity. Large department stores can and do carry the same merchandise as that offered in smaller shops, and small shops can, given sufficient resources, open mail-order businesses similar to those of catalogue companies. These dual qualities of diversity and fluidity suggest that the retail industry is highly competitive and fragmented.

A dominant response among retailers to these environmental constraints has been to pursue so-called strategies of 'enterprise-differentiation'. As it applies to retailing, enterprise-differentiation is a competitive philosophy '. . . by which each retail firm attempts to offer a unique set of goods and services to customers and at the same time make certain that these customers view that retail operation as different' (Duncan *et al.*, 1983, p. 8). In its most reduced form, the strategic pursuit of differentiation involves three interrelated tasks for the strategist. These are summarized in Figure 1.

First, the retailer must monitor the environment to ascertain the characteristics of other retail businesses. It is at this stage that the decision-maker must categorize the various retail businesses in the marketplace and identify 'the competition'. Next, he/she must discover, invent, or copy a business strategy involving a mix of merchandise, service, location, and other appropriate factors which profitably differentiates his/her own business from those of other retail firms. Finally, the differentiation strategy must be implemented successfully and impressed upon the mind of the consumer. Of course, these activities form a strategy-making cycle, since all three must occur continuously over time if the business is to keep pace with the marketplace.

The strategy-making cycle depicted in Figure 1 places major psychological demands upon retailers and has important implications for the identity of

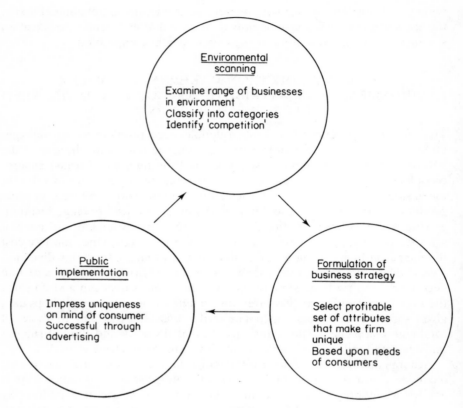

Figure 1.   The enterprise-differentiation cycle

retail firms. A strategy of enterprise-differentiation in a diverse and dynamic environment implies that the firm's identity is constantly being re-examined because of the ever-present need to change. Does, for example, a tavern-owner who has decided to differentiate her business from other pubs by adding a luncheon and dinner selection continue to view the business as a tavern, or does she begin to define the firm as a restaurant? Moreover, does the tavern-owner continue to monitor only other pubs to keep up with the competition, or does she begin to examine restaurant trends as well? Such questions are fundamental to establishing a relationship between the firm and its environment. In this way, the strategy-making cycle in Figure 1 demands a continual re-evaluation of the retail firm–environment interface.

From a psychological perspective, 'self–other' judgements such as these become descriptively more tractable by considering retailing businesses in their most fundamental form—as clusters of information-rich attributes presenting themselves to observers. Figure 2 illustrates schematically what

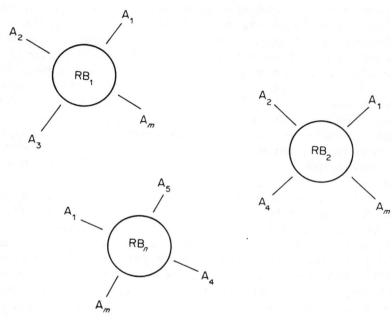

Figure 2.   Retail businesses as clusters of attributes. Any retail business
(R_B) can be considered a cluster of attributes (A_1 . . ., A_m). Businesses
can be compared on the basis of overlapping attributes, with some being
shared by more than one business (e.g. A_1) and some being unique (e.g.
A_5). The greater the degrees of overlap, the more similar the businesses
being compared. (See text for further discussion)

this sort of description entails. The strategically relevant differences among
retail establishments are essentially differences in the various attributes they
possess. For present purposes, the notion of 'attribute' can be considered
very broadly (but see Garner, 1978, for a more extensive discussion). Some
attributes are discrete properties, such as the presence or absence of a certain
type of merchandise or the availability of customer credit. Other attributes
are qualitative or quantitative dimensions along which a retail business
assumes a value, such as size of store, number of sales employees, or quality
of service. Some attributes are relatively concrete, such as store lighting;
others are more abstract and intangible, such as sales staff attitude. It is the
aggregate of its salient and relevant attributes which endows a retailing
establishment with a unique identity in the environment. Moreover, the
degree of attribute overlap between one business and another is a useful
metric for comparing their essential qualities.

   Using this analysis, the strategic cycle of enterprise-differentiation can be
recast in terms of the logic of the attribute-contrast approach. The environ-

ment presents itself to the retailing decision-maker as a collection of 'attribute clusters' (that is, retail establishments). It is the task of the strategist to scan the environment and decipher the degree of overlap between his/her own business and others in the focal marketplace. Retail business differentiation is evident when the decision-maker is able to add or subtract attributes from his/her own business in such a way as to satisfy *uniquely* a profitable customer need; in other words, in a way that establishes a profitable degree of attribute dissimilarity with other retail businesses. Hence, '. . . competition in retailing is related to the active pursuit of differences among what generally appear to be similar types' (Duncan *et al.*, 1983). Henderson (1979) terms this process 'isolating the battlefield' in the search for a strategic sector of competition.

Many of the psychological demands occurring in strategies of enterprise-differentiation stem from the need to conduct continual attribute comparisons in order to remain competitive. The simple case of contrasting one's own firm with another is not very problematic. Judgements of similarity and dissimilarity have been studied extensively (e.g. Tversky, 1977; Tversky and Gati, 1978), and binary contrasts between sets of attributes appear to be well within the range of human information-processing capacities. Hence, in an environment containing only a few other firms, attribute-comparisons should present no unwieldy informational burden. Unfortunately, the retail industry is not characterized by simplicity. Because the number of firm-by-firm attribute-contrasts multiplies as the number of firms increases, the massive number of binary comparisons required to monitor the typical retail environment makes such comparisons difficult, if not impossible. Well-known limits to human cognitive resources (e.g. March and Simon, 1958; Kahneman, 1973) would suggest that it is highly unlikely that a complete firm-by-firm attribute-analysis could ever occur in practice. Although the decision-maker might impose cognitively driven limitations on the number of firms being compared, a purely arbitrary selection of businesses to compare with his/her own is likely to be counterproductive in the long run. Pure random sampling is psychologically inefficient if there are enough similarities among firms in the environment to group them into informationally more reasonable clusters.

Instead, we suggest that retail decision-makers order their environments in sensible ways by using implicit classification schemes that group retail businesses into useful conceptual categories based upon firm similarities. Once formed, such schemes make it possible to compare and contrast the *typical* attributes of *classes* of businesses rather than the idiosyncratic attributes of all individual firms. Using *a priori* categorization schemes permits a simplification of the environment and allows the retailer to narrow the focus of environmental scanning to those classes of businesses that are most strategically related to his/her own. It is the nature of these cognitive categorization schemes that we examine next.

ORDERING THE RETAIL ENVIRONMENT WITH COGNITIVE TAXONOMIES: BASIC ISSUES AND EXAMPLES

The above analysis makes clear that the retailer is faced with the complex task of summarizing a diverse and often fragmented environment. As in all summarization tasks, the goal is to balance richness of information with simplicity of description. On the one hand, the varied assortment of retail businesses, each possessing a unique collection of potentially important attributes, presents a valuable source of information to the creative manager wishing to gain a competitive edge. Attending to as many idiosyncratic characteristics as possible of as many firms as possible would thus seem to be worthwhile. On the other hand, the infinite differences among large numbers of firms must be reduced in some way to cognitively usable proportions. It is in striking this balance that cognitive classification schemes become important.

Of course, the suggestion that firms are organized into categories of a more abstract nature is not new to strategy research. Many researchers (e.g. McGee and Thomas, 1986; Porter, 1980) have viewed an industry as a collection of strategic groups, with each group consisting of firms which are highly similar in their strategies. Hawes and Crittenden (1984), for example, used cluster analysis to form four major strategic groups for retailing strategies in the generic supermarket industry. However, instead of making sense of retail environments through the exclusive use of statistical cluster analysis, using the researcher's conceptions of attributes to be included in the sample, we argue that a combination of perceptual data drawn from individual decision-makers (e.g. Dess and Davis, 1984) and the economic models of competition should produce a more general framework for identifying competitive positions and the strategies that develop among retail firms.

The principles of cognitive categorization: Lessons from the human sciences

When examining the nature of cognitive categorization schemes in retailing it is necessary to confront two related issues. First, it is important to understand how it is that individual businesses are grouped into perceptually more abstract categories. If a 'cognitive category' is roughly defined as a collection of retail businesses that are identified as similar to each other and different from those not included in the category, then this issue reduces to formulating the rules which transpose similarity judgements into global groupings. Second, once categories are formed it is necessary to describe how they are related to one another within some cognitive framework. Because both these issues are fundamental to human categorization in any knowledge domain (and not just to retail decision-making), considerable psychological and anthropological research has been conducted during the past two decades to uncover the principles by which individuals classify aspects of their environment (see Rosch and Lloyd, 1978; Tyler, 1969). A general consensus about such principles has slowly emerged, and it is useful to review the essential findings.

With respect to the issue of how categories are formed, theory and research suggests that conceptual groupings are developed on the basis of the similarities and dissimilarities of the attributes possessed by the objects, persons, and events being classified. Using retailing as an example, forming the category of 'discount clothing store' might begin by recognizing that certain businesses have a number of attributes in common. These might be such things as 'low overhead locations', 'reduced sales staff', 'limited selection', etc. Using such attributes, individuals can begin to mentally group firms together into categories. Some attributes (e.g. 'low prices') might be common only to those firms that are in the 'discount clothing' category. These attributes have high informational value because they serve to demarcate a discounter from other types of clothing retailers. Other attributes (e.g. 'low overhead location') may be present in other types of clothing retailers as well, making such attributes less informative as a basis for classifying businesses. A category of business is likely to be formed when there are a number of attributes common and unique to a set of firms which can differentiate those firms from others not included in the category.

One important finding that has emerged in recent years from psychological research is that cognitive categories seem to be 'fuzzy sets' (Zadeh, 1965). That is, there is no clear and definite boundary between the members of one cognitive category and those of another. Indeed, cognitive categories have graded boundaries, with some members being considered more representative of a category than others. Thus, for example, the category of business 'French restaurants' might be considered a marginal member of the general class of 'retailers', while the category of 'department stores' might be considered very much of a retailer. Thus membership in the cognitive category 'retailers' would not be all or none but graded according to the degree to which a business possesses the attributes associated with retailing.

Rosch and Mervis (1975) suggest that those members of cognitive categories which are considered to be most typical of the category act as cognitive 'prototypes'. Category prototypes seem to share more attributes with other members of the category than more borderline cases. Category prototypes also seem to have a special status. When contrasted with less typical members of a category, prototypes are learned earlier (e.g. Posner and Keele, 1968), are identified earlier when individuals are asked to name objects (e.g. Rosch *et al.*, 1976a), and are more frequently mentioned by people when they are asked to specify category examples (e.g. Mervis *et al.*, 1976).

Thus, cognitive categories seem to be graded classes of membership based upon the possession of attributes which individuals consider common to the category. The second issue concerning cognitive categorization is how categories, once formed, are related to one another. There is evidence to suggest that categories differ in terms of how abstract they are. Abstract categories include members of less abstract categories such that cognitive categorization schemes form a 'cognitive taxonomy'. According to Rosch (1978), a cognitive taxonomy is

> . . . a system by which categories are related to one another by means of class inclusion. The greater the inclusiveness of a category within a taxonomy, the higher the level of abstraction. Each category within a taxonomy is entirely included within one other category (unless it is the highest level category) but is not exhaustive of that more inclusive category (p. 30).

Thus, for example, Kempton (1978) found evidence that individuals organize their knowledge regarding the common category 'cup' with a conceptual taxonomic grouping of five hierarchical levels of inclusion. The category 'utensils' was the most general grouping in the structure and specific types of cups such as 'Chinese teacups' were the least inclusive.

The existence of a taxonomic cognitive structure immediately raises questions concerning the level of abstraction used to refer to and understand the environment. If a taxonomy does, in fact, exist in the mind of an actor, then it is clear that any object could be referred to at more than one taxonomic level. A 'French restaurant' is also a 'restaurant'. It is also a 'place selling food'. If an individual is asked to classify a particular restaurant in a category (e.g. with the question: 'What type of business would you call this?'), which level of abstraction is used?

There is growing evidence to suggest that this issue is resolved by individuals relying upon one level of abstraction to describe everyday aspects of the world. That is, levels of a cognitive taxonomy are not used with equal frequency. It appears that one level of taxonomy is more informative and used more often than others (e.g. Rosch *et al.*, 1976b). Rosch *et al.* label this the 'basic level' of a taxonomy and suggest that

> . . . the basic level of abstraction in a taxonomy is the level at which categories carry the most information, possess the highest cue validity, and are thus the most differentiated from each other (p. 383).

They argue that the basic level of a taxonomy is usually of an intermediate degree of inclusiveness, although the specific basic level can vary across domains of knowledge (e.g. Dougherty, 1978). Very general and inclusive levels of a taxonomy are less informative because they are too general. To know that Harrods, for example, is a 'retailer' does not say much about the specific aspects of the business. Very specific categories are very redundant. To say that Harrods is a full-line department store is not that much different from saying that Harrods is a department store. According to *Rosch et al.*, intermediate levels of a cognitive taxonomy thus provide an individual with the most information about distinctions in the environment. Hence basic categories are more psychologically efficient and are, for this reason, more likely to be used in everyday situations.

When applied to the case of retailing taxonomies our outline review of cognitive theory would thus suggest that conceptual groupings of retail businesses would be organized as fuzzy sets of firms classified as equivalent by the decision-maker because they share some common attributes and are different from members of contrasting categories. Some members of each category of business should be perceived as more representative or more typical of the category than various borderline cases. In addition, conceptual groupings of retailers should appear to be related to each other in taxonomic fashion by means of class-inclusion. Although all levels of a retailer's taxonomic system should provide some information about similarities and differences in the environment, one level would be expected to be more fundamental. At this basic level, businesses should be perceived as most differentiated from each other. We examine the plausibility of these ideas in the next section.

Cognitive taxonomies in retailing: evidence and argument

Can the notion of a 'cognitive taxonomy' help to explain how retailers make sense of their competitive environment? Is conceptual knowledge about retailing businesses organized according to the principles discussed above?

We have recently been conducting research exploring the conceptual schemes of retailers in an effort to address these questions. We began with the assumption that common retail business categories such as 'department store', 'book store', and 'menswear shops' are primarily conceptual groupings that have been formed by retailers to make sense out of the diversity of retail businesses—i.e. they are grouped according to perceived similarities and differences among firms. As such, they should be organized in the mind of the retailer in terms of the general principles of cognitive categorization. Our research has attempted to ascertain whether this is indeed the case. Although our data are tentative, and at this time incomplete, they are sufficiently developed to illustrate the potential merits of studying the cognitive classification of retail businesses. Some of our findings are reported in this section.

The research was conducted in the community which serves as the home for the University of Illinois at Urbana–Champaign. The twin cities of Champaign and Urbana, Illinois, are located in the rural heartland of the USA. Total county population as of 1980 was approximately 160 000, most of whom live within 8 kilometres from the centre of the university campus. The concentration of the population around a stable university base has meant that the community is relatively prosperous, with low unemployment and supporting a considerable variety of retailing establishments. Most such firms are small shops privately owned by one or a few individuals. Because of its rural setting, the retail environment in the community is relatively isolated from outside competition (no communities of comparable size are located within a radius of approximately 60 kilometres). Therefore, area retailers compete principally among themselves for community business. Thus it can be assumed that environmental scanning and competitive strategy among the many merchants are focused locally, providing an excellent environment in which to study retail cognitive taxonomies.

As part of the study, local retailers (all of whom were owners, managers, or owner–managers of small firms) were contacted and asked to participate in a short interview concerning their 'perceptions of the retail environment' in the area. Most agreed, and those who did were interviewed in their place of business by a research assistant. The interview procedure itself was adapted from Kempton's (1978) work on the categorization of everyday objects. We began with the most general root category of 'retailer' and asked one sample of respondents to list the next most general *subtypes* of this more global class. Responses to this task were coded and summarized, and all unique subtypes were used as focal categories for another sample of respondents who likewise were asked to list all the specific subtypes of a more general class. These responses were again coded and summarized. The sampling procedure was repeated, with successive samples of respondents providing increasingly specific subtypes of more general categories, until several levels of a commonly accepted taxonomy of retail businesses in the area were uncovered.

Figure 3 shows a subcomponent of the complete cognitive taxonomy produced through the interview. The number of respondents listed in the right-hand column at any given level of the taxonomy is the size of the sample used to generate the subcategories immediately below that level. As can be seen in the figure, the root category of 'retailer' was cognitively separated by respondents into 'retailer of goods' and 'retailer of services'. The former category was subdivided into 25 more specific types of retailing businesses (see Table 1), three of which are reproduced in the figure: 'bar/tavern', 'grocery store', and 'confectionary shop'. Grocery stores were subdivided into nine subcategories, three of which were 'supermarkets', 'stop and shop convenience stores', and 'Oriental food stores'. Finally, convenience shops were classified into those that sell gasoline and those that do not. The

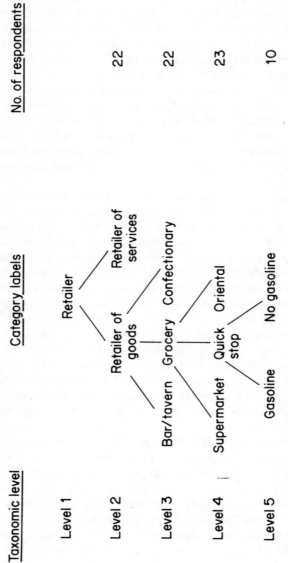

Figure 3. Cognitive subtaxonomy of retail businesses in Champaign-Urbana, Illinois. (At Level 3, respondents listed 25 business categories but only three are shown. At Level 4, nine categories were uncovered, but again only three are shown)

Table 1. Means, medians, and SDs of ratings of
categroy representativeness for twenty-five categories of retail businesses (based upon $N = 25$)

Category name	Mean	Median	SD
Department store	5.9	6.3	1.4
Book	5.8	6.0	1.2
Record	5.7	5.9	1.3
Drug	5.7	5.9	1.3
Variety	5.6	5.8	1.4
Hardware	5.6	5.8	1.4
Materials/supply	5.6	6.2	1.5
Gift	5.6	5.5	1.2
Sporting goods	5.5	5.6	.9
Shoe	5.5	5.8	1.4
Clothing	5.5	5.9	1.6
Grocery	5.4	5.7	1.7
Card	5.4	5.3	1.5
Jewelry	5.4	5.7	1.5
Electronics	5.3	5.6	1.3
Novelty	5.1	5.1	1.5
Confectionary	5.1	5.0	1.5
Furniture	5.0	5.5	1.8
Poster/art	4.9	4.4	1.7
Housewares	4.9	5.0	1.7
Fabric	4.8	4.5	1.7
Automobile	4.7	4.0	1.6
Gasoline	4.4	4.3	2.3
Bar/tavern	4.0	3.5	2.0
Real estate	3.4	2.8	2.4

structure in Figure 3 thus possesses five taxonomic levels of increasing specificity.

Figure 3 raises a number of questions related to the research and theory on cognitive categorization cited earlier. One question pertains to the internal structure of the categories in the taxonomy. In asking retailers to generate subtypes of more general cognitive categories we requested that they use as a basis for categorization those attributes related to merchandise offered, service, clientele, physical facilities, convenience, promotions, store atmosphere, and customer satisfaction. Thus, in generating subtypes, respondents presumably engaged in a number of attribute contrasts of various category members and segregated on the basis of some rough intuitive measure of cue validity. On this basis, the categories listed in Figure 3 are classes that differentiate members from dissimilar non-members. However, if conceptual categories possess indefinite boundaries (Rosch and Mervis, 1975), some members of the categories in the figure should be perceived as more typical of the higher-level category than others. That is, there should be perceived differences in how well the businesses at one level of the taxonomy represent the category at the next highest level.

We examined this issue empirically at Level 3 of the structure. We asked a separate group of 25 retailers to rate the degree to which they considered each of the 25 business categories identified at Level 3 in the taxonomy to be representative of the more general category 'retailer of goods'. One retailer from each of the 25 categories was included in the sample, and ratings were obtained on a seven-point scale varying from 1 = fits very poorly my idea or image of a retailer of goods to 7 = fits very well my idea or image of a retailer of goods. The means, medians, and standard deviations of these ratings are listed in Table 1. As can be seen, average and median ratings varied from a high of 5.9 (6.3) for the category 'department store' to a low of 3.4 (2.8) for 'real estate broker'. Clearly, differences in representativeness were perceived. This finding is even more striking given the fact that the subtypes of 'retailer of goods' were generated through interviews with retailers similar to those rating representativeness. Since frequency of mention of category members has been found to be positively related to the degree of member prototypicality (e.g. Mervis *et al.*, 1976), it is to be expected that the subtypes listed in Table 1 would be perceived as at least somewhat representative of a retailer of goods. This seems to be the case, since most of the 25 subcategories had mean ratings of '5' or more.

Somewhat unexpectedly, our data also indicated that, in general, respondents rated their own business category as more representative of a retailer of goods than did respondents from other businesses. Since each of the 25 types of retail firms was represented in the sample (this was verified by having respondents denote the one business type that most closely approximated that of their own), it was possible to compare self-ratings with the ratings of others simply by determining whether self-ratings were above or below the median ratings of the entire sample of 25 respondents. If no relationship existed between ratings of representativeness and one's own membership in a business category, by chance alone it would be expected that 50% of the ratings would be above the median rating and 50% below it. In fact, 17 of 25 ratings of own business representativeness were above the sample median ($x = 9.0$, $p < 0.05$). Perhaps the most extreme cases of this tendency are those of the automobile dealer and real estate broker. While both had very low median ratings of prototypicality in the total sample, the owners of the business rated themselves a '7' on this scale. Apparently, there is a tendency to perceive one's own business as representative of the category 'retailer of goods'. We have also obtained similar results at other levels of the taxonomy in Figure 3.

Another question raised by Figure 3 is whether all levels of the taxonomy are psychologically equivalent. According to theory, one level should be more 'basic' than others. Again, Rosch *et al.* (1976b) suggest that 'middle-level' categories provide the most information about the environment because of their high cue validities. Although we have yet to generate data necessary for a rigorous test of this assertion as it applies to retailer taxonomies, anecdotal evidence from our research suggests it to be reasonable. As part of our study, we asked groups of respondents to list as many attributes of the categories noted in Figure 3 as they could recall. Many of the respondents had difficulty listing meaningful attributes at the top two levels of the taxonomy, and those attributes that were mentioned were very general—such as 'sells things', and 'has customers'. Such difficulties and generalities could indicate that Levels 1 and 2 in the figure are not particularly informative of business similarities and dissimilarities in the environment. At the same time, Level 5 categories are highly similar to each other. In Figure 3, for example, the major differentiation between subtypes of convenience marts is the presence/absence of gasoline sales. It is not likely that this represents a very informative difference.

We suspect that the basic level in Figure 3 is one of the middle two levels (3 or 4). It is at these levels that clearer differentiations were often made between the attributes of the various business categories. Thus, for example, the category 'grocery store' was noted to have a 'wide selection of goods', 'shopping carts', and a 'check-out counter', while the category 'confectionary store' was perceived to have 'glass displays', to 'smell good', and to be located in 'small buildings'. These attribute differences are concrete and easily identified, much as would be expected if the categories 'grocery store' and 'confectionary store' are members of the basic taxonomic level in the minds of the retailers in our sample.

THE INFLUENCE OF COGNITIVE TAXONOMIES ON RETAIL COMPETITIVE STRATEGY: SOME GENERAL PROPOSITIONS

Earlier we raised the issue of how retailers scan the environment and engage in the firm-by-firm attribute comparisons necessary to pursue a strategy of enterprise-differentiation. We argued that, because of cognitive limitations, it is usually too psychologically unwieldy to make all possible comparisons among individual firms on a day-to-day basis. At the same time, we noted the desirability of using a mental classification scheme to simplify information-processing during competitive scans. Both cognitive theory and the initial results of our own research investigation give support to the view that such schemes are a component of a retailer's conceptual understanding of the business environment. It remains to discuss more specifically the influence of cognitive taxonomies on retail competitive strategy. We advance three general propositions.

Proposition 1: Retail decision-makers conceive of competitive strategy primarily at intermediate levels of their taxonomic understanding of the environment

This argument follows directly from the suggestion that middle levels of a cognitive taxonomy are more informative than others. In our derived taxonomy in Figure 3 we proposed that Levels 3 or 4 provide more useful and informative categories of businesses because of clearer differentiations among them. Following this line of reasoning, we would expect that decision-makers conduct their competitive strategy formulation primarily at these levels of generalization. If so, two fundamental aspects of competitive strategy would be affected.

First, a retailer's definition of his/her own business would take place using middle taxonomic groupings. Abell (1980) has pointed to the importance of business definition in the formulation of strategy by noting that before any strategy is set, a decision-maker must have some 'concept' of the business the firm is attempting to conduct. Restated in the terminology of the present analysis, a decision-maker must place his/her own business within the context of a cognitive taxonomy of the retailing industry. But at what level? Does, for example, a retailer selling foodstuffs to consumers consider the business to be 'retailing', 'goods retailing', 'selling groceries', 'quick-stop shopping', or 'quick-stop shopping with gasoline service'? Because of the class-inclusion relations implied in a taxonomic structure, all such definitions could theoretically apply to a business. However, our analysis suggests that middle-level definitions are used *most* frequently.

Second, once a retailer places his/her own business in a middle-level category it is likely that scans of other businesses in the environment will be focused primarily upon those within that middle category (and, of course, its subcategories). This implies, for example, that if the business is defined as a 'grocery store' the decision-maker will concentrate his/her firm-by-firm attribute comparisons only on those businesses subsumed by this category label (thus, convenience marts, supermarkets, etc.). Less attention would be given to members of alternative middle-level categories (such as taverns or confectionery shops). In this way, the use of an implicit categorization scheme permits the retailer to simplify environmental scanning by focusing resources on the routine of monitoring businesses in the same category. It also follows that any competitive moves will be aimed primarily at countering the tactics of firms within the same category rather than firms in categories not scanned. Of course, any shift in business definition would have implications for both environmental scanning of basic category businesses and the identification of strategic alternatives.

Proposition 2: Within a category, retail decision-makers focus competitive strategy primarily upon members of businesses that are most similar to their own

It was suggested that not all category members are considered equally representative of category membership, with some being considered more typical than others. Table 1 provides evidence for this assertion in retail taxonomies. Although Proposition 1 states that competitive strategy is focused upon firms considered to be in the same category as the decision-maker's own business, the varying degrees of representativeness of category members makes it psychologically inefficient to continually focus upon all category members with equal degrees of attention. It is tempting to posit that decision-makers resolve this issue by monitoring closely only those businesses that are most representative of the category, regardless of how similar such businesses are to his/her own. However, the evidence we cited above indicates that a general tendency might exist for retailers to consider their business to be the most representative of the category. We suggest that retailers use their own business definition as a 'cognitive reference point' (Rosch, 1975) and focus scanning and competitive strategy upon those category members most similar to themselves. Thus, for example, if the decision-maker has defined his/her business as a 'grocery store' it can be expected that monitoring and strategy *within* this category will be centred upon those subtypes of grocery stores most closely resembling the decision-maker's own. In this way, business definition acts to further reduce the potential set of firms that demand routine attention.

Proposition 3: Changes in retail business definition can be viewed as creative recategorizations of the business via vertical shifts to an alternative level in a cognitive taxonomy, horizontal shifts along the same level, or the creation of new categories altogether

Retail competitive strategy is a result of scanning and interpreting information from the environment in a creative problem-oriented way (e.g. Day, 1984). During such problem-solving a retailer's cognitive categorization scheme can act as both an inhibiting factor in the generation of unique approaches to the business as well as a source of much creative inspiration. On the one hand, once a business is defined in the mind of the retailer, at whatever taxonomic level, the focus of attention is relatively locked in by the cognitive structuring effect of the business category so defined. This structure provides the foundation upon which much of the environment is understood. Since new information about changes in the environment is interpreted from the perspective of a current business definition, the categorization scheme acts as a subtle filtering device which removes anomalous data. A certain degree of cognitive inertia is thus to be expected because of the fixation on a particular business definition at a particular point in time.

On the other hand, cognitive taxonomies develop over extended periods of time and contain much of what is important to know about a particular business environment. By actively using the entire array of conceptual knowledge at his/her disposal the retail decision-maker can gain creative insights into alternative ways of structuring the business to exploit profitable market opportunities. The motivation to look beyond an immediate business definition might come from events in the marketplace, from market data, from the suggestions of an expert consultant, or simply from personal reflection. However, because of the nature of mental categorization schemes, when such creative recategorizations do, in fact, happen, they are likely to take one of three forms.

First, the decision-maker might shift the definition of the business to a higher level in the taxonomic structure, thereby opening up the business to attribute-comparisons with a larger set of other firms (and also to a greater number of business opportunities). Levitt's (1975) analysis of the downfall of US passenger railroads is a particularly illustrative example of the possibilities inherent in vertical recategorization. Levitt argued that one problem at the time was the fact that railroad executives defined their business in a very limiting way—as a 'railroad' rather than as a 'transportation' company. In terms of the present analysis, railroad executives were psychologically constrained at one level of their cognitive taxonomy. If they had been able to shift their thinking to a more general taxonomic level, comparisons with a new set of alternative businesses could have been made (e.g. with airlines and bus companies), possibly with the result of a fresh look at profitable opportunities. Creative recombinations of the attributes of their business might then have been suggested.

Second, business definition can change horizontally along a taxonomic dimension. Using Figure 3 once again, such a recategorization would be apparent if an owner who defines his business as an 'Oriental food store' begins to reconsider this classification and shifts the definition to the category 'supermarket', perhaps because of the decision to carry more variety in groceries. Again, implicit contrasts with a new set of business firms could then take place.

Finally, entirely new conceptual categories can be invented by creatively recombining the attributes of different existing categories of businesses. A good example of such innovation is evident in the current restaurant business in Los Angeles, California. An article by Charles Keely in the October 1985 issue of *American Way* magazine describes two of the most popular restaurants in town as being renowned for their creative combinations of ethnic dining, 'La Petite Chaya', serving 'Franco-Japanese' cuisine, and 'Chaya Brasserie', noted for its 'Japanese–Italian–Californian' selections. In terms of the present analysis, 'French', 'Japanese', and 'Californian' restaurants could qualify as members of the more general category of 'ethnic restaurants'. The creative insight exhibited by the owners of these two restaurants was the intuitive leap of faith that a combination of various attributes of these subcategories would prove profitable in the long run. Although the initial resistance to thinking in such innovative ways is great (one owner noted that 'People said we were crazy. Stupid, maybe.'), successful recombinations of this sort will lead to permanent placement in a conceptual scheme when others begin to imitate their characteristics. Thus such hybrids would eventually become legitimate cognitive categories in their own right.

SUMMARY

We have suggested in this chapter that retail decision-makers are faced with complex information-processing demands in pursuing a strategy of enterprise differentiation. These demands stem primarily from the necessity of a constant re-evaluation of the relationship between the decision-maker's own business and others in the environment. We have argued that the infor-mation-processing load involved in this re-evaluation is reduced by organizing the multitude of businesses into conceptual categories based upon firm simi-larities and differences. Using grouping taxonomies permits the retailer to focus attention only upon a limited subset of businesses that have been defined, for whatever reason, as being strategically relevant to his/her own.

Although our arguments have been heavily oriented toward a psychological analysis of competitive strategy it is important to note that there exist parallels in the strategy literature which draw more heavily from the economic sciences. Of particular importance in this regard are the arguments by some theorists (e.g. Porter, 1980; McGee and Thomas, 1986) that a level of analysis between the aggregate industry and the individual firm is necessary to explain the competitive forces in an industry. In arguing that the industry level is much too broad to completely explain and/or describe firm competition, these authors have advocated the use of an intermediate level of analysis, clustering firms into 'strategic groups' based upon similarities in business strategies. Approaching the problem from a psychological perspective, we have argued that firm-by-firm analyses are pragmatically impossible for the decision-maker, and global categories of businesses such as 'retailing' are too general to be of much use in sorting our environmental complexity. We have suggested that decision-makers conceive of strategy by using intermediate levels of business aggregation that provide useful information about the differences among firms.

The principal difference between our arguments and those of other more popular approaches to competitive strategy thus centres upon our psychological orientation. We feel that analyses of decision-maker perceptions are important for at least two reasons. At minimum, an understanding of how retailers conceptualize their competitive domains is important as an aid to devising analytic models of firm competition. Since a major goal of such models is to help managers to formulate competitive strategy, knowing the psychological rules which structure a decision-maker's understanding of the environment will help to modify analytic models to fit with the retailer's own conceptual scheme. More importantly, however, knowing how decision-makers conceptualize their competitive environments will likely prove a useful source of information about the competitive forces in those environments. By sampling the conceptual schemes of industry participants and combining such schemes with those formulated on the basis of analytic criteria it should be possible to achieve a much more accurate description of the true competitive forces in the industry as a whole. Although at this point the methods and theories of the analytic approach are more developed, we have tried in the present chapter to provide the groundwork for equally useful developments in the measurement and theory of cognitive classification schemes. Our further research is focused upon identifying competitive groupings in retailing using both economic and perceptual bases to make sense of the complexities of the competitive environment.

REFERENCES

Abell, D. F. (1980). *Defining the Business: The Starting Point of Strategic Planning*, Englewood Cliffs, NJ: Prentice-Hall.
Day, G. S. (1984). *Strategic Market Planning: The Pursuit of Competitive Advantage*, St Paul, MN: West Publishing Co.
Dess, G. G., and Davis, P. S. (1984). Porter's generic strategies as determinants of strategic group membership and organizational performance.' *Academy of Management Journal*, **27**, 467–88.
Dougherty, J. W. D. (1978). 'Salience and relativity in classification'. *American Ethologist*, 66–80.
Duncan, D. J., Hollander, S. C., and Savitt, R. (1983). *Modern Retailing Management: Basic Concepts and Practices*, 10th edn, Homewood, IL: Irwin.
Garner, W. R. (1978). 'Aspects of a stimulus: Features, dimensions, and configurations.' In Rosch, E., and Lloyd, B. (eds), *Cognition and Categorization*, Hillsdale, NJ: Erlbaum.
Hawes, J. M., and Crittenden, W. F. (1984). 'A taxonomy of competitive retailing strategies.' *Strategic Management Journal*, **5**(3), 275–89.
Henderson, B. (1979). *Henderson on Strategy*, Cambridge, MA: Abt Books.
Hofer, C. W. (1975). 'Toward a contingency theory of business strategy.' *Academy of Management Journal*, **18**, 784–810.
Kahneman, D. (1973). *Attention and Effort*, Englewood Cliffs, NJ: Prentice-Hall.

Kempton, W. (1978). 'Category grading and taxonomic relations: A mug is a sort of a cup.' *American Ethologist*, 44–65.

Levitt, T. (1975). 'Marketing myopia.' *Harvard Business Review*, September–October.

March, J. G., and Simon, H. A. (1978). *Organizations*, New York: John Wiley.

McGee, J., and Thomas, H. (1986). 'Strategic groups: Theory, research, and taxonomy.' *Strategic Management Journal*, 7, 2.

Mervis, C. B., Catlin, J., and Rosch, E. (1976). 'Relationships among goodness-of-example, category norms, and word frequency.' *Bulletin of the Psychonomic Society*, 7, 283–4.

Porter, M. E. (1980). *Competitive Strategy: Techniques for Analyzing Industries and Competitors*, New York: Free Press.

Posner, M. I., and Keele, S. K. (1968). 'On the genesis of abstract ideas.' *Journal of Experimental Psychology*, 77, 353–63.

Rosch, E. (1975). 'Cognitive reference points.' *Cognitive Psychology*, 7, 532–47.

Rosch, E. (1978). 'Principles of categorization.' In Rosch, E., and Lloyd, B. (eds), *Cognition and Categorization*, Hillsdale, NJ: Erlbaum.

Rosch, E., and Mervis, C. B. (1975). 'Family resemblances: Studies in the internal structure of categories.' *Cognitive Psychology*, 7, 573–605.

Rosch, E., Mervis, C. B., Gray, W. D., Johnson, D., and Boyes-Braem, P. (1976a). 'Basic objects in natural categories.' *Cognitive Psychology*, 8, 382–439.

Rosch, E., Simpson, C., and Miller, R. S. (1976b). 'Structural bases of typicality effects.' *Journal of Experimental Psychology—Human Perception and Performance*, 2, 491–502.

Rosch, E., and Lloyd, B. (1978). *Cognition and Categorization*, Hillsdale, NJ: Erlbaum.

Tversky, A. (1977). 'Features of similarity.' *Psychological Review*, 84, 327–52.

Tversky, A., and Gati, I. (1978). 'Studies of similarity.' In Rosch, E., and Lloyd, B. (eds), *Cognition and Categorization*, Hillsdale, NJ: Erlbaum.

Tyler, S. (1969). *Cognitive Anthropology*, New York: Holt, Rinehart, and Winston.

Zadeh, L. A. (1965). 'Fuzzy sets.' *Information and Control*, 8, 338–53.

PART 2
Strategies and Strategic Positioning in Retailing

GERRY JOHNSON

An oversimplistic notion of strategy would be that businesses are simply reactive to the changing environment. This, of course, is not the case. Managers seek to formulate strategies which take advantage of a changing environment to the benefit of their business. To put it another way, they seek to tailor the strategies of their businesses to the opportunities they perceive in the environment. The chapters in this section of the book deal with strategies followed by retailers and, in particular, focus on the issue of strategic positioning in retailing. This needs some explanation.

Of all industry sectors, retailing is perhaps the closest, by definition, to the final consumer; and one in which the lessons of marketing are particularly apposite. In particular, the ideas of market segmentation and product and market differentiation are important in retailing and historically relevant. There has always been a highly differentiated approach to retailing. Historically this took the form of specialist shops, selling to particular communities—the local butcher or baker, the small grocery or hardware store. Today the strategies of differentiation are more sophisticated within a retail structure immensely changed. Nonetheless these strategies of differentiation persist, and in some respects are even more pronounced in the 1980s than they have been over the past two or three decades.

To some extent, with the transition from the small local specialists to the large multi-product retailer, retailing lost its character of specialization and differentiation. In many cases retailers became mass merchandisers. With the growth of supermarkets and the later introduction of self-service retailing in most of the sectors, strategies adopted by retailers focused primarily on methods of trading and the opportunity to grow bigger with wider ranges to cater for large volumes of customers. The later 1970s and the 1980s in the UK (earlier in the USA) have seen a more sophisticated approach to retailing develop. No longer do retailers expect to benefit simply by size and economies of sale. These do, of course, remain important parts of the retail equation but they are, in themselves, not seen to be sufficient. As we have seen in the previous section of the book, given a changing retail environment, successful retailers see the importance of positioning themselves carefully in terms of particular market segments and consumer expectations. In effect, the major chains are increasingly seeking for a more precise match between the strategies they are following and the consumer. Why should this be so?

Arguably, there are two bases upon which competitive advantage can be sought in retailing. One is essentially cost-focused and the other essentially product market-focused (see Figure 1). A cost focus seeks competitive advantage in terms of those elements of retailing on which the retailer can expect to exercise discretion over costs; on customer-handling, distribution, product-handling, the services and facilities offered, and on the ranges stocked and the volumes of products purchased. Most basically it was this focus which determined the growth of the supermarkets. They were able to offer not only vastly increased ranges of products but, through the design of the retail offering, much more competitive prices over the smallest specialist shops.

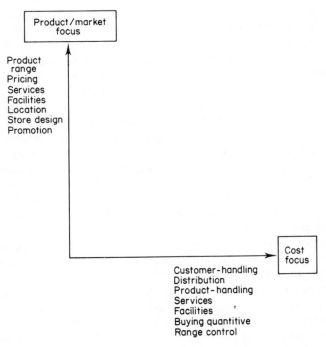

Figure 1.   Elements of competitive advantage in retailing

However, essentially this was a strategy to achieve competitive advantage over higher cost competitors. Whilst it provided the supermarket with a competitive advantage over the corner shop it was much more difficult for one supermarket to continue to achieve competitive advantage in this way over another. It could only do so through economies of scale and with increasing concentration in the industry. The danger was that such strategies reduced themselves in the marketplace to price wars.

The alternative was to seek competitive advantage through a product market-focus. Here the retailer seeks to provide an offering in terms of product range, pricing, services and facilities or store location, and design specifically tailored to consumer needs and essentially different from competitors. Here we have the basis of a market-positioning strategy.

Market-positioning

Market-positioning is the identification of particular customer expectations which provide opportunities to provide a specific retail mix which:

(1) Differentiates the business from competitors;
(2) Creates barriers to entry;
(3) Provides relative advantages over competitors and suppliers; and
(4) Serves as a base for further development of strategy.

As has been said, historically retailers have always segmented their markets. Traditionally this has been on the basis of geographical location of customers or of the product needs of customers; hence the local butcher, baker, etc. We have already seen, however, that retailers have learned that increasing size of operation does not necessarily mean that the benefits of segmentation must be lost. The identification of a clear market segment allows the retailer to tailor his retail mix precisely to that segment. His merchandise, pricing and location, store ambience and services can be planned around the central strategic thrust of satisfying particular consumer-expectations. In short, the opportunity is to adopt a precise positioning strategy, and this benefits from the advantages of differentiation shown to be so significant in achieving competitive success (Porter, 1980).

The benefits of a positioning strategy

By pursuing a positioning strategy the retailer aims to achieve a number of benefits:

(1) A positioning strategy may help to create a barrier to entry for competition. Once established and successful, it provides the retailer with a

unique image in the marketplace: competitors can only expect to imitate it, and must spend heavily, for example, in terms of advertising in order to convince the consumer that they can do better: or they must choose to find some other bases of positioning. So the retailer is in effect carving out a piece of the market for himself and, since he is first into it, benefits from the experience of operating in that part of the market. In retailing, where knowledge and understanding of customer expectations is so important, this experience is most valuable. It represents what has been called 'uncertain imitability' (Lippman and Rumelt, 1982). The effect is to reduce competition within part of the market.

(2) Market-positioning facilitates 'fine-tuning' of strategy. The experience gained by being close to the consumer helps in determining precisely what retail offering is required. The benefits of this are considerable:

(a) It reduces shopping around. If a retailer is able to design an offering to meet the particular needs of a market segment then it is quite likely that he will earn relatively high customer loyalty. Terence Conran observed of his Habitat operation that there would be many who might dislike it, but those who shopped at Habitat for furnishings would not wish to shop elsewhere.

(b) It can help reduce stock levels. The product range that is carefully positioned, targeted to specific customer needs, and planned with a thorough knowledge of those needs is also likely to be slimmer, item for item, than that of the retailer who relies on mass appeal. George Davies of Next, targeting a retail operation specifically at the 25–40-year-old fashion-conscious woman, launched a whole chain of shops with a limited product range; but one that changed frequently and left him with no more than a week's stock at the end of each cycle.

(c) It allows greater price-flexibility. A retailer able to provide very specifically for the needs of his customers and build up substantial customer loyalty can reasonably expect that customers may be prepared to pay slightly more for the merchandise.

(3) A positioning strategy may well increase the power of the retailer and reduce that of suppliers. In the UK in the 1960s, certainly, it was the manufacturers of consumer goods who prided themselves on knowing their markets. They claimed to be able to show retailers what the market required and how their products satisfied market needs. It was the era of mass branding, manufacturer-specified prices, and manufacturer-design promotions. Increasingly in the 1980s it is the retailer who can claim to know and cater for an identified market. Moreover, retailers, in seeking to position themselves differently from other retailers with whom they are competing, identify and demand that manufacturers meet the needs of specific market segments. Manufacturers can no longer enjoy the benefits of marketing to mass markets. They must meet the needs of

market segments for which the 'branding' may well now be more identified by the customer as the retailer than the product. No longer can
the manufacturer set the price; he may well have to negotiate and plan
promotional support with the retailer and, increasingly design products
specifically to meet the needs of that retailer.

There are, of course, problems and potential dangers in seeking to formulate positioning strategies. Perhaps the most fundamental is that the basis of
positioning may not exist at all; it may be that managers perceive an opportunity for differentiation which has no basis in commercial reality. The lesson
here, of course, is the need for careful and insightful analysis of market opportunity. However, even when there is a basis for differentiation the benefits
of precise positioning do need to be offset against some practical problems:

(1) How easy is it for competitors to imitate the strategy? Savitt, in the
chapter which follows, suggests that the ease with which retailers are able
to imitate others' strategies is increasing, and therefore the advantages of
positioning strategies are being reduced. This questions the extent to
which a given strategy really offers anything which is unique or to which
the skills or resources required to effect the strategy are difficult to
imitate without considerable expense or the investment of large amounts
of time. Skills and resources are, of course, in retailers often bound
together in individuals; often the successful strategy is largely dependent
on the executives who have launched and planned it. It is perhaps not
surprising, then, that those competitors who seek to imitate the strategies
of others may well see a basis for imitation in the acquisition of just
those executives.
(2) A very precise positioning strategy may entail the acceptance of shorter
time-horizons for the life of that strategy. The retailer who tries to hang
on to a successful formula may find that, not only have competitors
learned how to imitate it but that customer needs have changed, if only
marginally, and the formula is no longer appropriate. Ralph Halpern of
Burtons takes an aggressive view towards this problem; he regards it as
necessary to 'institutionalize change' in Burtons so that managers are
expected to change even a winning formula. Life-expectancy of one of
his womenswear shops would be no more than three or four years.
(3) Positioning strategies may be costly strategies. High costs may be associated with the continual change, with the high costs of research to establish
and meet market needs, of design and refilling, and of image-building
through promotion.
(4) There may be significant problems in re-positioning. It may be that
the strategy adopted by the retailer becomes so fixed in terms of the
infrasturcture of that retailer that the ability to re-position becomes very

Business Strategy and Retailing

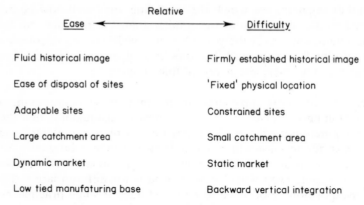

Figure 2.   Ease of re-positioning

difficult. Figure 2 highlights some of the problems of re-positioning in terms of relative ease and difficulty. A relatively fluid historical image is more likely to enable re-positioning than an image established over many years which has become fixed in customers' minds. There may be physical limitations of sites; if sites can be easily disposed of or adapted then the ability to re-position strategies is greatly increased over the retailer who is faced with relatively more fixed sites. So, for example, whilst small city-centre or precinct sites may be easy to dispose of or refit, a five-storey department store in a city centre may be neither easy to dispose of nor flexible to adapt. A large catchment area may also help re-positioning; the larger the catchment area, the more likely it is that the market can be segmented. A retailer with a small catchment area may be forced by default into relying on wider customer appeal for an essentially geographic market. Changing market conditions rather than static market conditions are also likely to help since they imply changing customer-tastes which is the basis of positioning strategies. Finally, the retailer that is vertically integrated into manufacturing is more likely to be under pressure to meet the needs of the manufacturer rather than the customer; this, too, is likely to reduce the possibility of re-positioning.

The contention here is that the logic of positioning strategies can be discerned in the strategic activity of many retailers. In the chapters which follow the issue is raised and discussed in various ways.

The chapters which follow

John McGee (Chapter 6) provides a useful introduction to this section. He places the strategic developments of UK retailing into existing frameworks of business strategy and discusses retail strategy at three levels—in terms of competitive strategy, functional and operational policies, and the business portfolio. In so doing he addresses the logic of different retail strategies. This is followed by a discussion of competitive positioning and diversification in retailing.

Leonard Berry and Julie Barnes (Chapter 7) build on the idea of 'positioning strategies' and argue that successful retailers in the USA have been those that have been able to achieve just the sort of clarity of purpose implicit within the notion of positioning. They develop a taxonomy of positioning strategies on the basis of their observations of successful retailers; specifically, identify *value retailing, time-efficient retailing, high-contact retailing*, and *sensory retailing*, and discuss the nature and benefits of these generic types.

Ronald Savitt (Chapter 8) reviews growth strategies employed by US retailers and suggests that although there is increasing evidence that they need to employ diversified positioning strategies, they are finding this increasingly difficult to achieve. He shows how the breakdown of traditional product bases of positioning has occurred in the USA with the growth of life-style retailing and the blurring of traditional retail boundaries. He concludes that new bases of positioning must be found and suggests that a 'production orientation' is a likely development. By this he means that retailers are likely to move into the provision of total processes of service to the consumer.

Retail image is an important aspect of a retailers positioning, but what does 'image' mean and how can it be measured? Gary Davies (Chapter 9) looks at positioning in terms of a market research approach to the mapping of comparative images of retailers. He shows how, within the context of the Manchester department store market in the UK, image-positioning was achieved and changed over time by various retailers.

The problems of re-positioning are reviewed in Joshua Bamfield's analysis of the problems of the UK Co-operative Retail movement (Chapter 10). He shows how the management 'recipes' and traditional values of the society, together with their ownership structure and decision-making processes have prevented the Co-Op from pursuing either an effective cost-reduction strategy or an effective re-positioning strategy, leaving them 'caught in the middle'. Building on this case study of the problems of strategic change he also draws some general lessons for retailers at the end of his chapter.

REFERENCES

Lippman, S. A., and Rumelt, R. P. (1982). 'Uncertain imitability: an analysis of interfirm differences in efficiency under competition.' *Bell Journal of Economics*, **13**, No. 2, 418–38.

Porter, M. (1980). *Competitive Strategy*, New York: The Free Press.

Porter, M. (1985). *Competitive Advantage*, New York: The Free Press.

CHAPTER 6
Retailer Strategies in the UK

Templeton College, Oxford

STRATEGY IN RETAILING

Traditionally, retailing has not been of interest to analysts of corporate strategy. It has not, at least until recently, shared in the dramatic productivity growth of manufacturing industry. It has remained low value added, for the most part quite fragmented with a very large proportion of working proprietors. Retailing is traditionally a way of life rather than an occupation, and its fragmentation has proved resilient in the face of change. A strategist would observe that this is an industry with few degrees of freedom: entry is easy, suppliers are relatively large, and competition appears to be spatially constrained but nevertheless intensive. Economists have for a long time regarded retailing as the prime example of monopolistic competition. Although there are substantial entry barriers in the form of locational advantages, a prime source of profits is operational efficiency—'retail is detail'.

This depiction of retailing is clearly a caricature. For a long time it has been clear that economies of scale have been available in purchasing, stock turnover, and skilled merchandising. Innovations in retailing have been plentiful—hire-purchase, self-service, mixed merchandising in supermarkets, and now electronic point-of-sale systems. Large retailers have long ranked high in UK corporate performance rankings (although this might reflect the tribulations of manufacturing industry as much as retailing virtue). However, now retailers in the UK are becoming the talk of the City with the recent take-over activity and the subject of new retailing concepts and the 'retailing revolution'.

Clearly, there is something strategic about retailing, and this is beginning to be reflected in recent journal articles and books (e.g. Baden Fuller, 1984; Blackwell and Talerzyk, 1983; Knee and Walters, 1985). Knee and Walters provide a survey of the application of strategic management concepts to retailing, together with case study illustrations of strategic moves by retailers. The building-blocks for their very useful and well-informed contribution are

89

Ansoff's (1965) product market matrix, Porter's (1980) competitive-strategy popularization, and market segmentation. This is a natural triumvirate in that the market is represented as the vital shaping force and strategic decisions are reflected in competitive strategy and diversification moves. From this, Knee and Walters build an array of strategy types in retailing, namely specialty conglomerates, consolidation and productivity, re-positioning, growth, diversification, entry, and specialization. These are intended to be illustrative rather than exhaustive of all possibilities.

Recent history and continuing trends reinforce the need for a strategic perspective. An earlier chapter in this volume (Segal-Horn, 1986) outlines the fundamental changes taking place in the market and the nature of changes in retailing. Step-changes in technology are set to make irreversible changes in the way retailers manage their (traditionally) centralized functions and their product range and mix. The availability of sites in the UK for out-of-town development is becoming problematic, although the prospect for systematic centre of town redevelopment looks somewhat brighter. The persistent buoyancy of consumer spending has favoured the income-elastic products (for example, non-food retailers). In general, the theme is one of 'change'.

This chapter introduces a framework for understanding strategy in complex organizations (Vancil, 1976) and shows how ideas of competitive strategy, competitive positioning, and product market strategy are evident in retailing. It explores particular ways in which generic cost and differentiation strategies are deployed and looks at the economics of related product lines. Finally, it reviews the nature of acquisitions in retailing and the economics of diversification.

A STRATEGY FRAMEWORK

Strategy within a company can be represented at three levels (see Figure 1): corporate, business unit, and functional (Hofer and Schendel, 1978; Pearce and Robinson, 1985). At the top, the corporate level is responsible for the overall performance of the firm in relation to the concerns of shareholders and society at large. In particular, it determines in which businesses the firm should be involved and provides the organization structure and financial context within which these businesses operate. The second level is concerned with defining how each business should compete and translating this into functional objectives for the third level. Business units are designed to focus on particular product-market areas within which can be identified specific market segments. The third level is composed of managers of product, geographic, and functional areas. It is their responsibility to develop objectives and strategies in such areas as manufacturing, marketing, finance and

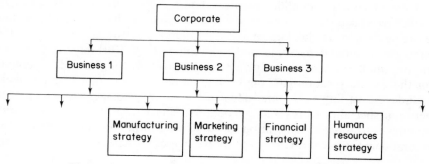

Figure 1.   Levels of strategy in multi-business firms

accounting, etc. Their prime responsibility is the execution of these functional strategies in support of the business/competitive strategy.

COMPETITIVE STRATEGY

The basic building-block in this framework is, of course, competitive strategy—the question of 'how to compete'. As is now well known, this derives from essentially economic concepts of the structure of markets, the configuration of buyers and sellers, and the nature of entry barriers. When put alongside underlying market characteristics and consumer buying behaviour we obtain the familiar prescriptions about cost-based and differentiation-led strategies moderated by the degree of 'focus' of the firm's operations (see Figure 2).

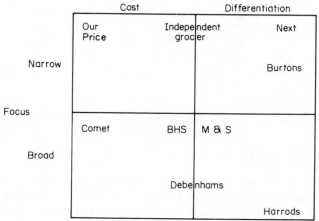

Figure 2.   Examples of generic competitive strategies of UK retailers

This, of course, simplifies greatly, if not excessively. It does, however, enable us to see distinctions between cost-based productivity and efficiency strategies (such as the largest food retailers) and the specialist, targeted strategies exhibited by some non-food chains (e.g. Burtons). Evident also are the small retailers whose forte is local focus but at higher cost. Claimants for the central position (the pig-in-the-middle slot) are many, and probably include the variety stores and department stores who seem to be squeezed between speciality stores and discounters. The virtue of these simple dichotomies is to force consideration of the driving forces and points of leverage behind competitive strategy—a point we elaborate below.

Competitive positioning

However, it is important to consider competitive positioning within specific sectors, e.g. grocery retailing within the industry. Unhappily, there is considerable and systematic overlap between apparently separate groups. For example, Marks & Spencer is officially classed as a 'mixed business' but it is the seventh largest food retailer. Incorporation of the obvious 'funnies' is not difficult but the interpretation of their underlying economics (facilities and operations shared with other product groups) may be less easy. Figures 3 and 4 illustrate competitive positioning in grocery retailing and in clothing.

Behind these two axes lie more variables than can reasonably be summarized. The persistent increases in market share of the large grocers (turnover in excess of £8 million), the relative sizes of stores opened and stores closed (see Tables 1 and 2), and the large number of closures of small units are a prime indication of the sources of cost efficiencies. If market coverage (number of stores and geographic coverage) and store size dictate the cost base, then differentiation is fuelled by product factors such as range and mix (for example, own-label versus private brands, 'value-added' products versus standard products), and by targeted customers (for example, local shops and convenience stores). However, differentiation can also come through the image presented by newer and larger retail outlets (for example, the 'style of trading' at Waitrose, Sainsbury, Tesco, Bejam, and Kwik-Save as well as local majors such as Morrisons and Hillards). This can be further reinforced by advertising of the store and its own brands (as opposed to manufacturers' brands). However, the classic example of differentiation must be Marks & Spencer with 'value-added' food products.

In menswear and womenswear the variety of strategy seems greater. The ability to secure scale economies is less pronounced with smaller store sizes and lower volume per product line. More important, the market probably segments more finely and on more dimensions enabling a wider range of targeting and store-presentation possibilities.

Table 1. Average size of grocery store openings and store closures: Multiples

	Openings	Closures
1974/5	11 200	1 500
1975/6	14 400	1 300
1976/7	16 000	2 200
1977/8	22 800	1 800
1978/9	21 400	2 200
1980	20 600	3 600
1981	20 850	4 000
1982	21 523	3 400

Source: IGD Research Service.

Table 2. Number of grocery outlets

	1971	1982
Multiples	10 973	5 430
Independents	86 565	44 174
Co-operatives	7 745	4 630
All	105 283	54 234

Source: IGD Research Services, Department of Industry.

Competitive positioning and the securing of competitive advantage is central to any discussion of strategy. However, strategy is concerned with the development and deployment of 'distinctive assets' (following Rumelt, 1981, assets which can only be imitated by competitors with uncertainty and at high cost), against specific market opportunities to achieve competitive advantage and longer-term superior performance. These generic descriptions catch the flavour of competitive position but do not reflect patterns of resource deployment. Nor do they lead to an unambiguous statement of strategy.

Product-market strategy

The firm's activities are constructed around a set of product markets. Its 'strategy' can be identified from the resource configurations in and around product markets. The principal variables which drive and shape resource deployment are the customer base, the physical configuration of markets and customers, the products/services offered, and the operations structure of the company (see Figure 5).

Strategy requires that these four variables are jointly determined with balance, consistency, and fit between them. Changes in markets may provoke

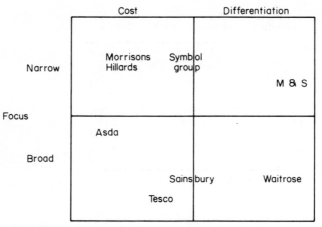

Figure 3. Author's perceptions of grocery retailers' competitive positions

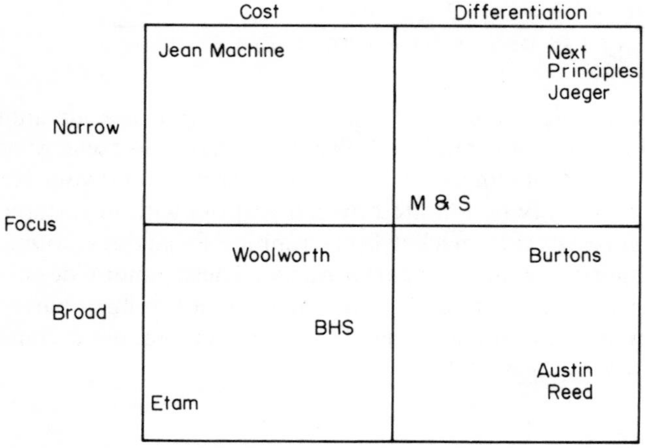

Figure 4. Author's perceptions of clothes retailers' competitive positions

resegmentation, a reorientation of the product-offering, changes in the structure of production and buying, and changes in merchandising and marketing. The distinguishing characteristics of alternative cost and differentiation strategies can be seen in the *identifiable assets*, *policies*, and *procedures* which lie behind these four variables. There are some fairly obvious lessons which follow from this. Resegmentation does mean changing the structure of operations. Growth through market (i.e. geographic) extension does require

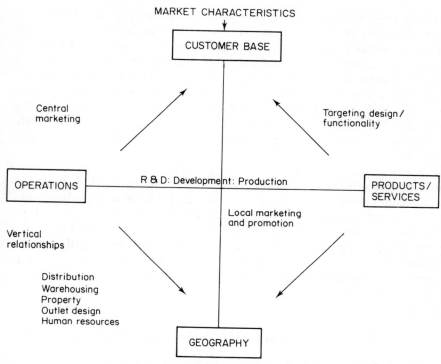

Figure 5.   Product market strategy

extensions to the existing infrastructure of distribution and the necessity for a property acquisition and management function. Operations technology changes will affect the cost-base and enable adjustments to the price–performance ratio offered for the customer and therefore perhaps some adjustments in the targeting.

Strategic fit

Taken more generally, there is a wider lesson: the idea of 'strategic fit'. First, there is the fit between the size of the target markets and the scale of the company. Small firms find it difficult to gain a competitive edge in large markets if only because the resource requirements to keep up with the markets in advance of competitors are too great. Smaller companies are increasingly at risk as markets become larger and more homogenous. This leads to the second point, that size and scale of the company limits the number of customers and accounts that can be efficiently serviced. 'Too many' accounts leads to a spreading thin of the assets and long lead times.

Third, there is advantage to be gained from a fit between the philosophies of the customer and those of the company. This amounts to a very high degree of customer orientation in terms of procedures such as the level of personal and direct contact (consumer clinics, for example) and in terms of empathy which enables customer issues to be identified and addressed with speed. Along with an extreme customer orientation goes flexibility in operations, the ability to redesign, retarget, present new ranges, adapt sites and stores, etc. This kind of orientation therefore has strong implications for the way in which operations are organized and conducted down to levels of quite fine detail.

In a recent speech on Burton's strategy (Scrimgeour, Kemp-Gee, 1984) Ralph Halpern blended together longer-term objectives with short-term management priorities: for example, 'a clear understanding of business planning', 'constant feedback of results', 'continuous interest in new things', 'focus our attention on change'. These are operational requirements of a clearly defined market position—'the policy is to develop tightly focused speciality chains catering for a specific target market'. The value therefore of an explicit statement of competitive strategy lies in its specific implications for the key operations of the business.

FUNCTIONAL (OPERATIONAL) POLICIES

Strategic fit implies some balance between the company and its target markets and the desired competitive position. Strategy can be identified by assessing the configuration of resources but is implemented through specific functions of the business, some of which play a key role with others taking minor parts.

Table 3 outlines for selected functional areas some of the key (strategic)

Table 3. Key functions in retailing

	Food	Department stores	Non-food
Property	Out-of-town sites	Refurbishment	Refurbishment
IT	Growing quickly	Some take-up	Limited take-up
Distribution and stockholding	Centralized	To/on site	Some centralization (carpets, furniture)
Product policy	(1) Diversification within food	Designer labels	(1) Specialization of ranges and/or
	(2) Non-food diversification (e.g. Tesco)	Broad lines	(2) Broadening of range
Stores	Superstores	Stores within stores	Redesign

issues and the ways in which they differ between food, department stores, and non-food. Finer categorization of stores would give more detail but the broad outlines can be seen. The food business is (relatively) capital-intensive. Its key functional policies reflect this and show the drive for productivity gains, scale increases, and low costs. Future developments in electronic point-of-sale systems are more likely to be seen first in food retailing because of the scale of potential cost savings (labour, stock control, sales information). As these systems are interfaced with distribution, additional savings should be available. Food is a price-competitive business and is set to become even more capital-intensive. However, entry by entrepreneurs (for example, Iceland, Cartier, Sperring) remains easy. Although economies of scale are the driving force there is no indication of oligopoly control even though concentration is rising (Baden Fuller, 1984).

Sources of differentiation

Non-food retailers show a different and more diverse set of functional policies. To the extent that specialization is the flavour of the times, most functional policies reflect the need to 'target' and therefore elicit operations with specific, tailored attributes. Figure 6 uses a value-chain structure (Porter, 1985) to illustrate the many possible sources of differentiation. The bottom half of the figure shows the sequence of retail operations and the ways in which they can convey distinctive and 'differentiating' characteristics. The top half shows how central functions can also create differentiating characteristics within each of the operational areas. Differentiation, therefore, arises in many different ways, and stems both from operations and from firm infrastructure. The essence of successful differentiation lies in its size and in its defensibility. The firm is investing in specific assets which perform distinctive functions, and which competitors find difficult to imitate. A characteristic of retailing and target marketing in particular is the layering of many sources of differentiation together. Individually these may be minor in effect but collectively are substantial. As a deterrent to imitation, targeting requires that many functions be reshaped in a particular fashion. Thus effective differentiation lies in the nature of the organization (compare Halpern's call to institutionalize change) rather than in one or two distinctive attributes, which can provide a focal point for competitors' attentions.

Product policy and the cost-base

Product range and mix are identified in Figure 6 as sources of differentiation. In addition, judicious choice of product mix can lower the cost-base by maximizing the amount of resources in the value chain that are shared by different product lines. In other words, the incremental cost per product line

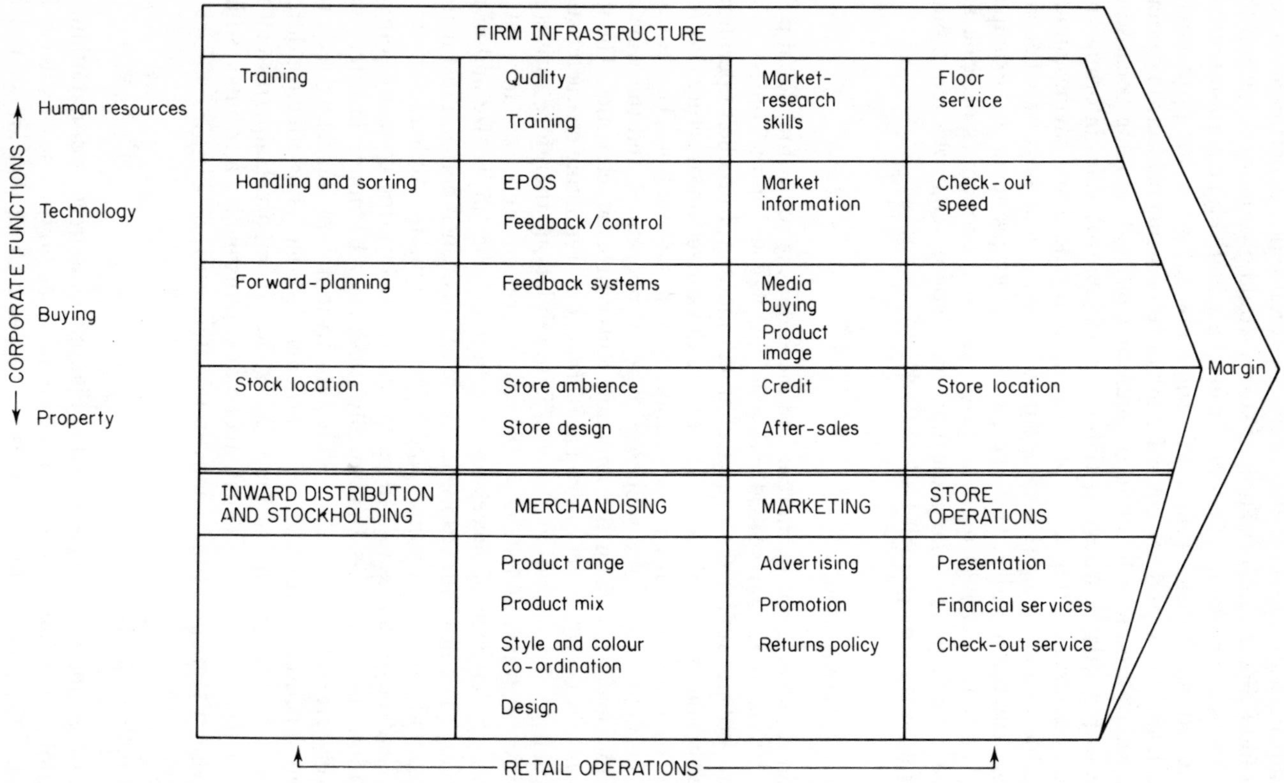

FIRM INFRASTRUCTURE

CORPORATE FUNCTIONS

- Human resources
- Technology
- Buying
- Property

RETAIL OPERATIONS

Margin

Human resources	Training	Quality / Training	Market-research skills	Floor service
Technology	Handling and sorting	EPOS / Feedback / control	Market information	Check-out speed
Buying	Forward-planning	Feedback systems	Media buying / Product image	
Property	Stock location	Store ambience / Store design	Credit / After-sales	Store location

INWARD DISTRIBUTION AND STOCKHOLDING	MERCHANDISING	MARKETING	STORE OPERATIONS
	Product range	Advertising	Presentation
	Product mix	Promotion	Financial services
	Style and colour co-ordination	Returns policy	Check-out service
	Design		

Figure 6. Possible sources of differentiation

is lower the more interrelated are the lines. Experimentation with the product mix can yield more attractive customer value to cost ratios by increasing the usage of fixed capacity and common systems, such as stock control. Figure 7 illustrates this. Offsetting these benefits are the costs of co-ordination, compromise, and inflexibility.

Co-ordination simply reflects the greater complexity of multiple products (and perhaps multiple segments). The temptation is to weaken the focus of target marketing by broadening the line and the segmentation in order to spread fixed costs more widely. Cost savings from shared resources are more securely achieved from product-diversification than segment-diversification. Compromise costs occur when the design of the value chain (i.e. the nature of the operations) is not optimal in serving the product or segment mix. This cost is the greater when the ability to serve the market need is also compromised. Inflexibility arises when shared functions inhibit adaption to changes in particular product markets (even though technical economies of scale might not be exhausted).

Implications for retail sectors

Many retail sectors are following a cost-based, scale-led strategy. We see the growth in superstores located out of town, with huge stockholding depots, computerized control, and modern distribution (for example, food, carpets, and furniture). Increasingly, DIY seems to be moving to the edge of town—63% of DIY outlets are now superstores and specialists (Key Note, 1985). Perhaps electrical goods retailers will develop in this direction? Clothing and footwear lie much more in the High Street comparison-shopping game, but where scale effects are less pronounced we see a variety of responses. There are downmarket, sometimes discount, operations, especially in electricals, furniture, and DIY, where price-comparisons are readily made and where there are potential scale effects. The traditional High Street multiples tend to be moving upmarket, emphasizing quality and service. Smaller chains and some multiples are target marketing and specializing in a dramatic way. Are the traditional variety stores getting caught 'pig-in-the-middle' with neither low cost nor distinctive differentiation? Given the size and location of their stores and the structured nature of their organizations, is it possible for them to re-position themselves? This applies also to department stores, but their store characteristics might more readily permit various experiments—stores within stores, galleria, etc.

THE RETAIL BUSINESS PORTFOLIO

The recent spate of acquisitions in retailing in the UK has brought to the fore the issue of the composition of retailers' business portfolios. Early

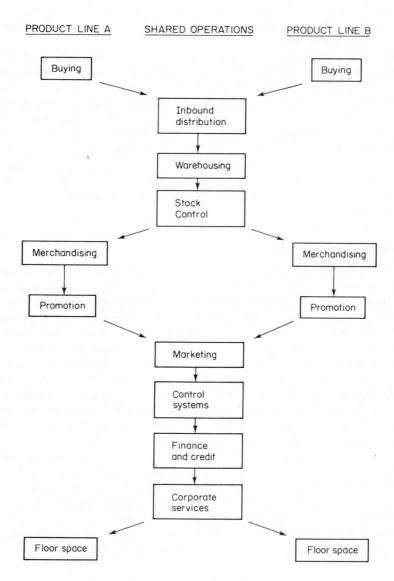

PRODUCT LINE A   SHARED OPERATIONS   PRODUCT LINE B

Figure 7.   Interrelated product lines

expositions of corporate strategy (e.g. Ansoff, 1965) blurred the distinction between corporate and business unit strategies by using the product-market matrix.

Although this claimed different degrees of risk inherent in the broad options of product development and market development it said little about ways in which competitive advantage might be constructed and risks managed. The Rumelt (1974) and Wrigley (1970) research introduced us to not just the terminology but the calibration of related and unrelated diversification. Supporting the strategy-structure stream of research (Chandler, 1962), it emphasized the importance of the organizational arrangements appropriate to the degree of relatedness among business units.

Additions to the existing business structure

The Ansoff matrix does have the advantage of showing alternative expansion paths. In the context of retailing, Knee and Walters (1985, p. 36) attach higher degrees of risk to moves further away from base (see Figure 8). However, this seems to beg a number of questions about the nature of these decisions. Moves into related products and related markets can be implemented in a number of ways (Figure 9). Product and market extension can be fostered within the existing business structure. For example, Asda's move south and Dee's acquisitions create growth through geographic market extension with attendant cost efficiencies from increased scale and buying-power. Similarly, product-range extension is shown by grocery retailers and, more dramatically, by Marks & Spencer's entry into food. Relatively risky

		MARKETS		
		Existing	Related	New
PRODUCTS	Existing	Internal growth	Asda Sainsbury	M & S France
	Related	Grocers – range extension	Principles for Men	Supermarkets – wines and spirits
	New	M & S – food	Dixons microwave	Sainsbury – Homebase

Figure 8.   Expansion patterns: retailing examples

diversification can thus be fostered within the existing business structure. The driving force here is the existence of a set of shared resources (for example, brand name, store operations, and buying infrastructure) and a property bank.

Similar to this is the use of the existing trading business, its infrastructure, control systems, and store operations to encompass new distinctly targeting activities alongside the traditional core business. Additional brands are the simplest example (C & A's Clockhouse, Sixth Sense, and Rockferry Trading Co. Brands). The distinctive targeting implied by this branding indicates that this is more than simple product-range extension. According to *Time* Magazine (1984) the Sears Roebuck attempt to lure younger, wealthier shoppers, offering them higher-priced, more stylish merchandise under the Sears brand name was a failure. The Sears 'stores of the future' now contain fashion labels endorsed by big names (for example, Arnold Palmer, Joe Namath, Evonne Goolagong).

More radical is the partitioning of large stores into smaller, better-targeted operations offering specialization along with a 'one-stop' appeal. Again the availability of resources with excess capacity is essential, but in this instance the existing business does not carry sufficiently strong or well-enough targeted appeal: an additional and distinctive competitive positioning is needed. These kinds of responses within existing business structures reflect the marked changes in the marketplace but, in addition, point to the inflexibility of the inherited stock of assets. Marginal or even incremental changes in the market appear to offer profitable opportunities, but can large retailers easily abandon their hitherto stable segments? The temptation to broaden the appeal to cover more segments can lead to a squeeze between pricy speciality stores and discounters (the classic dilemma for variety multiples). The more attractive route is therefore new branding and segmentation within existing sites, serviced by existing infrastructure.

New business units

New business units seem to offer a better solution to the segmentation challenge; at least, that is implied by the growth of and enthusiasm for 'speciality chains' such as Burtons, Hepworths (and now Dixons–Currys?). Although offered as a new concept in retailing, it is very familiar elsewhere. The keys to success are effective market-segmentation and targeting of the business coupled with the opportunity for business units to share some common resources and management skills.

Relatedness between old and new business units arises from common senior management, marketing, and control systems. However, the choice of separate business units rather than new in-house branding rests on the added market focus and pulling-power obtainable from distinctive marketing

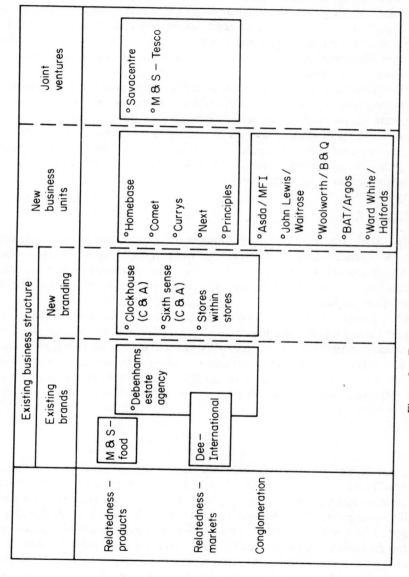

Figure 9. Examples of diversification in retailing

channels (stores primarily) and a dedicated operations structure. A weaker argument is the absence of suitable space in the premises of the existing business. In practice the development of new business units has been by acquisition (for example, Burtons) or development from scratch. The choice rests in part on the availability of High Street property. The existence of a suitable property bank is a *sine qua non* for speciality chains. However, other initiatives requiring scale are more suited to out-of-town sites where only new growth is practical.

In conglomerates the degree of interrelationship is much lower. Conglomeration sometimes results from the possibility of making once-for-all changes such as the turnaround of inefficient operations or the matching together of a limited number of complementary attributes (for example, Asda–MFI). In the extreme, conglomerate positions represent an investment in the underlying profitability of a new unit with limited possible enhancement of its competitive position from the parent.

Joint ventures

Finally there are an increasing number of joint ventures (Savacentre, Marks & Spencer–Tesco). In retailing, joint ventures seem to take place between producers of complementary goods. The aim is to tap new segments by creating a new infrastructure the costs and risks of which can be conveniently shared.

With a need for large scale, the expense of constructing out-of-town sites, and the difficulties of obtaining planning permissions the sharing of complementary expertise and costs seem very attractive. The danger for the partners is the (tacit) invitation of potentially dangerous new competitors into their own markets: i.e. Tesco entered the clothing market within its own store structure, whereas Sainsbury are positioned adjacent to this market through Savacentre.

SUMMARY

This chapter has been concerned with the nature of strategy in retailing. The traditional caricature of retailing and indeed the attitudes of retailers themselves suggest that retailing is predominantly the management of finely detailed operations. The proposition in this chapter is that retailing contains much that is strategic and that the retailing revolution itself requires a deal of strategic thinking for retailers. We have reviewed the notion of competitive strategy, noting the need for its explicit statement, and explored its meaning in terms of functional policies and its implications for the structure of operations. The discussion was then broadened to ideas of corporate strategy in which different kinds of business portfolios were examined. The underlying theme is the benefit obtainable from interrelationships—between products, product lines, brands, and businesses. Interrelationships are based on shared resources—shared elements in the value chain. These effects are seen first at operational levels as fixed-cost functions get filled to capacity first within the store (for example, shelf-space), then in the control and scheduling infrastructure, further then into marketing, merchandising, and positioning skills, and eventually in the role of top management. The extent of these common functions and therefore the importance of interrelationships may be the distinctive feature of retailing. As market conditions continue to change and as elements of the value chain continue to be transformed by information technology, the future for retailers looks like being even more 'strategic'.

The theme of this chapter has been the late arrival of strategy to retailing. The retailing revolution has significant strategy dimensions in terms of the scale of resources required, the commitment of companies to specific directions and the inflexibility in use of the specific assets employed, and the preemption of alternative investments. The types of strategy issue have been organized and presented under familiar headings of corporate, of business unit, and of functions and operations. A common theme of 'interrelatedness' is evident at each of these three levels. Interrelatedness allows the sharing of common assets, both tangible and intangible, between elements in a product line, within a business unit, and between business units. Retailers will find familiarity in the product-line discussion but a new dimension has begun to emerge in the last few years in the construction of well-defined business units and interrelated business portfolios. As the level moves from 'functional' through 'business' to 'corporate' the more important becomes the infrastructure and the managerial components of retailing. The traditional characteristics of retailing are changing. Capital intensity is growing; value added is increasing; the product/service definition is broadening and segmentation within this is increasing. Strategic decisions are more evident and more frequent.

Challenge for the future?

UK retailing companies have been extremely successful, but they have also been largely protected from direct competition. There is as yet no equivalent in retailing to the tough Japanese competitors cutting into UK manufacturing. As international competition increases, national shelters are, in general, weakened. However, UK retailing is quite well positioned to take advantage of the globalizattion of markets. Although conventional wisdom and certainly stock-market preference has it that retailing formulae and service concepts do not travel well (for example, Marks & Spencer in Canada, although the French outlets have now turned round), there are some examples of successful UK international retail operations. Laura Ashley, Habitat, Ward White—all have established themselves in the North American market.

The next set of strategic challenges for UK retailers may be expansion abroad or even incursions into UK markets from foreign retailers.

NOTE

This chapter has benefited from extensive discussion with Susan Segal-Horn. It was presented originally as part of a longer paper, 'Strategic Issues in UK Retailing', by McGee and Segal-Horn at the Workshop on Retail Strategy in November 1985.

REFERENCES

Ansoff, H. I. (1965). *Corporate Strategy*, New York: McGraw-Hill.
Baden Fuller, C. W. F. (1984). 'Rising concentration in the UK grocery trade, 1970–82.' In Tucker, K. (ed.), *Firms and Markets*, London: Croom Helm.
Blackwell, R. D., and Talarzyk, W. W. (1983). 'Lifestyle retailing: competitive strategies for the 1980s.' *Journal of Retailing*, **59**, 4, Winter, 7–27.
Chandler, A. D. Jr (1962). *Strategy and Structure: Chapters in the History of Industrial Enterprise*, Cambridge, Mass.: MIT Press.
Hofer, C. W., and Schendel, D. E. (1978). *Strategy Formulation: Analytical Concepts*, St. Paul: West Publishing Co.
Johne, F. A. (1983). 'How to lead by innovation.' *Management Today*, September, 90–5.
Key Note Publications Ltd (1985). *Do-It-Yourself*.
Knee, D., and Walters, D. (1985). *Strategy in Retailing: Theory and Practice*, Oxford: Philip Allen.
Pearce, J. A., and Robinson, R. B. J. (1985). *Formulation and Implementation of Competitive Strategy*, Homewood, Ill.: Irwin.
Peters, T., and Waterman, R. (1982). *In Search of Excellence*, New York: Harper and Row.
Porter, M. E. (1980). *Competitive Strategy*, New York: Free Press.
Porter, M. E. (1985). *Competitive Advantage*, New York: Free Press.
Rumelt, R. P. (1974). *Strategy, Structure and Economic Performance*, Cambridge, Mass.: Harvard University Press.
Rumelt, R. D. (1981). 'Towards a strategic theory of the firm.' Paper prepared for a conference on Non-Traditional Approaches to Policy Research, Graduate School of Business, University of Southern California.
Scrimgeour, Kemp-Gee & Co. (1984). *Retail Review*, No. 13, October.
Segal-Horn, S. L. (1986). 'The retail revolution.' In Johnson, G. (ed.), *Retailer Strategies in the UK*, Chichester: John Wiley.
Tichy, N. M. (1982). 'Managing change strategically: the technical, political and cultural keys.' *Organizational Dynamics*, Autumn, 59–80.
Vancil, R. (1976). 'Strategy formulation in complex organizations.' *Sloan Management Review*, Winter, 4–10.
Wrigley, L. (1970). *Divisional Autonomy and Diversification*. Unpublished DBA thesis, Harvard Business School.

CHAPTER 7
Retail Positioning Strategies in the USA

LEONARD L. BERRY
Center for Retailing Studies, Texas A&M University
and
JULIE A. BARNES
College of Business Administration, Texas A&M University

The immediate future holds some of the greatest challenges the retailer in the USA has ever faced. Although a myriad of factors are involved, three prominent environmental changes account for a great deal of the mercurial nature of the retail business in the USA today.

(1) *Economic conditions* in the USA have forced retailers to re-examine their corporate strategies. The days when success was dependent upon an ever-expanding market are gone. Among the economic developments directly affecting retailing are the following:

(a) 1985 retail figures indicate a real growth of only 3% and there does not seem to be any reason to predict a great variance from this figure for some time (*Kiplinger Washington Letter*, 1986);
(b) Consumer savings are low and indebtedness is high (*Chain Store Age Executive*, 1986a);
(c) High housing, utility, and medical costs take up more disposable income, and spending on general merchandise has dropped 24% since the mid-1970s (Main, 1985).

(2) *Saturation of the retail market* has evolved as a particularly vexing problem of the 1980s. As a result of the population and economic growth in sunbelt states in the late 1970s and early 1980s, US retailers aggressively expanded into this part of the country, often without regard to the plans of competitors to do likewise. 'Too many retailers are chasing the same customer,' say James Williams, President of the National Retail Merchants Association (Main, 1985).

According to *Shopping Center World*, the number of shopping centers in the USA increased by 70% and square footage by 80% from 1974 to 1984, whereas the population only rose by 12% (*Wall Street Journal*, 1984). Consequently, many large retailers are today sharply curtailing their expansion activities and are instead stressing the efficiency of each of their stores. Return on investment has become more significant than sales revenue alone.

Additionally, an ever-increasing number of foreign investors are competing for the same market. For instance:

(a) Laura Ashley, a women's fashion and home furnishings chain, opened 23 units in 1985 alone and reported US sales in excess of $52 million (*Chain Store Age Executive*, 1986b).
(b) Biggs, a French hypermarket selling food and non-food items, opened its first store in the USA in October 1984 and in 1985 enjoyed $100 million in sales (*Chain Store Age Executive*, 1986b).

(3) *The demographics of the American buying public* are in a constant state of change. Retailers cannot expect to simply mass merchandise, and, indeed, the rise of specialty retailing in the USA is a clear indication that many retailers recognize the strategic significance of a more heterogeneous population. Speciality retailers in the USA experienced sales growth of 56% from 1977 to 1982. This is in contrast to a 37% increase for department and variety stores during the same period (Buchsbaum, 1985). Identification of target markets has become increasingly vital to the survival of any firm. The most salient characteristics of American demographics include the increasing number of senior citizens, childless couples, Hispanics, and the shrinking pool of 18–24-year-olds. The following figures (Koehn, 1986) serve to underline the importance of these demographics.

(a) Couples without children make up 30% of American households.
(b) There are 42 million people in the over-55 age segment: 77% of all financial assets belong to those over 50.
(c) In 1984 there were more than 17.6 million Hispanics with a combined earning power of $70 billion a year.
(d) There will be 2–3% fewer 18-year-olds each year until the year 2000.

The implications of these numbers are numerous and will require a great deal of analysis by US retailers. For instance, senior citizens will spend some of their discretionary income on leisure items and services, whereas the decreasing number of 18-year-olds will impact upon the number of entry-level personnel available to many retail operations.

All these factors combine to create an intensely competitive atmosphere. Marketing strategies which profited the American retailer in the past are no longer sufficient. In fact, most industry experts predict a general 'shakeout' in the late 1980s, allowing only the most aggressive and creative firms to remain.

Retailers surviving this shakeout will be effectively positioned along one or more of four dimensions: *value retailing, time-efficient retailing, high-contact retailing*, and *sensory retailing*. These dimensions, which could be pursued in various combinations, seem to offer the best opportunities in retailing's turbulent world (Berry, 1982).

VALUE RETAILING

Value retailers focus on providing, and being perceived as providing, a 'package' with better value than that of competitors; they stress the strong benefits-to-cost ratio of their products. Best Products, Walmart, Target, and K mart all exemplify the potential of positioning along the value-retailing dimension. Although value retailing has long been important, it became more important during the decade of the 1970s with inflation rates at or near double-digit levels. Today, a vast number of American consumers are cautious and value-oriented when they shop; they want to get their money's worth. These value-conscious consumers want—and increasingly insist upon—good value, not merely low prices.

A case in point is the K mart Corporation. After successfully inundating the US retail market with discount outlets which reached 80% of the American population, K mart found its earnings slumping in the early 1980s (*Business Week*, 1984). Subsequent research pinpointed the problem—consumer preference had shifted. Buyers were attracted to newer, more creative discount stores which offered more brands, flashier merchandising, and emphasized value over price.

The retail warehouse

Value retailing is applicable to many lines of trade and retail formats. One format likely to grow in prominence in the 1980s is the retail warehouse. The true warehouse outlet has the following characteristics:

(1) Large, low-cost physical facilities;
(2) Vertical rather than horizonal merchandise displays and warehouse fixturing;
(3) Elimination of all non-essential services;
(4) Reliance on price as the primary appeal (Berry, 1982).

One company which has successfully incorporated these principles is IKEA—a Swedish-based furniture retailer in Philadelphia, Pennsylvania. Offering knock-down furniture at low prices, their customers select furniture from showrooms and pick up their purchases in the warehouses with an oversized shopping cart. Few managers and minimal services are available. Housed in a sprawling two-storey building, the store covers 165 000 ft² and is located on reasonably priced real estate. The potential success of this format is evidenced by the fact that IKEA's store was attracting 30 000 customers a week during its first year of operation.

Warehouses which cater to members of various consumer groups (also known as wholesale clubs) have also shown a great deal of promise as a retailing format. Restricting their market to small businesses and consumer 'groups' (such as government employees), these stores offer no amenities and advertise very little. However, low overheads, membership fees, and rapid inventory turnover allow them to feature big bargains that are 20–40% below supermarket/discount store prices.

Another novel application of warehouse retailing is the warehouse home-improvement centre. Operating on warehouse principles, this appeals to value-conscious consumers in two ways: it underprices competition through low-cost operations and it sells DIY merchandise that may lead to further economies for the consumer.

Off-price retailing

Another value-retailing format that has grown rapidly in the 1980s is 'off-price' retailing. These stores emphasize brand-name merchandise procured at below wholesale costs and sold to consumers at significantly discounted prices.

Although off-price retailing is most common in apparel, it has spread to other lines of trade (for example, pharmacies, optical shops, and bookstores). Off-price footwear and apparel sales grew from $3 billion in 1979 to $8.5 billion in 1984. More than 300 malls dedicated to off-price retailing of items ranging from linens to furniture were in existence by mid-1985 (*Marketing News*, 1986).

The growth of off-price retailing is having several effects. One is a shakeout among off-pricers—the market simply cannot bear the overwhelming number of off-pricers competing within the same formats. Consequently, it is 'survival of the fittest' time, and many off-price competitors will be leaving the market. Second, department stores have been forced to respond, and have done so with more private branding, aggressive price-promotion of brand merchandise, and upgraded commitments to customer service. Additionally, because of the intensely competitive nature of the industry and its phenomenal growth, the amount of quality merchandise available to off-price firms is limited.

In spite of these complicating factors, the future of off-pricing is good. In fact Management Horizons, a leading retail consulting firm, projects that the off-price sector will capture almost 13% of the total apparel and footwear sales in the USA by 1990 (*Retail Control*, 1985).

TIME-EFFICIENT RETAILING

Time-efficient retailers seek to help time-poor consumers to save time when shopping. Retailers positioning themselves along the time-efficiency dimension attempt to make their stores more convenient to get to and through or to make shopping possible without going to a store at all.

Time-efficient retailing is becoming increasingly important as a large and growing number of consumers become 'time-buyers' (Berry, 1982). In short, consumers may be more protective of their time than their money.

Food retailing

The biggest winners of the 1980s in food retailing have been larger warehouse stores and superstores. The most likely explanation for the performance of these types of stores is their ability to combine time-efficient retailing with value retailing. These large stores tend to be quite price-competitive while allowing consumers to find all the items they need under one roof. Today, there are 5 000 superstores in the USA, and while they represent only 3% of the 160 000 food stores, they account for 30% of sales. A Newspaper Advertising Bureau report, *Toward Tomorrow*, predicts that by the year 2000 the total number of food stores will decrease to 120 000, but the number of superstores will double to 10 000 and will account for 50% of sales.

Catalogue retailing

Another form of time-efficient retailing that should continue growing strongly is catalogue retailing; few sectors of retailing have been as dynamic in recent years. The synergy of computer, credit card, and telephone technology and the consumer's need to save time has encouraged more shopping without stores. In fact, American consumers spent over $41 billion in 1984 and over $45 billion in 1985. It is estimated that 8.5 billion catalogues were mailed in the USA in 1985 (*Business Week*, 1985).

Two aspects of catalogue retailing that bear examination are 'catalogue overload' and increasing catalogue specialization. 'Catalogue overload' is a condition brought on by the profusion of catalogue mailings in the USA. Since catalogue retailers build their mailing list on the basis of past purchase behaviour, households buying from catalogues get bombarded by even more catalogues. Also, a recent study by Stone and Adler, a Chicago advertising agency for direct marketers, found that 43% of US household surveyed are downright anti-catalogue (*Fortune*, 1986b). Consequently, many firms are beginning to cull their mailing lists to identify unresponsive clients. Efforts are then intensified towards those consumers who have been responsive in the past.

Specialization (or targeting) has also changed the complexion of the trade. The preponderance of mail-order houses in the USA today market to very precise, well-defined niches. General merchandising, once the principal form of catalogue retailing, is no longer cost-effective. Montgomery Wards, a department store chain will a 113-year-old tradition of cataloguing is a prime example. In August 1985 they ceased publication of their annual mailing, citing $50 million a year in losses.

Electronic catalogue retailing

Recently developed, this form of catalogue retailing has the potential to save both the consumer and the retailer considerable time and money. Unfortunately, only one manifestation of the genre, in-store electronic kiosks, has been widely tested to any practical degree. Very simply, these systems employ free-standing terminals which allow the consumer to order a variety of hard goods at discounts of usually 20–40%.

Currently, several supermarket chains are testing consumer reactions to this application of electronic retailing. In fact, one supermarket executive remarked 'We look at electronic shopping as another extension of the supermarket industry' (*Chain Store Executive*, 1985a). The value provided to the consumer is just one of the more appealing aspects of electronic shopping in retailing centres. The space saved which merchandise such as appliances and housewares would otherwise occupy and the ability of the retailer to offer a greater assortment of goods would seem to render the concept irresistible.

An electronic teleshopping revolution in American retailing is not imminent, however. The rest of the 1980s should be characterized by considerable experimentation with electronic teleshopping; eventually the winners and losers will become clear. In 1990, however, the telephone should still be the dominant technology for ordering merchandise from the home, and most consumers will still shop at stores most of the time. Reading about experiments with electronic teleshopping around the country is intoxicating. It is easy to forget that electronic teleshopping is a discontinuous innovation, requiring consumers and retailers alike to learn new behaviour. In fact, a recent survey conducted by *Chain Store Age Executive* (1985b) found that only 12% of those with current access to cable television shopping channels are 'at least somewhat likely' to make a purchase through electronic in-home shopping systems.

HIGH-CONTACT RETAILING

Whereas value retailing focuses on the economics of transactions, and time-efficient retailing on the convenience of transactions, high-contact retailing focuses on human performance in the form of considerable contact between retail personnel and the customer. Service becomes part of the product; service is what makes the difference. For many retailers—especially those handling ego-intensive merchandise lines—the best opportunities in the 1980s will be in adding service rather than eliminating it. These retailers will be responding to still another evolving consumer orientation; namely, the 'I am an individual' consumer. Fostered by rising educational levels and emerging quality of life values on the one hand, and by institutional bigness, depersonalization, and service reductions on the other, a very large number of consumers today are fiercely protective of their individuality.

With high-contact retailers there is often considerable contact between store personnel and customers during the crucial search and decision-making stages. Accordingly, the competence and attitude of its personnel can figure prominently in a high-contact retailer's image and sales. Matters such as personnel selection, training, supervision, and compensation are especially important for high-contact retailers.

We can expect more high-contact retailers to attempt to serve smaller numbers of people extremely well at a premium price. Individual customer records will be kept, customers' names will be known (and used) by store personnel, and more personalized methods of promotion (for example, a personal letter) will be emphasized. Sales personnel in these stores will be better trained in product knowledge and in selling skills than is customary in retailing. Retailers offering merchandise that is ego-intensive and that is purchased on a recurring basis (for example, fashion apparel, home furnishings, and art work) are the most likely to adopt this positioning strategy.

Nordstrom's, a highly successful department store chain on the West Coast of the USA, has its sales personnel keep notebooks on 'client' dress, shoe, and lingerie sizes. They will also assemble co-ordinated outfits from various departments in the store while the client runs errands or relaxes. An average sales per square foot of retail space in 1983 of $248 would seem to confirm the advisability of their high-contact marketing strategy (Bellew, 1984).

In addition to adding services designed to 'facilitate' the sale of merchandise, many high-contact retailers are also adding 'revenue-generating' services, i.e. services for sale. These retailers are attempting to capitalize further on existing resources (reputation, personnel, and facilities) and increase store traffic, sales of related merchandise, and institutional distinctiveness. A growing number of general merchandise and specialty retailers have been adding such revenue-generating services as beauty-care systems, colour analysis, aerobics classes, weight-control clinics, dental care, tour packing, restaurants, financial services, and gourmet cooking classes.

SENSORY RETAILING

Still another important positioning dimension is sensory retailing. This focuses on the shopping experience itself. The attempt is made to inject excitement and novelty into the shopping experience; indeed to make shopping more than shopping.

Although sensory retailers sometimes use sound and smell for sensory stimulation, their chief tool is the stunning visual effect—a collage of architectural and lighting effects, graphics, display techniques, and merchandise assortments—that makes the store unique. Sensory retailer trade on the unusual; they view themselves as being in showbusiness.

In fact, one of the latest developments in merchandising—the fashion video—requires a great deal of cinematic talent. Featuring sophisticated visual effects, miniplots, and sound tracks, these films are shown on television screens in department and speciality stores to advertise ready-to-wear apparel. 'It is the single most influential selling tool of the 80's', according to one vice-president of Associated Merchandise Corporation (*Newsweek*, 1985).

Although sensory retailing is especially suited to fashion merchandise retailing, this is not its only application. For example, independent food chains like Byerly's in Minneapolis, Minnesota, have successfully used sensory strategies. One of Byerly's newer suburban stores has 90 000 ft^2 of retail space, carpeting throughout, multi-coloured wallpaper, and a 80-ft^2 chandelier hanging from the ceiling. The store carries about 18 000 items, including many specialty food items.

Clearly, however, fashion goods retailers are the most active proponents of sensory retailing. Many are attempting to combine efforts in sensory retailing with efforts in high-contact retailing. They are trying to appeal to the consumer's senses and ego.

Despite the sky-high costs of constructing new stores and a general slowing of new-store development, we can expect to see more architecturally innovative retail facilities like the downtown retail centre in Indianapolis, Indiana, that will include a concert hall as one of its anchors. As pointed out by the builder of the project, 'The draw of theaters, museums and other cultural attractions provides a strong environment for the sale of goods and services' (*Chain Store Age Executive*, 1986).

SUMMARY

Positioning-identifying and occupying an available market position is a key strategic response to the intense competition retailers are experiencing. The most successful retailers in the USA are positioning themselves along one or more of these four dimensions: value retailing, time-efficient retailing, high-contact retailing, and sensory retailing. These are the principal positioning opportunities for today and tomorrow. Retails need to be very good in at least one of these dimensions to survive the tough competitive realities characterizing the American market. Retailing's winners all stand for something; they are distinctive, 'first choice' companies. They have a *raison d'être*.

REFERENCES

Bellew, P. A. (1984). 'Nordstrom strategy of coddling shoppers facing challenge in california expansion.' *Wall Street Journal*, 10 May, 33.
Berry, L. L. (1979). 'The time-buying consumer.' *Journal of Retailing*, Winter, 58–69.
Berry, L. L. (1982). 'Retail positioning strategies for the 1980's.' *Business Horizons*, November–December, 45–50.
Buchsbaum, S. (1985). 'A nation of shopkeepers.' *Inc.*, November, 66.
Business Week (1984). 'K Mart: the No. 2 retailer starts to make an upscale move—at last.' 4 June, 50.
Business Week (1985). 'A shakeout has mail-order houses aiming at smaller targets.' 9 September, 98.
Chain Store Age Executive (1985a). 'In-store retailing goes video.' October, 5.
Chain Store Age Executive (1985b). 'Shopping by TV or PC: is it Viable?' October, 12.
Chain Store Age Executive (1986a). 'Analysts cherry picking retail stocks.' April, 48.
Chain Store Age Executive (1986b). 'The new immigrants.' February, 16.
Fortune (1986a). 'Shopping Swedish-style comes to the US.' 20 January, 63.
Fortune (1986b). 'Catalog fallout.' 20 January, 63.
Gilman, H., and Weiner, S. (1984). 'Oversupply of retail outlets is seen as big cause of holiday price cuts.' *Wall Street Journal*, 8 December, 33.
Higgins, K. T. (1986). 'Retail strategies always evolving.' *Marketing News*, 31 January, 6.
Kiplinger Washington Letter (1986). 17 January.
Koehn, H. E. (1986). 'Historical and future perspectives on consumers.' *Zale Retailing Issues Letter*, **1**, No. 3.
Main, J. (1985). 'Merchants' woe: too many stores.' *Fortune*, 13 May, 62–72.
Newsweek (1985). 'Dressing up with FTV.' 7 January, 37.
Wintzer, F. W. (1985). 'The future of off-price retailing.' *Retail Control*, January, 21–3.

CHAPTER 8
American Retailing Strategies and the Changing Competitive Environment

RONALD SAVITT
School of Business Administration,
The University of Vermont

INTRODUCTION

The complex relationships between American retailing and the changing competitive environment are massive and a comprehensive understanding of the issues would go far beyond the present discussion. Yet even a discussion of selected issues can be informative for students of retailing in their attempts to understand change in retailing and in their needs to develop relevant retail strategies. The present discussion is limited in several ways. First, the period has been limited to the decade of the 1980s; this decision has been arbitrary and the reader is advised that many of the trends discussed have their origins in previous eras. Second, the discussion focuses on the large, corporate mass-merchandise retailers including department stores, 'discounters', drug chains, variety stores, etc. These retailers cut across geographic areas, product lines, and management practices. Third, the competitive environment is viewed at a macro level which is concerned with structural changes of firms and general competitive activities. Fourth, little attention has been paid to the whole host of environmental factors which directly and indirectly shape competitive practices. It is not that these are unimportant, there is simply limited space. Finally, the dynamic interrelationships between the large mass merchandisers and the small retail firms are not considered, in spite of the fact that they are important in understanding the competitive processes.

The analysis is built around a central theme, the new-growth strategies of these retailers. Such strategies are aimed at increasing profits and return on assets and they are pursued basically through market development, expansion, and diversification. The first is the strategy of growth through the expansion of operations into new geographic markets. The second represents a new definition of the retail function, including the incorporation of production-oriented functions. The third incorporates growth through new retail ventures in present markets or in new ones. While growth is not new in retailing, the present growth strategies are more clearly focused and reflect formal market planning, a process not extensively used in retailing up to now. Underneath these strategies is a realization that market penetration, expansion of present operations in current markets, will not sustain desired goals. An underlying principle driving many of these retailers is their goal to obtain greater and greater proportions of individual consumers' expenditures for, but not limited only to, retail goods and services.

These forces require that retailers must pursue growth strategies which provide greater differentiation from their competitors. Within the search for differentiation one finds a diffusion of competitive techniques as a result of new technology. Retailers of all sizes can almost instantaneously imitate the competitive activities of others. As a result, retailers are finding it increasingly difficult to differentiate themselves. Product-line programmes, promotional price programmes, and location decisions have not been as successful as hoped. Retailers are searching for means of more fully differentiating themselves and thus realizing their goals.

This chapter has three sections; a discussion of retailing and the new competition, general evaluation of these new retail strategies, and a discussion of retailing and production orientation. The last section discusses this retail strategy that might possibly evolve as the result of the present competitive conditions.

RETAILING AND THE NEW COMPETITION

Overview

One of the most dynamic sectors of every economy from least developed to most developed is retailing. Although competition among American retailers has always been substantial, the competitive environment is rapidly changing. While many of the changes have been taking place over the past two decades, they have been accelerating at the same time that other competitive practices are diffusing throughout retailing. The clear boundaries which were once helpful in understanding types of retailers and their competitive behaviours have all but disappeared. Not so many years ago it was possible to conduct meaningful analysis of inter-market and intra-market competition by focusing on size of firm, products sold, markets served, and marketing practices. Simply, that is not the case; inter-market competition has become the order of the day.

Intensive competition among similar firms has been replaced in part by competition among diverse types of retailers in large well-defined market segments (Westbrook and Black, 1985). Retail management has recognized that consumers do not spend their money in a single firm nor do they concentrate their purchases in any class of retail establishments. High-income and high-status consumers have been found to purchase certain items in K mart rubbing shoulders with lower-income, lower-status consumers. Retailers have realized that they are also in competition with non-retail establishments and they have become involved in intertype competition that exists, for example, between restaurants and supermarkets (Ingene, 1983).

There are some important exceptions. Some firms have pursued policies which avoid direct competition. Wal-Mart Stores, Inc., one of the major discount retail chains in the USA, has concentrated its growth by focusing most of its 745 stores in communities with populations of less than 25 000. Others employing the small-town strategy include Ames Department Stores, Duckwall–Alco Stores, and Family Dollar Stores (Ozment and Jones, 1985). While these firms have had significant impact on the small independent retailers in the small communities, it will be interesting to see what happens when they compete directly with each other and with larger firms who eventually seek business in smaller, secondary markets.

Throughout this period there has been little innovation in retail types such as the supermarket. What has taken place has been a widening and deepening of competitive methods. Department stores, for example, have traditionally reduced prices in an orderly fashion during well-defined periods in the sales year and used strictly developed mark-down policies. The variety of competitive activities has expanded greatly, so that department stores actively pursue price-competition. Also, retailers have expanded the number of tactics within each marketing variable. 'Down-market' retailers have systematically increased the quantity and quality of their product assortments and 'up-market' retailers have engaged extensively in price-based promotional programmes.

A major force behind these changes is the more sophisticated managers who have adopted and implemented well-planned strategies. They have concentrated their efforts on understanding market conditions and developing marketing strategies aimed at affecting their markets. Such management have not given up 'the old ways' but have moved from an emphasis on tactics to one on the management of market position. What we see is a shift in managerial philosophy from the operation of a narrowly focused retail store to a business firm whose survival and profitability will come from a diverse set of activities. Within this change, responses to competition have been more sophisticated. For example, department stores became active participants in direct mail marketing in contrast to mail order and have set up specific departments to compete with firms such as L. L. Bean and Land's End. The driving strategy behind these activities has been differentiation, attempting to create the conditions by which consumers concentrate more of their purchases with a single retailer. The most obvious case of this is Sears Roebuck, who has expanded beyond traditional products and services into financial service with acquisition of Dean Witter in financial markets and Caldwell Banker in real estate (James, 1984, p. 16). The 'new Sears' offers the traditional assortment of appliances, clothing, sporting goods, etc. but also offers almost everything for the house and in many instances the house itself, along with insurance, building products, plumbing, and property maintenance. Although Sears' management has not been able to bring all of these offerings together, once it does the company will certainly be a formidable competitor.

Environmental factors and retail responses

The ultimate consumer market in the USA has gone through important changes in the past two decades. Among these changes are an increase in purchasing power, shifts in employment pattern (especially those related to the role of women in the workforce), changes in the structure of family life-cycle (with the importance of the elderly and family-formation), and shifts from formal to informal life-styles. There has also been a democratization of consumption. This is a process in which consumers at most levels in society consume products and brands basically identified with limited segments. Designer clothes, prestigious automobiles, and exclusive photographic and stereo equipment once marketed to exclusive market segments are in demand by other segments. Ethnic foods once limited to groups with specific heritage spread across most consumer groups. Historical rigidities in consumption have broken down and provided retailers with new opportunities. Many reorganized their operations to meet the new purchase conditions and consumption patterns and developed a strategy known as 'life-style retailing' (Blackwell and Talarzyk, 1984). This became visible as supermarkets moved to carry automobile accessories, hardware items, garden equipment, and clothing; drug stores offered similar items and added a wide number of food items (*Chain Store Age Executive*, 1985). Other types of retail establishments added products and services, extended hours of operation, and changed their locations to meet changes in consumer wants. The result of these actions was to blur the traditional distinctions that once were present. While these shifts did not create duplicates, they affected the criteria used by consumers' in-store choice (Rosenbloom, 1983). While much of this took place in the area of product offerings, it was also present in other areas. Retailers such as K mart, Wal-Mart, and Zayres, for example, upgraded their product assort-ments and at the same time engaged in aggressive price competition with the so-called 'off-price retailers'. These firms began to acquire retailers in a wide variety of lines of commerce and in diverse geographic markets. They have begun to upgrade their locations and have engaged in significant remodelling activities by using state-of-the-art equipment; and they promote themselves as low-price leaders with the same brands found in traditional department stores (*Chain Store Age Executive*, 1985a, p. 15).

There are several underlying factors which have led to this blurring effect and the resultant intensity of competition among these retailers. First, retailing firms have grown in size and have adapted the management practices found in other large American corporations. Long-run retail planning and strategy have replaced the traditional yearly planning horizon, and as firms have grown in size they have had to seek expansion funds in traditional financial markets. Hence their operations and management have come under the scrutiny of financial institutions and investors (Cronnin and Skinner, 1984). Second, in spite of increase in personal income levels, the total demand for goods and services has not grown at projected rates. Part of this has been a result of a slowdown in the growth of population, the recessions of the past several years, the shift in consumer wants from retail goods to services, including personal services, travel, and the like. Finally, retailers have begun to exhaust the set of tactics which allow them to differentiate themselves from one another and have not developed others. Retail-differentiation efforts have been narrowed as many large retail firms discovered that they could all follow the competitive practices of the others. Many retailers accepted the general belief that there was a large mass market, and they attempted to reach it by becoming similar in terms of the products offered, competitive techniques (especially price promotion), and location. While retail competition had worked well when the competitive advantages were difficult to imitate, the last two decades have shown that imitation is easily undertaken and hence implemented. Instead of a retailer having a competitive advantage over competitors for a season or for a year, competitors could reach out into markets and purchase reasonably similar merchandise, rearrange stores, drop prices quickly, and even expand the number of locations with great ease. The diffusion of innovation of competitive techniques has assumed rates beyond anyone's belief (Higgins, 1986).

Product, price, and service

Product-expansion and imitation has become easier to undertake as a result of manufacturers' greater interest in expanding their markets, often without regard to effects in the retail market in so far as they saw their profits tightly tied to retailer's whims rather than to market expansion. This behaviour on the part of manufacturers of a wide set of goods, including clothing, electronic goods, and household products, accelerated during the 1980–3 period, when they saw that they could not rid themselves of high inventories through traditional retail channels. One means of dealing with these inventories was to place them in 'off-price' markets, which allowed many of the end-of-the line retailers and the 'off-price' affiliates of major retail chains to offer nationally branded items not that dissimilar from their 'up-market' cousins. These outlets were successful in attracting consumers who were 'brand-conscious' rather than store-loyal and who, because of the economic times, could not afford to purchase in the traditional retail establishments. While a good proportion of these customers realized that the products were last year's merchandise or seconds, these goods were still valued because of the brand they carried. The net result of the large surpluses of known branded goods and their availability through the 'off-price' retailers was the minimization of the perceived differences between the 'up-market' and 'down-market' stores. During this process two other things took place. The traditional retailers, the department stores and speciality stores, became more active in price-promotions, and the stores at the other end of the spectrum added more and more of the traditional services of their full-price competititors. Once again, congruence between types did not take place, but differences became less clear.

Department stores have begun to increase the level and quantity of services as one approach to bring customers back from other competitors. As a means of combating the diffusion of national brands throughout the mass retailers, department stores have begun to develop their own private-label brands. Dayton Hudson, the Minneapolis-based firm, introduced 'Boundary Waters' as a brand for its line of casual clothes. Dayton has not extended the name to other products. It is not clear as to whether their efforts will be successful enough to leave a permanent impression on the minds of customers in contrast to the already well-known national brands (Dunkin, 1985, pp. 66–7).

The 'down-market' retailers are also adapting many of the same image-building and promotional techniques used by 'up-market' firms. Boutique departments have been taken from the major department stores and have been introduced into all levels of retailing. Some catalogue showrooms, for example, put in kitchen boutiques for dishware, silverware, and kitchen accessories and appliances on the same principles as found in major department stores such as Bloomingdale's.

Extensive promotional pricing, once the domain of the so-called discounter, has become an important competitive weapon for most retailers. In part this has come from aggressive, specialized retailers' areas who are pursuing their growth strategies by increasing their market share at the expense of general-line retailers. Such retailers have often disregarded and rejected mark-up pricing principles and have substituted in their place demand-oriented pricing schemes. These schemes incorporate low retail prices and pressures on suppliers for lower costs. Toys 'R' Us have pursued this policy, which has created a low-price image for itself by selling 'hot products' at little or no profit (Gilman, 1985, p. 26). The adaptation of price-promotion activities means that in order to be competitive more emphasis must be given toward the development of 'price images'. Retailers, regardless of market position, want to be known as the low-price leader, whether it is true or not. Many department stores and speciality stores who had avoided aggressive price tactics have begun to employ them, although without the brassy blare found elsewhere. Management discovered that aggressive price policies have not disrupted their quality image; they also saw that mark-downs had other benefits. Merchandise turnover increased and lower prices (or the image of lower prices through more frequent sales and greater promotion of sales events) attracted new consumers.

More intense competition is found throughout the country, although some of the more interesting examples are on the West Coast. In the Los Angeles market, The Broadway, the May Company, Robinsons', and Bullocks' are competing for the upper end of the department store market. Bullocks' and Robinsons' are at the higher level. However, they have not been able to dismiss the activities of the Broadway and the May Company. These stores have directed their energies toward creating fashion images and have attempted to increase the quality of their services. Although these retailers are natural foes, they have formed a bond in holding customers in their stores and out of others (Kristof, 1985, p. D-5). A recent entrant in the Los Angeles market is Nordstrom, the Seattle-based retailer, known for its service orientation. Nordstrom has opened seven stores in the Los Angeles market and is aiming at the same market segment of the four majors. It has many of the same brands, competitive prices, and good locations, but has focused on services to differentiate itself. According to recent reports, its customer-service policy has been well accepted by consumers, who view them as having a 'superior sales force'. Nordstrom's management reportedly pays its sales force 20% or more than its immediate competitors, and compensates these expenditures by spending less on promotion (*Chain Store Age Executive*, 1985b, p. 17).

Not all of the competitive activities have been successful (Norman and Dunkin, 1985). Some product-expansion suggests that management skills and the benefits of economies of scale are not transferable among different retail product areas. One area in which major operators are having difficulties is hardware. Basically, the problem stems from the intensity of competition between major firms which, in spite of lower prices, has affected consumers' preferences for service.

The major chains are competing heavily with one another in size and complexity of product lines, promotion, and price-leadership. This type of competition has led to massive advertising costs and intensive price-cutting:

> When Builders Square opens a store, it launches a $500 000, three-week adver-tising blitz. And standard industry practice calls for a new store to offer as much as 20% off a competitor's prices for a limited time. In addition, to reinforce their low-price image, the stores provide hundreds of loss leaders, sold at or below cost, to build traffic (Davis, 1985, p. 84).

While the major hardware chains fight the expensive battle, they are basically affecting one another and not the small independent chains or independent stores, whose success in great part is based on service. Their success in great measure stems from a more comprehensive knowledge of the products they market and from their ability to recognize needs, an issue which will be developed later in the discussion.

Retail location

The competition for space still remains one of the major problems facing American retailers, in spite of the beliefs of many that the problems have been solved. Population shifts, decay and regentrification of central business districts, the growth of the number and variety of shopping centres and overstoring continue to challenge retailers. At the management level, methods of selecting store location have advanced at rapid levels in the past decade. However, the changes in the environment have come at even faster rates, often making rational decisions unprofitable. Space remains the scarcest resource, and proper space the rarest of them all. Retailers are aware of the need to acquire adequate space, operate it effectively, and then move on when market conditions change. They have also recognized the need to engage in policies to block their competitors from such space. Numbers of retailers operate in real-estate markets, purchasing land or taking options on property as a specific means of changing access to others. Some purchase retail firms in other parts of the country in order to obtain the property for expansion rather than for the value of 'on-going' firms.

The large regional shopping centre as well as other types of shopping malls has dramatic effects on retail competition. They have opened up vast amounts of retail selling space for which retailers have bid up prices to enter. Because of the complex nature of shopping-centre planning, development, and oper-ations, forecasted use and actual consumer patronage have varied greatly. Often the new space has not been amenable to retailers' desires (Resener, 1985). Some shopping centres have not been able to create and maintain images compatible with retailers' needs, and many malls have been too successful in so far as they have tended to have homogenizing effects. Retailers in shopping centres have limitations placed on them, and find themselves having to adopt to mall objectives and strategies rather than their own (Savitt, 1985a). At the same time, they have found less than perfect matches between the space created in malls and the individual requirements for the establishment.

What is clear is that many retailers have become more sensitive to the location decision of their overall strategy and are beginning to use and apply more sophisticated spatial performance measures. BAT Industries, the giant British company, which owns Saks Fifth Avenue, Marshall Fields, Gimbels, and other department stores, is reorganizing its operations on the basis of floor-space performance (Barmash, 1985). How such analysis and strategic decisions will fold into competitive activities is difficult to estimate. What is clear is that the competition for retail location is on the increase.

Acquisitions and mergers

Within the past several years the merger movement in the USA has grown, and this has greatly affected retailers and competition in retailing. In previous merger movements the retail sector was not greatly affected. However, there has been great interest in retailing in the present merger wave. For a variety of corporations, domestic and foreign in a number of industries, retailing investments provide them with important opportunities to fulfil their own growth strategies. Such firms have eagerly sought retailers as a means of diversifying their own holdings.

As major American retailers entered financial markets to pursue their own growth and development programme they exposed their assets and operating statements to a wide variety of investors (Higgins and Kerin, 1983). Economic conditions encouraged investors to actively pursue retail firms for several reasons. First, retail stock prices have generally been low and many retailers exhibit high cash flows and undervalued assets. Second, most retail chains have substantial real-estate assets, including wholly owned properties and long-term leases far below market value. The shortage of proper space has become a major consideration. Third, retail firms are generally loose, unfederated organizations, and groups within them can be sold off to finance the purchase. This is especially important, because there is a 'second market' for retail establishments. This is unlike the conditions in manufacturing, where the assets sold often have limited or no market value and are written off taxes for retailers wanting to enter a specific geographic market, line of trade, or desirous location. Fourth, the once tightly controlled retail enterprise with family ownership and management eroded as the result of earlier expansion drive, hence, allowing takeovers to become easier.

Among the most prominent cases of aggressive and successful growth by merger are The Limited, managed by Leslie Wexner, who has recently absorbed Lane Bryant and Lerner Stores, and Petrie Stores, managed by Milton Petrie, who took over Miller–Wohl (Schultz, 1985). Others, including K mart, F. W. Woolworth, and Associated Dry Goods, have been active as well. Some of the acquisitions have focused on secondary markets, typically smaller markets, where, as a result of the mergers, the retailers can claim a dominant position. These are often reviewed as prime targets, because the smaller markets typically have fewer competitors and are easier to operate in as a result of lower labour costs, property taxes, etc. (Mason and Mayer, 1984, p. 229). Most prominent of these is Wal-Mart Stores, Inc., which has pursued smaller markets (Mason, 1985, pp. 142–7). There has also been an interest in backward vertical integration, though at present the number of mergers back into wholesaling have not been significant to draw implications about their impact on competition (Bivins, 1985).

Of great importance has been the increased interest of foreign firms in American retailing. The acquisition of American retailers by foreign firms continues to grow at a steady rate. These acquisitions have been across the board and include such take-overs as (1) Marshall Field and Co., by BAT Industries of Great Britain; (2) Spiegel, by Otto Versaud GMBH of West Germany; (3) Shoppers Drug Mart, by Imasco Ltd of Canada; and (4) Gimbel Brothers, by British American Tobacco–United States (BAT) (Mason and Mayer, 1984, pp. 224–5). Each of these and the other acquisitions by foreign firms have affected competitive activities by style of management, new operating requirements, and access to foreign products.

One of the more important outcomes of the merger movement in retailing is the increase of the size of retail firms. To be certain, there have always been large firms composed of several major operating divisions, each of whom had general managerial integrity. What is taking place now is the concentration of strategic decisions in retailing, and as a result of this retailers should be able to exercise more influence on wholesalers and manufacturers. What is important is the growth of retail size on the manufacturers, who now have to deal with fewer but larger retailers. Many major retailers have already begun to put new pressures on them through a number of strategic policies, including private branding, active price-competition both in the traditional store and by 'major-owned' off-price outlets, and greater access to worldwide supplies. As the intensity of competition increases among the larger and more highly horizontally and vertically integrated retailers there will be an extension of the competitive processes up the marketing channel. Simply, retailers will pursue sources of supply more actively and will use whatever they can to diminish the success of their retail competitors from those suppliers.

THE NEW RETAIL STRATEGIES

The previous section has examined an important cross-section of competitive behaviour in American retailing. Even with limitations we can begin to see some important patterns which can be helpful in understanding other aspects of retail competition in the USA and can be used in evaluating competition in other economies.

What is seen is the development, implementation, and management of sophisticated strategies by retailers. Some of these represent some of the most sophisticated and well-thought-out programmes to be found in all of marketing. This is especially significant, because retailers in general, even the largest of all firms, were never known to have engaged in the systematic development of strategy. They have made significant strides in a short period of time, given their newness to the process, and their achievements stand head and shoulders above many of their suppliers in terms of understanding their environment and developing the means to shape and control it.

These new retailing strategies stem from retailers addressing the competitive process in new and startling ways. In part this has been a reflection of changes in their environment and in part in examination of traditional assumptions about the role of retailing in the production–marketing–consumption continuum. Extensive study of retail behaviour (of which only a small part has been presented here) suggests that retailers are pursuing competitive strategies more extensively than ever before. The new retailing competition has become an active process of rivalry which takes place between firms for the custom of consumers and between consumers, in this case the retailers themselves, for access to suppliers. What has taken place is that the retailer is becoming a more active participant in the marketing channel. Not only are they expanding to serve more and more of consumers' wants (the process of transforming consumers into customers), they are also placing significant efforts into making their suppliers aware of the retailers' importance.

These competitive strategies are developed in the context of the occupation of all of the consumer's scarce resources—time, space, and financial; namely, they want customers to spend more time in their stores, allocate more of their space to their products, and concentrate more of their total expenditures with a specific retailer. As we have seen, these retailers have extended their operations in order to make customers increasingly dependent on them. Finally, these strategies have a strong entrepreneurial orientation. They are designed to mould and affect present and future environments by creating and exploiting market discrepancies and opportunities. While these have been aimed at consumers, they have also been clearly directed at their competitors. Retailers have actively expanded the number and variety of stores, engaged in purchasing practices such as buying entire outputs of producers, and extensive consumer financing as a means of disrupting their competitors' ability to complete their own programmes. They are purposefully using tactics to block competitors from customers and the resources required to compete (Savitt, 1985b).

These retailers are actively engaging in market-shaping. Common wisdom in marketing and retailing has handed down incorrect premises about what is controllable and what is uncontrollable in marketing strategy. The new strategies have disregarded such notions and have substituted for them assumptions about the need and the ability to shape markets. They have put into action the long-standing, but not adhered to, proposition of Edith

Penrose (1958): 'Firms not only alter the environmental conditions necessary for their actions, but, more important, they know they can alter them and that the environment is not independent of their own activities' (p. 42).

RETAILING AND PRODUCTION ORIENTATION

Overview

As a further recognition of the ability to shape environment takes place in retailing, new competitive forms will come to the surface as retailers pursue their new strategies. One which is very much in its infancy is production orientation. This is representative of the type of retailing strategy which might evolve as the present competitive activities run their course. Production orientation refers to the restructuring of the basic production–marketing–consumption functions by the integration of these three in the context of the retail firm. The production orientation means that retailers will become more concerned with the production and distribution of new sets of utilities which will radically affect consumption activities of consumers. For example, garden-supply firms will provide 'total garden care' rather than the assortment of items, plants, hoses, equipment, etc. which they now offer. Retailers adopting this strategy will absorb the management function of the consumer in the consumption process and allow the consumer simply to enjoy the garden. A production-orientation strategy is consistent with the goal of dominating consumers' resources.

Production orientation is more than retail services

More will be said about production orientation. However, it is necessary to clearly differentiate it from the traditional retail services. Most retailers provide and have provided some set of services at specified levels for some time. Among these are found alternations, wrapping, deliveries, complaints, adjustments, and returned goods, repair, credit, bridal registry, and personal services ranging from food to haircuts (Duncan *et al.*, 1983, pp. 495–6). To most retailers the concept of services really represents things that have been part of retailing and whose intensity and quality have been part of the competitive process. These services are normally regarded as part of the elements required to complete a transaction with normal degrees of consumer satisfaction. They do not represent a commitment (with rare exceptions, such as home decorating) to production orientation. They represent an assembly of products with services. Production orientation represents the creation and performance of activities which relieve consumers of some or all of the demands of the consumption process.

Production orientation requires products and services. However, the end-result is the combination of these major elements in a way the retailer exercises their application for the customer. Instead of simply offering hardware products and some advice, as many hardware departments do at present, they could transform themselves into retailers who are part and parcel of the consumer's home-maintenance operations. This perspective is not simply the sleight of hand in a magic show but a clear extension of Theodore Levitt's marketing myopia (Levitt, 1960). Retailers are becoming part of their customers' consumption system. A household-maintenance system will obviously be a combination of products, services, and labour, either bought on the market or supplied by the customer. This system may include everything from gardening services to house-maintenance and repair. Garden services could include plants, their care, cutting of grass, watering gardens, cleaning of garden areas, said preparation, and even the clearing of snow in winter. The 'garden department' of the store may shrink in space or even disappear in the traditional sense, leaving more space for other types of merchandise or in-store services.

In hardware, a similar scenario can be sketched. The thousands of retail stock-keeping units at retail become part of maintenance services in which retail inventory can be moved back in the marketing channel. Retailers are beginning to consider contract services in plumbing or other household repairs in which customers pay monthly fees for belonging to a home-maintenance service. Such a service provides 'on-call' service on a 24-hour basis. What this does is to expand the retailer's contact with its customers from the store into the residence. This, of course, has significant implications for retailers in industrial and governmental markets.

Management of the production-orientation strategy

Production orientation provides important benefits for retailers but also requires an increased commitment to basic marketing principles. The benefits are as follows:

(1) Retailers will be able to capture a greater proportion of the expenditures of each consumer through the creation of a store-loyalty or bonding of the customer to the store.
(2) Retailers will be able to gain higher profits to the degree that mark-ups on the 'labour-plus product' content of the service will be higher than that of products alone. Consumers are less able to evaluate cost-value relations of labour than they are with products.
(3) Production services will lead to economies in the traditional management of inventory and physical distribution. Such benefits will not accrue without expenditures, primarily, in the development of production systems highly attached to customer-service premises and the investment

in human resources. Both of these represent areas to which retailers need to pay great attention.

The implementation of production-oriented services by retailers means that retailers will have to engage in much more extensive consumer research than undertaken heretofore. What needs to be known is more than what purchases are made and what trends may be occurring, both short-run phenomena. Long-run oriented research requires a greater understanding of how consumption takes place. This is more than understanding the relevant 'life-styles' of how people live their lives; it includes comprehending specifically how consumers 'produce' and use goods. Indeed, this may be an important new area for all of marketing to undertake. While we have produced significant models of the factors that influence choice and of the buyer processes, little is known about how consumers use the products and services they purchase. Retailers who undertake such research and implement the results will have an advantage in their ability to shape markets and in the occupation of consumer resources.

In order to implement service production, retail management must make a firm committment to the development of human resources. No retailer would ever admit to a lack of attention being paid to sales employees. However, the truth of the matter is that less attention is paid to employees than to any other part of the competitive elements. Labour costs are high, but a great part of the problem stems from high labour turnover and the lack of high productivity. The retail selling force is undertrained, undersupported, and underpaid to accommodate the conditions of full service activities. The reasons for the generally poor state of human resource management in retailing stems from a wide variety of factors; in reality, excuses which need a complete examination and revision. The central premise is that there is high mobility, a fluctuating labour force, and a low-skill supply of employees. With labour costs a high proportion of operating expenditure any increase will make most marginal operations unprofitable and many profitable ones marginal.

Unfortunately, this view prevails, and for many retailers it has become entangled with highly seasonable operations, with a net result that attempts to invest in employees whose activities could lessen the dependence on seasonal trade by providing services year-round gets pushed aside. The human resource problem in retailing is much like the solution to inflation; if one firm would not increase prices, a second might follow, and so on: the same applies to labour wage demands. It is always risky for the first firm to make such a decision, but then taking risks is what business is all about. Taking the risk of moving forward a service orientation is based on the requirement of developing new human resources policies. The reason is simple: the provision of services in the manner defined then requires both a production and marketing component in retail employees. They can no longer be viewed and compensated solely on how much is sold; straight commission is anathema to production-orientation retailing. It also requires substantial training, since retail sales employees are now part of production and they must know about the product and its applications. Also, of course, once trained it means a commitment to fuller employment rather than on the current seasonal basis. Furthermore, it means that management must become *entrepreneurial* in the development of a production-oriented strategy, that is, fostering an awareness of market discrepancies.

SUMMARY

Competition among retailers will continue to follow differentiation strategies. As has been shown, there is a readjustment of the various elements among American retailers. Associated with these changes have been increases in the rapidity in which practices can be adopted and used by others. Greater rates of diffusion of competitive practices leave retailers with increasingly shorter time-horizons in which to gain operating goals. The continual flux among them, given greater pressures to be price-competitive, means that there are greater pressures on operating margins. Creation of in-store boutiques or private labels are expensive, and their lasting value is still to be determined, so that retailers, in the quest for larger market shares, may be doing so at the cost of profits. While expansion by acquisitions and merger affect overall corporate growth, profits still come from the operation of individual stores which exist in these different competitive environments. Competitive behaviour will take new dimensions as retailers attempt to occupy more consumer resources. An important means of reaching that goal will come from strategies which attempt to shape and mould the retail environment. A major means of reaching such ends will be the implementation of a production orientation strategy by retailers. The success of this will require new perspectives on the performance of basic functions, including research and management of human resources.

REFERENCES

Barmash, I. (1986). 'BAT's paragons of retailing.' *The New York Times*, 5 February, D1 and D8.

Bivins, J. (1985). 'Store wars: is America big enough for all?' *Chain Store Age Executive*, August, 15–17.

Blackwell, R. D., and Talarzyk (1983). 'Lifestyle retailing: competitive strategies for the 1980's.' *Journal of Retailing*, **59**, 7–28.

Chain Store Age Executive (1984). 'Drug chains find fuel in auto aftermarket.' September, 21–3.

Chain Store Age Executive (1985a). 'Discounters maneuver for market position.' March, 15–17.

Chain Store Age Executive (1985b). 'Nordstrom's impact: how big the wallop?' September, 15–17.

Cronnin, J. J., and Skinner, S. J. (1984). 'Marketing outcomes, financial conditions, and retail profit performance.' *Journal of Retailing*, **60**, 9–22.

Davis, J. E. (1985). 'Hardware wars: the big boys might lose this one.' *Business Week*, 15 October, 84–8.

Duncan, B., Hollander, S. C., and Savitt, R. (1983). *Modern Retail Management*, Homewood, Ill.: Irwin.

Gilman, H. (1985). 'Retail genius.' *The Wall Street Journal*, 21 November, 1, 26.

Higgins, K. T. (1986). 'Retail strategies always evolving.' *Marketing News*, 31 January, 6.

Higgins, R. C., and Kerin, R. A. (1983). 'Managing the growth—financial policy nexus in retailing.' *Journal of Retailing*, **59**, 19–48.

Ingene, C. A. (1983). 'Intertype competition: restaurants versus grocery stores.' *Journal of Retailing*, **59**, 49–75.

James, F. E. (1984). 'Sears a powerhouse in many fields—Now, looks into new ones.' *Wall Street Journal*, 10 February, 16.

Kelley, P. J. and George, W. R. (1982). 'Strategic management issues for the retailing of services.' *Journal of Retailing*, Summer, 26–43.

Kerin, R. A., and Vararya, N. (1985). 'Mergers and acquisitions in retailing: a review and critical analysis.' *Journal of Retailing*, **61**, 9–34.

Kristof, N. D. (1985). 'The retail war in Los Angeles: a 4-way fight.' *The New York Times*, 12 December, D1, D5.

Levitt, T. (1960). 'Marketing myopia.' *Harvard Business Review*, **53**, July–August, 60, 24–47.

Mason, J. B., and Mayer, M. L. (1984). *Modern Retailing: Theory and Practice*, Plano, Texas: Business Publications, Inc.

Mason, T. (1985). 'Sam Walton of Wal-Mart: just your basic homespun billionarie.' *Business Week*, 14 October, 142–7.

Norman, J. R., and Dunkin, A. (1985). 'How Bobby Saleonitz took an escalator to the basement.' *Business Week*, 19 August, 55.

Ozment, J., and Jones, M. A. (1985). 'Growth of discount retail chains in rural communities: an analysis of issues.' Working papers.

Penrose, E. T. (1959). *The Theory of the Growth of the Firm*, Oxford: Basil Blackwell.

Resener, M. (1985). 'How real estate dominates retail.' *ADWEEK*, 16 December, RR4.

Rosenbloom, B. (1983). 'Store image development and the question of congruency.' In Darden, W. R., and Lusch, R. F. (eds), *Patronage Behavior and Retail Management*, Amsterdam: North-Holland, pp. 146–63.

Savitt, R. (1985a). 'Issues of tenant leasing arrangements in shopping centres.' In Dawson, J. A., and Lord, D. (eds), *Shopping Centre Development: Policies and Prospects*, London: Croom Helm.

Savitt, R. (1985b). 'Time, Space and Competition. Formulations in the Development of Marketing Strategy.' *Managerial and Decision Economics*, **7**, 11–18.

Schultz, D. P. (1985). 'Retail Expansion.' *Stores*, August, 19–22.

Westbrook, R. A., and Black, W. C. (1985). 'A motivation-based shopper typology.' *Journal of Retailing*, **61**, 78–103.

CHAPTER 9
Monitoring Retailing Strategy by Measuring Customer Perception

GARY DAVIES
Manchester Polytechnic

INTRODUCTION

Why do shoppers pass one food or department store but visit others? What makes one store a first-choice store for one group in society? The questions are easy enough to ask; in fact the first one must be being asked regularly by every store manager eager to maximize his traffic at the expense of his local competition.

One key factor in the decisions shoppers make about which outlets to visit and which to visit most often is the image which each store presents. Image is a complex factor. Tangible components such as merchandise and store layout blend with less tangible ones such as store ambiance. Image can be reinforced, modified, or changed through advertising and promotion, although most radical changes can only occur through a substantial change in many elements of the retailer's marketing mix.

The image that a store presents is therefore a component of, and a consequence of, that store's overall business strategy. Senior marketing management will select a target image and will often monitor their image and those of their competitors in regular market-research surveys. A common approach is to ask shoppers to rate competing stores against a list of key attributes (Brooks, 1986). For example, a food retailer might ask 1 000 shoppers to give a rating for their stores and their main competitors for 'ease of shopping', 'good car-parking', 'fresh produce', etc. Different retail chains will receive different ratings and these can be used to identify the profile of each retailer and, if the survey is repeated over time, to see how the profile changes.

The problem in using this approach is that it is difficult to see how important each factor is to shoppers and to grasp a clear picture of the marketplace as a whole. To simplify matters, marketers tend to classify factors into groups. Lindquist (1974), for example, reviewed work by 26

133

researchers into the specific area of retailer-image and categorized the attributes examined in all these earlier studies into nine areas: Merchandise, Service, Clientele, Physical Facilities, Convenience, Promotion, Store Atmosphere, Institutional Factors, and Post-transaction Satisfaction.

Even with this level of simplification, it is difficult to obtain a clear picture of any one market. An alternative approach has been to differentiate between two types of retailer marketing: price-led and image-led.

The 'Wheel of Retailing' concept emphasizes price- and image-led promotion at either end of a life cycle for the individual retailer (see, for example, Hollander, 1960). It implies that adopting an image-led approach is a precursor to decline, as being image-led will mean higher margins. This view has been challenged and will be again in this chapter. However, one value of the wheel concept is that it introduces the idea of price- and image-led strategies as being different and at different ends of a continuum.

One problem with a price-led strategy is that it depends upon a technical or other advantage over competition that can often be matched. Few retail sectors contain a dominant retailer who can negotiate consistently superior prices from suppliers, even if the law of the land allows preferential discounts.

Many retailers have sought to avoid direct price-comparison by developing strong own-label ranges and by emphasizing 'value for money' rather than 'low price' in their promotion. Margins can be better protected, but, even so, the customer cannot be asked to accept that competing retailers each with their own product ranges offer different 'value' in the longer term. Price is consequently a difficult factor to use in differentiating one retailer from another. Retail marketers have to search for some other method of defining what Rosser Reeves first described as a 'unique selling proposition', or USP for short.

The value of a USP, a coherent image unique to the one product or company, is that customers value the image over and above the price–quality equation of their purchases. They are willing to pay extra in some circumstances and in others to buy more when they relate to a particular USP. It may well be that adopting this approach to marketing limits the target market for the store. Nevertheless, a strong and unique appeal to a specific segment has been shown time and again to be preferable to a more general appeal to the whole market.

As both markets and shoppers' perceptions are by no means static, a retailer's image may have to change over time. There is a need therefore to develop market-research techniques that can help develop USPs for retailing and that can measure changes in shoppers' perceptions of competing retail images within a market. Moreover, it would clearly be advantageous if any techniques were straightforward in application without losing the necessary detail to ensure reliability.

This chapter therefore has two objectives; (1) to outline a method of analysing any retail market using the approach of asking customers to rate competing retailers against selected image factors and (2) to illustrate the general value of analysing retail strategy by measuring customer perception by examining one market, that of department stores in Manchester.

THE METHODOLOGY

The method used here involves a number of stages. First, a large number of potential image factors are developed using one or more qualitative market-research techniques (for example, by holding group discussions among shoppers, by brainstorming and word-association, or by analysing the advertising of competing retailers.)

Typically, 30 or 40 image factors are generated in this way. Traditionally, these could all be used to rate competing retailers, as explained earlier. This number of image factors is, however, unnecessarily large, and two methods are used to reduce the number to manageable proportions. The first is to group factors together under Lindquist's nine areas (see above) to check for obvious duplication. The second is to screen all potential factors in a market-research survey.

In the market-research survey shoppers are asked to rate each factor against their view of the 'ideal' store in the sector on a monadic scale, with a rating of one meaning that the factor describes their 'ideal' store perfectly and a rating of seven meaning that it is totally undesirable.

Certain factors can be eliminated because they are confusing. Others are consistently rated as describing the 'ideal' store. The first group can be eliminated and the second can be subsumed into one composite image factor—the 'ideal' store itself. The remaining concepts are meaningful to the shopper but do not describe the general view of what is an 'ideal' store. However, they are the most valuable concepts in that they are capable of identifying why actual retailers are not seen as being the same as the 'ideal' store.

The final part of the methodology is to conduct a survey where shoppers are asked to compare all the selected image factors (including the 'ideal' store) one with another and to all the competing retailers in the sector under study. Stores are also compared one with another. The comparison is done normally on a seven-point scale from one to seven, asking respondents to rate pairs (store–store, store–concept, or concept–concept) on the scale where one means similar and seven means different.

The output from the final survey is more complex than that from a simple rating of stores against concepts. It takes the form of a semi-matrix, an example of which is given in Table 1 for the Manchester department store market.

Table 1.   Manchester department stores (1982): semi-matrix of arithmetic means

	Debenhams	Lewis's	Marks & Spencer	Kendals	British Home Stores	Woolworth	Boots	The ideal store	Wide range	Polite	Expensive	Comfortable	Traditional
Debenhams	1												
Lewis's	2.50	1											
Marks & Spencer	4.08	4.29	1										
Kendals	4.13	3.39	4.16	1									
British Home Stores	3.64	4.09	3.21	5.12	1								
Woolworth	4.76	4.80	5.38	6.38	4.17	1							
Boots	4.75	4.65	4.57	5.22	4.12	4.66	1						
The ideal store	3.44	3.15	2.85	3.20	4.36	5.32	3.52	1					
Wide range	2.70	2.22	3.23	2.32	3.67	3.32	3.36	2.00	1				
Polite	3.05	2.52	1.92	2.46	3.07	4.22	2.81	1.97	5.08	1			
Expensive	3.59	3.36	3.34	1.82	4.26	5.11	4.00	4.43	5.01	3.86	1		
Comfortable	3.55	3.35	2.88	2.76	3.73	4.79	3.10	2.09	4.77	3.76	4.06	1	
Traditional	3.81	2.96	3.53	2.25	3.96	3.63	3.68	3.85	4.15	3.14	3.98	3.91	1

(*NB*: A scale of 1–7 was used)

Data in this form can be analysed using a computer technique termed Multi-Dimensional Scaling (MDS). The simplest explanation of MDS is to liken the semi-matrix to the mileage chart in a map book where the distances between towns are displayed in a similar way. An MDS program takes these data and produces a map of the country with each town in its correct place relative to one another. When used with the market-research data, the towns become retailers, or concepts. The map is a model of how shoppers see competing retailers, how near they are in image or otherwise.

MDS is a relatively new technique. Kruskal (1964) developed the first of a number of similar mathematical approaches, many of which have been drawn together by Davies and Coxon (1982). Stefflre (1971) was, however, the pioneer in exploiting the approach as a market-research tool. He argued (Stefflre, 1967) the value of mapping perceptions of competing products or services by claiming that people behave in similar ways to products or services that they perceive as being similar.

Translating this into general business terms and returning to the questions which formed the first two sentences in this chapter, retailers who are seen as closest to the shopper's view of the 'ideal' retail outlet will be preferred. Retailers who are seen as being close together will be used as alternates and will share customers.

Further discussion of the marketing value of the methodology is left to later. It must be emphasized, however, that MDS provides only a means of illustrating a pattern in data which is not easily discernible even to the trained researcher. The market-research data are therefore only those in the semi-matrix.

How well the MDS program is able to fit its map to those data is measured by what is called 'stress'. Conventionally, a stress figure of 0.1 or less is held to be acceptable. However, any stress figure above zero implies that the MDS map is not a perfect fit to the semi-matrix data. A more precise representation of the semi-matrix is normally possible in three dimensions. These three-dimensional maps, or models, are both difficult to represent in an essentially two-dimensional book, but later figures do attempt to do so. As in the two-dimensional maps, the relevance of the model is only in the relative distance between points (this time in three dimensions). There is little relevance to any orthogonal direction, i.e. any traditional axes.

THE MANCHESTER DEPARTMENT STORE MARKET

The city of Manchester is the centre of a large conurbation in the North-west of England. While the resident population is quite small in number the city and its shopping centre provide a focal point for around 3 million people in the surrounding suburbs.

The shopping centre is relatively concentrated. A main street, Market Street, runs between two large department stores, Lewis's and Debenhams at one end, and the Arndale Centre, which is Europe's largest covered shopping area, at the other. Close by is Britain's third largest branch of Marks & Spencer and a few hundred yards further, Kendal Milne, part of the House of Fraser group. Woolworth was at the time of this study a similar distance from the other end of Market Street and in Market Street itself are Littlewoods and British Home Stores, with a large branch of Boots opposite the Arndale Centre, which incorporates many departments not normally associated with 'Boots the Chemists'.

Lewis's is part of a small chain of traditional department stores based largely in the North of England. It forms part of the Sears Group. Debenhams is one of a national chain of again traditional department stores, noted, at the time of the study, for a large number of in-store concessions. Marks &

Spencer is arguably Britain's most successful retailer, a large national chain, sometimes labelled as a variety chain store rather than as a department store. Kendal Milne (or Kendals, as it is referred to locally) is the third traditional department store in the city and is generally regarded as the most up-market one. Woolworth, now largely unassociated with the original American parent company, is a large national chain which had been struggling somewhat to return to earlier popularity. Many of their stores nationally are relatively small but the Manchester site was relatively large and carries a wide product range. Woolworth could be categorized as a variety chain store but does not fit easily into any one retailing type nationally. Littlewoods and British Home Stores (BHS) present a similar image, similar in turn to Marks & Spencer but with generally lower-priced merchandise. Boots has two branches in the centre of Manchester, a traditional chemists, representing the company's origins, and a much larger store operating along similar lines to BHS and Littlewoods, with the addition of a pharmacy.

The retailing environment is, as might be expected with such concentration, very competitive. During the period of the work reported here (1982–5) certain stores invested heavily in refurbishment and local promotion. Others benefited from national campaigns.

One objective of the Manchester study was to monitor any changes in shopper perception of the main stores that could be said to be competing in the department store sector. While practitioners and academics appear able to define the term 'department store' quite closely, preliminary work suggested that shoppers were less precise in their perception of which stores should possess that label. In the first study therefore at the end of 1982 it was decided to include not only Debenhams, Lewis's, and Kendals who would generally be classified as department stores, but also Marks & Spencer, Woolworth, Boots, and British Home Stores.

The initial stages in the research—the concept-generation and screening stage—yielded the terms 'efficient service', 'honest', 'courteous', and 'helpful' as concepts describing the 'ideal' department store. Other relevant concepts (which were included in the second stage) were 'wide range', 'polite', 'expensive', 'comfortable' and 'traditional'. As described earlier, these concepts, the 'ideal', and the seven stores were used in the final survey asking shoppers to compare all possible pairs drawn from the list of concepts and stores and to rate each pair on a seven-point scale to assess how similar (mark of 1) or dissimilar (mark of 7) each pair was in their perception. The average mark given was calculated and the results are shown in Table 1.

Before considering the MDS analysis of the semi-matrix it is worth analysing the raw data in Table 1 one stage further. Tables 2 and 3 show the rank order of stores against first, concepts and second, other stores.

Table 2. Stores compared with concepts

Concepts	Stores						
	Debenhams	Lewis's	M & S	Kendals	BHS	Woolworth	Boots
Wide range	3	1	4	2	7	6	5
Polite	5	3	1	2	6	7	4
Expensive	4	3	2	1	6	7	5
Comfortable	5	4	2	1	6	7	3
Traditional	6	2	5	1	7	4	3
The ideal	4	2	1	3	6	7	5

Table 3. Manchester department stores (1982): store rankings. Stores compared with stores

Base store	Compared against						
	Debenhams	Lewis's	M & S	Kendals	BHS	Woolworth	Boots
Debenhams	–	1	3	4	2	6	5
Lewis's	1	–	4	2	3	6	5
M & S	2	4	–	3	1	6	5
Kendals	2	1	3	–	4	6	5
BHS	2	3	1	6	–	5	4
Woolworth	2	3	5	6	1	–	4
Boots	5	3	2	6	1	4	–

Kendals' image profile was, for example, relatively close to all the concepts except the 'ideal', while Marks & Spencer—not normally classified as a department store—ranked closest to the 'ideal'. Table 3 shows that Lewis's and Debenhams were close together in shoppers' perceptions in 1982 and that Woolworth and Boots were consistently ranked well away from all the other retailers being considered.

When just the stores and the ideal store data were analysed by the MDS programme the two-dimensional map confirms the observations from the ranking data (Figure 1). Woolworth and Boots, despite their merchandising policies in Manchester, are excluded from shoppers' perceptions of the department store market while Marks & Spencer is quite definitely included.

The full models[1] in Figures 2 and 3 show that Marks & Spencer was close to the 'ideal' store (efficient service, honest, courteous, helpful) and was in a sector described as 'comfortable', which was shared partly by Kendals, whose main point of differentiation was 'expensive'. Kendals, in turn, shared the concepts of 'wide range' and 'traditional' with Lewis's and Debenhams. British Home Stores was in the same overall sector as Marks & Spencer but, being further from the 'ideal', was not going to be the first-choice store in that sector.[1]

In marketing terms, Kendals was the one highly differentiated store. Even though it was some way away from the average perception of the 'ideal', it

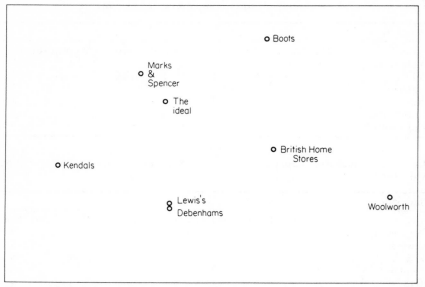

Figure 1.   Manchester department stores, 1982: seven stores. (Stress = 0.00)

had no closely competing stores. That sector of the population who valued a Kendals' type offering had no easy alternative to consider.

To improve a retailer's market share through improving their image could, logically, imply moving closer to the average perception of the 'ideal' store. Kendals, however, provides a good example of a differentiated offering which, although it was positioned quite far from the 'ideal', had no competition within its own sector. Lewis's and Debenhams were both as close to the 'ideal' store but far too close together in marketing terms. The danger is that shoppers will have no real loyalty to one or the other, and that the two stores share both the same sector and the same customers equally.

When there is no perceived difference in image terms (in other words, the two stores are not adopting image-led promotion in their competition) the tendency must be to adopt price-led strategies. This was apparent at this time with first Lewis's and then Debenhams claiming increasingly attractive bargains and launching ever more frequent 'sales'. Nationally Debenhams' promotional effort was highly concentrated around 'sales', labelling its own as 'The Sale'.

Further down Market Street, Marks & Spencer rarely (if ever) indulged in price-promotion. Indeed, while Marks & Spencer had clearly adopted an image-led strategy very successfully, their promotion of this image was hardly overt. Instead it had been evolved mainly through merchandising and recruitment and training policies over many years. The largest potential threat to

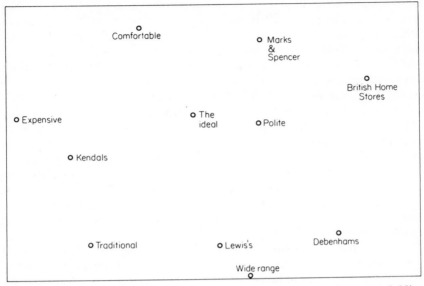

Figure 2. Manchester department stores, 1982: 11 stimuli. (Stress = 0.23)

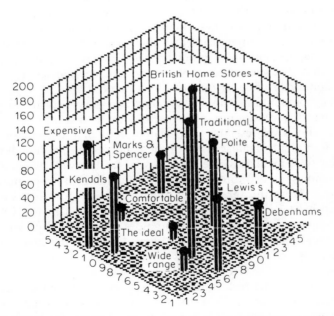

Figure 3. Manchester department stores, 1982: 11 stimuli.
(Stress = 0.13)

Marks & Spencer seemed to be from British Home Stores. However, BHS's strategy again appeared to rely on price rather than image. The presence of Littlewoods close by (not included in the exercise but believed to have a similar image to BHS) provided a further spur to price-led competition.

At the end of 1984 the study was repeated and a slightly different set of initial concepts were derived. This time the 'ideal' department store was described by 'reliable products', 'knowledgeable staff', 'efficient staff', 'a quality store', 'good refund policy', and 'satisfaction with previous products'.

The concepts included in the 1984 model were 'competitive prices', 'specialist departments', 'wide range of products', 'suited to planned shopping', 'in-store comfort', 'up-market store', 'good for browsing', and 'well laid out'. The relevant semi-matrix is shown in Table 4. The two-dimensional map (of stores only) is shown in Figure 4. Boots and Woolworth had been omitted as they clearly were not part of the same market in shoppers' perceptions. For comparison, Figure 5 is constructed from the 1982 data excluding Boots and Woolworth.

The fact that the model has rotated has no practical significance. The relative locations of the stores have, however, changed significantly. Marks & Spencer was no longer notably close to the ideal (although it still ranked first against the ideal), Kendals had moved closer, and Lewis's had moved away from Debenhams and towards Kendals. Interestingly, Kendals had spent a substantial sum on refurbishment in 1983 and Lewis's even more on both refurbishment and on promoting a new image under the banner of 'The New Lewis's'. Lewis's PR emphasized that their aim was to 'become the most fashionable department store group in the country'. Their trading policy explained that 'Lewis's does not intend to be the cheapest in our markets—neither in price or quality'. This marked an end to the price-led promotional competition with Debenhams and gave way to an image-led approach, which succeeded in differentiating the two stores.

Tables 5 and 6 express the semi-matrix data in the form of rankings. Lewis's scored highly against many of the concepts and, although it was still most similar to Debenhams, the latter scored far less well by comparison.

Figure 6 shows the two-dimensional map, including all stores and concepts, and Figure 7 shows the three-dimensional version. The stress on the two-dimensional model is fairly high but the main pattern in the 1984 data is clear. Debenhams have been left in the more price-led sector also occupied by British Home Stores as Lewis's has moved towards the image-led sector, where concepts such as 'in-store comfort' and 'good for browsing' emphasize the ambience-related nature of image promotion.

Table 7 compares the results of the two surveys, grouping similar concepts together between surveys. The rank order on most factors has not changed much: however, the relative scores have changed more (for example, Lewis's moved significantly on comfort).

Table 4. Manchester department stores (1984): semi-matrix of arithmetic means

	Debenhams	Lewis's	Kendals	British Home Stores	Marks & Spencer	The ideal store	Competitive prices	Specialist departments	Wide range of products	Suited to planned shopping	In-store comfort	Up-market store	Good for browsing	Well laid out
Debenhams	1													
Lewis's	2.66	1												
Kendals	3.13	2.89	1											
British Home Stores	4.53	4.92	5.42	1										
Marks & Spencer	4.89	4.68	4.66	3.78	1									
The ideal store	4.19	3.04	3.00	4.80	2.80	1								
Competitive prices	3.24	3.62	4.42	2.87	3.12	1.62	1							
Specialist departments	3.04	2.45	2.55	4.45	3.80	2.00	4.46	1						
Wide range of products	2.84	2.09	2.52	4.16	3.52	1.40	3.63	3.38	1					
Suited to planned shopping	3.38	2.76	2.95	3.95	3.09	1.99	4.23	3.19	3.04	1				
In-store comfort	3.75	2.87	2.61	4.07	3.00	1.74	4.63	3.55	4.02	3.39	1			
Up-market store	4.01	3.02	2.15	5.03	2.82	2.81	5.23	2.96	3.73	3.85	2.17	1		
Good for browsing	3.40	2.64	2.48	3.84	2.84	2.01	4.45	3.00	2.49	3.79	2.46	3.05	1	
Well laid out	4.09	2.75	2.91	3.60	2.77	1.47	4.01	2.90	3.18	2.05	2.75	2.86	2.17	1

(*NB*: A scale of 1–7 was used)

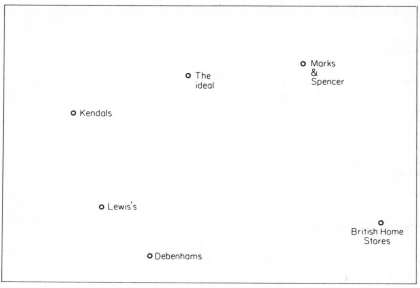

Figure 4.   Manchester department stores, 1984: stores only. (Stress = 0.00)

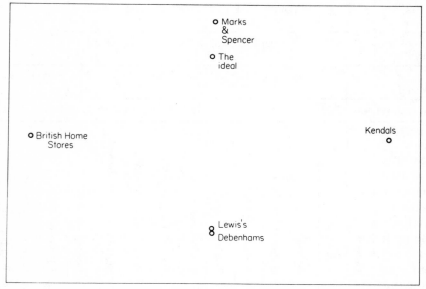

Figure 5.   Manchester department stores, 1982: five stores. (Stress = 0.00)

Table 5. Manchester department stores (1984): store rankings. Stores compared with concepts

Concepts	Stores				
	Debenhams	Lewis's	Kendals	BHS	M & S
Competitive prices	3	4	5	1	2
Specialist departments	3	1	2	5	4
Wide product range	3	1	2	5	4
Planned shopping	4	1	2	5	3
In-store comfort	4	2	1	5	3
Up-market store	4	3	1	5	2
Good for browsing	4	2	1	5	3
Well laid-out	5	1	3	4	2
The ideal	4	3	2	5	1

Table 6. Manchester department stores (1984): store rankings. Stores compared with stores

Base store	Compared against				
	Debenhams	Lewis's	Kendals	BHS	M & S
Debenhams	–	1	2	3	4
Lewis's	1	–	2	4	3
Kendals	2	1	–	4	3
British Home Stores	2	3	4	–	1
Marks & Spencer	4	3	2	1	–

Just after the 1984 study Marks & Spencer increased their floor area substantially and remodelled their Manchester store. They had been losing ground in fashion goods nationally, although food, a relatively recent introduction, had proved remarkably successful. In 1985 Marks & Spencer reorganized their Head Office, giving greater emphasis to formal marketing. Fashion leaflets were made available at store level as part of a general attempt to retain its premier position, which was being attacked by both the department stores and the newer fashion shops, including Next and Principles. The slight fall away in Marks & Spencer's position between the two measures is probably indicative of their position nationally.

In 1985 the Burton Group succeeded in a take-over bid for Debenhams. One of their promises was to rejuvenate Debenhams' image. As the second model in particular demonstrated, there was a need to shift promotional emphasis away from price and towards a definable and differentiated image. The options facing Debenhams are to differentiate along image lines or to move towards the 'ideal' ('reliable products', 'knowledgeable staff', 'efficient staff', 'a quality store', 'a good refund policy', and 'satisfaction with previous products' for the 1984 study, and 'efficient service', 'honest', 'courteous' and 'helpful' from the 1982 study). The image options fall into moving further

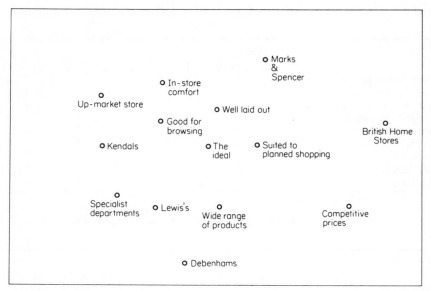

Figure 6.   Manchester department stores, 1984: all points. (Stress = 0.19)

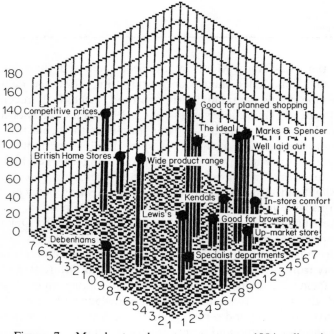

Figure 7.   Manchester department stores, 1984: all points.
(Stress = 0.13)

Table 7. Comparison of image factors, rankings, and average marks

Image area	Debenhams	Lewis's	Kendals	BHS	M & S
(1) Price					
M1 Expensive	4 (3.59)	3 (3.36)	1 (1.82)	5 (4.26)	2 (3.34)
M2 Competitive prices	3 (3.24)	4 (3.62)	5 (4.42)	1 (2.87)	2 (3.12)
(2) Product range					
M1 Wide range	3 (2.70)	1 (2.22)	2 (2.32)	5 (3.67)	4 (3.23)
M2 Wide product range	3 (2.84)	1 (2.09)	2 (2.52)	5 (4.16)	4 (3.52)
Specialist depts	3 (3.04)	1 (2.45)	2 (2.55)	5 (4.45)	4 (3.80)
(3) Store interior					
M1 Comfortable	4 (3.55)	3 (3.35)	1 (2.76)	5 (3.73)	2 (2.88)
M2 In-store comfort	4 (3.75)	2 (2.87)	1 (2.61)	5 (4.07)	3 (3.00)
Well laid out	5 (4.09)	1 (2.75)	3 (2.91)	4 (3.60)	2 (2.77)
(4) Store ambience					
M1 No concepts	–	–	–	–	–
M2 Good for browsing	4 (3.40)	2 (2.64)	1 (2.48)	5 (3.84)	3 (2.84)
Suited to planned shopping	4 (3.38)	1 (2.76)	2 (2.95)	5 (3.95)	3 (3.09)
(5) Personnel					
M1 Polite	4 (3.05)	3 (2.52)	2 (2.46)	5 (3.07)	1 (1.92)
M2 No concepts	–	–	–	–	–
(6) Store reputation					
M1 Traditional	4 (3.81)	2 (2.96)	1 (2.25)	5 (3.96)	3 (3.53)
M2 Up-market store	4 (4.01)	3 (3.02)	1 (2.15)	5 (5.03)	2 (2.82)
(7) The Ideal					
M1 Efficient service; honest, courteous, helpful	4 (3.44)	2 (3.15)	3 (3.20)	5 (4.36)	1 (2.85)
M2 Reliable product, quality store, efficient staff, knowledgeable staff, good refund policy, satisfaction with previous products	4 (4.19)	3 (3.04)	2 (3.00)	5 (4.80)	1 (2.80)

towards BHS and emphasizing price or towards one of the less price-led concepts. 'Wide range of products' is a feasible USP but not that practical without extending store area. A better positioning strategy would be a shift towards 'good for browsing', not associated closely with any one existing store. This would bring Debenhams well into the high-ambience sector, a difficult move for a store with a number of in-store concessions where imposing a coherent image requires the co-operation of a number of concerns.

Interestingly, the publicity issued by Burtons prior to their take-over of Debenhams offered the 'galleria' concept as their proposed method to rejuvenate Debenhams. This would presumably retain the in-store concession approach but involve a substantial redesign of individual stores. It would make Debenhams in fact 'good for browsing' and emphasize the diversity of products through the galleria concept, thus enhancing their 'wide range of products'.

Finally, at the time of writing, House of Fraser had clearly identified that being seen as 'expensive' was limiting their marketing appeal and were using television advertising to try to convince shoppers that 'Kendals are not expensive'.

USING PERCEPTUAL MAPS

The work reported here forms a small part of a much larger project where a number of different retail sectors have been modelled on a local, regional, or national scale. The value of such models seems to lie mainly in their ability to represent market research data in a way which is more meaningful to the retail strategist. Compare, for example, the models in Figures 2 and 5 with the same data presented in a more traditional way in Figures 7 and 8. Figures 8 and 9 present data in a monovariate form in a way which, it was suggested earlier, that many retailers would use in assessing image. Profiles for each store can be obtained and some insight can be gleaned into how the image of one store differs from that of another. However, Figures 2 and 5 show how each store is perceived in relation to its competition, offering better guidance on how to use image in strategic planning.

The role of the 'ideal' concept is an interesting one. The MDS program has no way of *knowing* that the 'ideal' has an additional significance compared with that of other points. Yet the 'ideal' usually appears in the centre of any model surrounded by various retail sectors. When models are made using the responses from subsamples from the market research survey, all retailers and concepts tend to remain in the same relative position except for the 'ideal'.

It seems that everyone can agree that Lewis's is similar to Debenhams and different from Woolworth but that each has his or her own view of the position of the 'ideal'. Not surprisingly, the woman who shops regularly at Kendals sees the 'ideal' as closer to Kendals. However, she does not redefine the concepts that are subsumed within the 'ideal'; she merely sees the concepts that all shoppers see as ideal as being closest to her favourite store—which is why it is her favourite store.

It is tempting to suggest that the ideal concepts are better regarded as things that every retailer in the given sector should seek to include in their image, at least in the perceptions of their target market. It is also interesting to see how quite simple-sounding concepts can be used effectively to label such complex entities as retail outlets. How marketers use these labels to position or re-position their stores is sometimes less simple. The example of Burton's views on Debenhams show how a practical concept, the galleria,

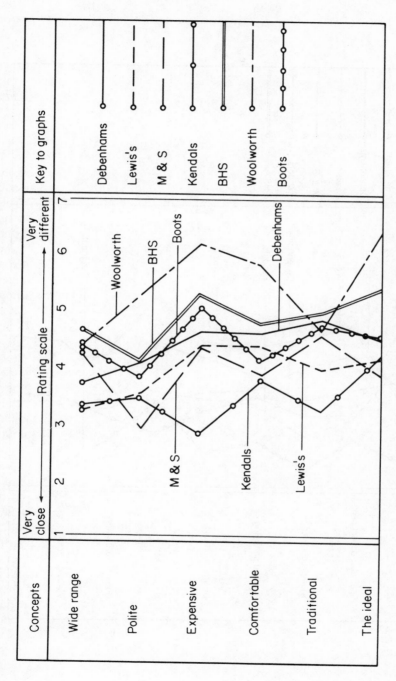

Figure 8. Manchester department stores, 1982: store profiles

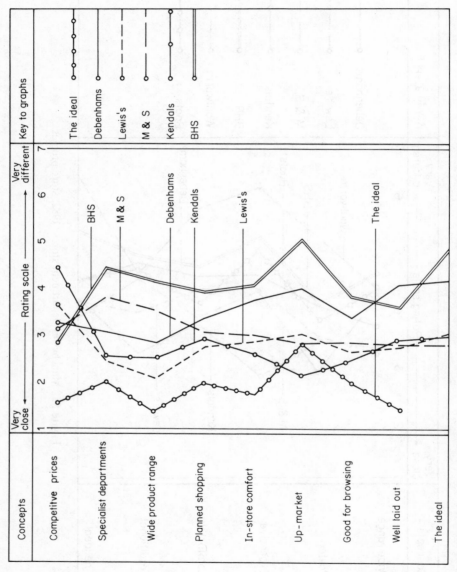

Figure 9. Manchester department stores, 1984: store profiles

which most retailers would relate to immediately down to some level of detail, can be compatible with more diffuse concepts such as 'wide range' and 'good for browsing'.

However, translating concepts into practical reality is rarely that straight-forward. In practice, store design, product range, staff and their training, and advertising have all to be changed to effect a substantial change in image. This needs to be established in each and every store. Even so, the more successful retailers are often those who adopt a formula for their businesses which is imposed strictly on each store. Further market research is often necessary to test whether the proposed changes can and do translate into the desired image-change in the perception of the customer.

CONCLUSION

The two studies demonstrate how the methodology can establish a realistic representation of a retail sector, explain why stores are seen as different or similar, and finally how it can monitor changes in image caused by the action of the retailer or changes in consumer taste and perception.

The general lessons on store-image strategies include the advantages of measuring competing images at the same time as one's own. Defining and executing an image strategy in isolation is clearly dangerous if that strategy results in narrowing rather than widening the degree of differentiation with competition. Similarly, image strategies do not have to aim for what has been labelled here as an 'ideal' position in the marketplace. In fact it can be assumed that this will form at least part of the strategy of all competing retailers. By inference, each successful image strategy will contain its own point or points of differentiation. Finally, a store's image is a complex factor. Measuring it in monodimensional form is less likely to offer the strategist a valid picture of the market he is seeking to influence. Multivariate techniques, while more complex, offer the potential for more realistic measurement.

NOTE

1. When the concepts are included the stress in two dimensions is high enough at 0.23 to distort the representation slightly (Figure 2). A three-dimensional model (Figure 3) has a lower stress at 0.13 but is more difficult to comprehend.

REFERENCES

Brooks, J. M. (1985). *The Marketing of Retailers*. PhD thesis due for presentation in 1986, Manchester Polytechnic.
Davies, P. M. and Coxon, A. P. M. *Key Texts in Multidimensional Scaling*, London: Heinemann: see also Coxon, A. P. M. *The Users Guide to Multidimensional*

152 *Business Strategy and Retailing*

Scaling, London: Heinemann, and the associated manual to the MDS(x) Program Suite.

Hollander, P. (1960). 'The wheel of retailing.' *Journal of Marketing*, **25**, July, 37–42.

Kruskal, J. B. (1964). 'Multi-dimensional scaling by optimising goodness of fit to a non-metric hypothesis.' *Psychometrika*, **29**, 1–27: see also Kruskal, J. B., and Wish, M., *Multidimensional Scaling*, London: Sage Publications.

Lindquist, J. D. (1974). 'Meaning of image.' *Journal of Retailing*, **50**, No. 4, Winter, 29–38.

Stefflre, V. (1967). In *Maxwell House Division (A)*, a case study published by Harvard College, 1967, revised 1970.

Stefflre, V. (1971). *New Products and New Enterprises. A Report on an Experiment in Applied Social Science*, PhD Thesis, University of California, 1971.

CHAPTER 10
Rationalization and the Problems of Re-positioning: UK Co-operatives Caught in the Middle

JOSHUA BAMFIELD
City of Birmingham Polytechnic

There is no proposition which meets us in the field of political economy oftener than this—that there cannot be two prices in the same market. Such undoubtedly is the natural effect of unimpeded competition; yet everyone knows that there are, very often, two prices in the same market. Not only are there in every large town, and in almost every trade, cheap shops and dear shops, but the same shop often sells the same article at different prices to different customers; and, as a general rule, each retailer adopts his scale of prices to the class of customers whom he expects (J. S. Mill, *Principles of Political Economy*, 1848, p. 174).

In this chapter we discuss some of the strategic issues and problems relating to business decline and retail companies whose performance is unsatisfactory compared with their competitors. The discussion covers three main areas. First, the options facing a declining firm are outlined in the context of a choice between general *cost reduction* and *re-positioning* the company (these options are outlined below). Second, the experience of the British retail Co-operative Movement is analysed in relation to these key strategic options, demonstrating the problems of using a cost-reduction strategy as the basis for a sustainable recovery. Finally, we look at the wider implications of this study for retailers of all kinds.

THE MAJOR RE-POSITIONING OPTIONS

Competition, as Mill states above, does not mean there can only be one price. Similarly, in any one market there can be more than one strategy—even in markets that are apparently price-dominated, such as grocery or electrical durables. The diversity of the tastes, needs, and disposable incomes of consumers creates several market segments. Moreover, locational factors and

differences in consumer perceptions and in consumer loyalty can provide the
basis for a choice of distinct and effective strategies.

Porter (1980) argues that whilst there are many possible business strategies
for firms, worthwhile strategies are those which aim to produce *sustainable
competitive advantage*. Competitive advantage is essentially the ability to
earn above-average profits—*sustainable* competitive advantage arises from
creating a defensible long-term position in the market which reduces the
firm's vulnerability to competition. Companies face many pressures, including
new types of competition, intensified competitive rivalry, new cost structures,
technological advances, or changes in the pattern of demand.

The key to sustainable competitive advantage is positioning in the market.
By 'positioning' or 're-positioning' is meant the orientation of the company
to meet a precise and defined market need (see Kotler, 1984). Porter (1980)
argues that there are three generic positioning strategies for companies: cost
leadership, industrywide differentiation, and market-segment focus.

Cost leadership

The cost leadership approach would require the firm to become *the* low-cost
retailer, finding and exploiting all sources of cost advantage, including scale
economies and experience benefits in both procurement and store operation,
applying technical/technological innovation to reduce costs, using its muscle
in the scale of its marketing activities, and typically operating in a standard
no-frills manner. Locational factors in retailing mean that there could be
more than one cost leader: but this situation may not, of course, be sustainable in the long term if both companies seek to grow.

Industrywide differentiation

The differentiated firm seeks to be unique in its industry along some dimensions that are widely valued by many buyers and are perceived to be
important. Differentiation can be based on the range and type of goods sold,
the quality and variety of retail provision, the marketing approach, and a
series of other factors.

Market-segment focus

This strategy is quite unlike the others because it rests on the firm's selecting
a segment or group of segments within the industry and tailoring its strategy
to serving the segment(s) to the exclusion of others. Even though it does not
possess a competitive advantage *overall*, the focuser seeks above-average
returns in its target market segment. Its strategy can be based on meeting
the needs of its segment at low cost (e.g. Kwik-Save) or, perhaps more
typically, by exploiting the special needs of its niche markets which are not

being met by more broadly targeted competitors. Examples of the latter approach in the UK include the well-publicized Next and Habitat operations.

In contrast to the three generic strategies of cost leadership, industrywide differentiation and focusing is a policy of general cost reduction.

Cost reduction

Trading problems usually show through in reduced profits. Thus an attempt to reduce costs in relation to sales is a natural response to a problem that may originate in poor positioning. For that reason it can be wholly inappropriate for anything except short-term benefits. The danger is that a firm may use cost reduction to implement an unsustainable strategy rather than generating a new strategy. A cost-reduction strategy will normally consist of rationalization of stores, asset-reduction, labour-force reductions (e.g. by quota), improvements in cost structures (via store refurbishment), as well as new store development and improved marketing. Net margins improve because of the fall in total costs overall; any increase in sales volume from the reduced number of outlets will lower *percentage* costs against sales.

Whilst most, if not all, companies adopt cost-reduction policies at various times, in this context a 'cost-reduction strategy' is differentiated from a re-positioning strategy because it is seen by the firm as a fairly complete means of restoring profitability and increased sales—i.e. as a substitute for clear re-positioning.

THE NEED FOR RE-POSITIONING

The fundamental basis of above-average performance is *low costs* or *differentiation*. A firm should either have the low-cost structure to earn above-average profits (setting the reference frame for prices within the industry), or, if that cannot be achieved, Porter argues that the firm should avoid direct cost/price competition with mass merchandisers. This can be done by strategies of *industrywide differentiation* or *focusing* on an individual market segment.

Firms that are unwilling or unable to position themselves clearly may become what Porter terms 'stuck in the middle'. This is a poor strategic position: 'The firm lacks the market share, capital investment, and resolve to play the low-cost game, the industrywide differentiation necessary to obviate the need for a low-cost position, or the focus to create differentiation or a low-cost position in a more limited sphere' (Porter, 1980, p. 41). Obviously this is not a sustainable position.

Up to now, multiples have grown mainly at the expense of the independent sector and, of course, Co-operatives. In 20 years their share of retail trade has risen from 29.2% (1961) to 50.2% (1982). Moreover, as Walters and

Knee (1985) argue, multiples are tending to converge on the same markets—C1/C2 groups aged between 25 and 44. The boundaries between retail businesses are coming down as shops diversify into other kinds of business. It is clear that in the 1980s the growth needed to sustain many multiples will only occur at the expense of other multiples. In grocery, for example, where the trade share of multiples has risen in the four years 1980–4 from 57% to 67% (EIU, 1985), there has been a major shakeout which has led to the disappearance of many weaker retail multiples. This trend will be accentuated by the increasing importance of superstores; for these units are highly specific retail premises with few easily available substitute uses. Thus exit barriers are high and we can expect fierce competition to continue. The same trend of domination by a few rapidly growing firms are seen in other retail markets, though the characteristics that incorporate these trends vary between industries.

Substantial profits can be made in the most competitive industries. In 1983 Norkett (1985) showed that the upper quartile (i.e. the best 25%) of grocery retailers earned 3.1% profit on sales compared with the average of 1.8% for the sector as a whole and 0.5% received by the lower quartile. In this situation, companies following an 'average' strategy (which may have been perfectly effective in a fragmented market) rather than a clear generic strategy may become vulnerable to accurately positioned competitors. Similarly, the growth rate of larger multiples will mean that there may not be room in the market for several firms following the same strategy on an industrywide basis. This is particularly true for a strategy of cost leadership, which is only sustainable if the firm has the lowest costs, or at least similar costs to the cost/price leader.

Thus re-positioning should become increasingly central to strategy-formulation as a means of providing firms with a distinctive role in the market as competition becomes more intense and a 'shakeout' occurs in many sectors of the retail industry.

CO-OPERATIVE STRATEGIC POSITION

We now turn to consider the strategy of the British retail Co-operative Movement in the light of these options. First, we consider the strategic position of the retail Co-operatives, and in the following section the specific retail strategies adopted by UK Co-operative societies are analysed. Discussion of the recent experience of the UK Co-operative Movement can be seen in Arnott (1983), Bamfield (1977), and Elliot (1985).

The UK retail Co-operative Movement is a voluntary group of a hundred autonomous Co-operative societies, each of which is a multi-purpose retailer operating a variety of shops in most retail trades. They have major strengths in their absolute market share, physical assets (1984 book value of £763

Table 1. Profile of the retail Co-operative Movement, 1984

Co-operative Retail Societies

Turnover	£4 460 million
Net profit	0.5% turnover
Net assets	£802 million
Reserves	£341 million
Membership	8 463 000
Employee numbers	86 000 (FTE)
No. of shops	5 826

Largest Co-operatives	*Turnover (£m)*	*Employees*
CRS	£969	17 000
CWS Retail	£428	7 200
United Co-op	£234	4 200
Greater Nottingham	£231	5 100
N. Eastern	£226	4 000
Central	£179	4 000
CWS	£2 251	21 000
Co-op Bank	£1 195	3 700
Co-op Insurance	£2 269	10 500

Major retail competitors	*Turnover (£m)*
Marks & Spencer	£3 088
Tesco	£2 744
Sainsbury	£2 689
Boots	£1 833
Asda	£1 755
Woolworth	£1 269
John Lewis Partnership	£1 072

Source: Company accounts, Co-operative Statistics.

million), financial assets, and a high degree of consumer loyalty: 8.5 million members jointly provide share capital of £171 million.

Although they have been in decline since the 1950s, the retail Co-operative societies are still collectively the UK's largest retailer, with a 1984 turnover of £4 614 million. Their core business is grocery, providing about one-half of Co-op sales, but they are extensively diversified with almost 6 000 shops, ranging from superstores to convenience shops, and also department stores, food specialists, general stores, clothing, electricals, etc. There are major funeral, dairy, and motor trades businesses. The Co-operative Movement is profiled in Table 1. Each society is autonomous and has its own directors and management. Concerted action between societies is therefore voluntary. Societies collectively own the CWS, which provides wholesale, buying, and marketing activities for Co-operatives and is a substantial manufacturer and food processor in its own right.

The high-water mark of UK Co-operatives was 1957, when their share of total retail trade was 12.3%. In food they held 19.7% of total UK retail business. At that time, the share of all multiple traders was only 20.4%.

Co-operatives declined because they were unable to respond to the rapid changes in retailing. Their original trading formula of selling standard goods at high gross margins through a network of mostly small, neighbourhood shops was successful in an environment where there was little price-competition. High profits were returned to members as the 'Dividend' (1.0¼d in the £1 in 1958, for example). However, multiple supermarkets using new promotional techniques, higher retail standards, and the development of newer and better shops (whose sites took advantage of the rise in car-ownership) made Co-operative trading practices unattractive (Stacey and Wilson, 1966). Since then, although Co-operatives have changed in many ways they have generally been unable to configure their operations in ways that matched the effectiveness of multiples.

The problems of Co-operatives over the past 20 years have shown through in two main areas: declining profitability and falling sales. To deal with these problems, Co-operatives have undertaken extensive cost reduction and modernization of their businesses, starting in the mid-1960s. Since 1968 this process has reduced the number of their shops from 24 500 to 5 800 (a fall of 76%) and Co-operative employees have fallen by 58% (full-time equivalent (FTE)) from 203 000 to 86 000.

However, although there was a Co-operative revival in the mid-1970s, cost reduction did not preserve either Co-operative profitability or their sales. Table 2 reveals a pattern of a steady fall in the rate of net surplus since the 1960s (although in part the high rates of the 1960s were due more to high prices than to efficiency). In the 1980s profitability has been marginal, the rate of profit as a percentage of sales in 1984 being 0.5%

Table 2.   Retail Co-operative Societies, 1963–84

	1960	1963	1968	1971	1978	1984
Retail sales volume	109.0	100.0	83.5	73.8	77.1	65.7
Employees FTE (000s)	262	260	203	162	129	86
Membership (millions)	13.0	13.2	12.8	11.3	10.5	8.5
Net surplus (percentage sales)	5.8	4.6	3.2	2.8	2.1	0.5
Dividend (percentage sales)	4.7	3.8	2.6	1.8	1.0	0.4
Capital employed (£m)	415.8	429.5	404.0	353.7	608.8	781.0
Share cap (£m)	254.1	247.5	203.9	142.2	159.2	171.0
Reserves (£m)	39.3	43.5	49.0	70.2	255.1	333.0
No. of retail Co-op societies	895	708	495	271	197	112
No. of shops	29 000	28 500	24 500	16 500	10 500	5 800
Share retail trade	11.0	9.5	7.8	7.0	6.8	5.2

Source: Derived from Co-operative Union, Census of Distribution, Retail Inquiry.

The Co-operative trade share in 1984 of 5.2% was 40% of that achieved in 1957; but, as well as losing trade share, the Co-ops have lost volume sales. Since 1968 their volume of trade has fallen by 20%.

In terms of positioning, the Co-operative Movement aims to be a mass merchandiser selling standard branded and Co-operative own-label goods to compete on price, particularly from its superstores and large supermarkets. Reflecting this, its share of the packaged grocery business is particularly high, although the wide variety of its shops and standards makes its actual positioning stance rather fuzzy. Its approach in non-foods has been down-market, based on the price-conscious rather than fashion-conscious person and having little appeal for the young. The only major success has been in electrical consumer durables, where national buying of a standardized number of lines and low retail margins have given Co-operatives a significant role in this sector.

CO-OPERATIVE DISTINCTIVENESS AND VALUES

Co-operatives have always seen themselves as representing distinct moral attitudes in retailing as opposed to their competitors—whom they saw as being primarily profit-motivated. By the 1950s and 1960s Co-operative 'values' were viewed as involving 'profit sharing' (high dividends for members), 'consumer service' (the cross-subsidizing of products and shops, acceptance of loss-making outlets as a consumer service), 'fair prices' (the dislike of selective price-cutting or modern promotional methods), and 'equity' (targeted on lower-income consumers). These values were seen as fundamental and organic, particularly by lay directors.

However whilst the *principles* were fundamental, the particular application was merely the trading formula used by Co-operatives until the 1950s. Societies resisted changes in their trading formula; this would have affected the integrity of the entire system. Price-cutting to meet multiple competition reduced gross margins and therefore the dividend rate and would have increased the number of loss-making small shops. Co-operatives were particularly anxious not to reduce the dividend: this was not only the major inducement to trade for most members but was seen by Co-operatives as their prime claim to consumer-orientated distinctiveness.

Thus for a long period of time Co-operatives tended to discount the increasingly successful experience of multiple retailers as inappropriate to the needs of Co-operatives. Changes in retail techniques were applied in ways that did not threaten established values. Co-operatives had introduced self-service shops into the UK; by 1961 42% of all self-service and 26% of all supermarkets were Co-op-owned. However, the supermarkets were run like corner shops—even as late as 1968, 73% of Co-op supermarkets had the same price structure as corner shops, would make up orders, and provide a delivery service (CU, 1969). Self-service/supermarkets were seen by Co-operatives as modern shop layouts rather than methods of capitalizing on the (hitherto slight) economies of shop size, and so lowering percentage personnel costs by using new promotional and price-cutting techniques to boost volume sales.

Grinyer and Spender (1979) term the distinctive culture and pattern of beliefs developed by a firm a 'managerial recipe'. The managerial recipe (or what Co-operatives called 'values') reflects the accumulated experience of the industry and what can, and cannot, be done. They argue that each firm has its own recipe, determining how managers perceive their environment and the range of options they are likely to consider as solutions to problems. Whilst the Co-operative managerial recipe as described can be regarded as virtually a pathological condition, preventing effective responses to environmental change, this is just an extreme example of managerial conditioning through the 'managerial recipe.'

CO-OPERATIVE STRATEGY

The Co-operative aim in the 1960s, when finally the Movement realized the seriousness of its position, was first to survive and then to regain its former situation in retailing as a mass merchandiser based on Co-operative values. With some exceptions, Co-operatives did not think in terms of a new strategy incorporating re-positioning. They were enforcing the existing recipe using different techniques.

Initially, Co-operatives ignored their growing trading problems, declining real sales being masked by inflation. It was felt that current trading conditions were both exceptional and untypical. By the mid-1960s Co-operative societies had introduced tight budgetary control. Uneconomic operations were cut back and about 4 000 shops were closed. Although trade volume fell by 16.5% between 1963 and 1968, the policy was successful in restraining the fall in profitability. Net surplus fell only from 4.6% to 3.2% in the same period.

However, a rapid deterioration in performance after 1968 forced societies to introduce rapid cost reduction strategies or face the danger of collapse. The continuous erosion of profitability and sales for more than 10 years had left them financially weak. Poor liquidity, high dividend to retain custom, and the continued existence of large numbers of highly marginal Co-operative shops left them vulnerable to a downturn in trade or a rise in operating costs. Both these problems occurred during 1968–70. Cash-flow problems created serious difficulties, particularly when unfavourable publicity prompted widespread share withdrawals by members—£50 million was taken out of societies between 1968 and 1970 (or 12% of total capital employed).

The major strategies for recovery were as follows:

Cost- and asset-reduction

This was the most important part of the strategy, involving the closure of one third of their shops and shedding over one quarter of their employees in three years. Asset sales during 1969–71 raised about £65 million. Although most retail societies sold off their processing and manufacturing operations, cost- and asset-reduction represented a fairly equal retrenchment for all Co-operative activities. Specialist shops, particularly food specialists, were hit most of all, but there was no evident policy to sell off or leave particular retail business activities; on the contrary, Co-operatives preserved their spread of business operations very much as before.

Improved cost structure

Policy here involved modernizing existing shops and developing new stores. *Store modernisation* was astonishingly successful. Previously most Co-operative shops were rather outdated and often poorly run. Investment in new interiors, refrigeration, self-service conversion, repainting, and remodelling the exterior produced substantial increases in trade. The original store-modernization programme, 'Operation Facelift', only cost £50 million to convert 5 000 shops. This gave a new lease of life to many older shops, and may have been perverse because the success of the programme convinced Co-operative societies that smaller shops could be run profitably.

New store development played a major part in reducing cost structures after 1972. During the 1970s and 1980s Co-operative capital spending has been about the industry average, though at a lesser rate than that of the major multiples.

Marketing and merchandising

Market research had shown that Co-operative shops appealed mainly to older and to lower-income consumers. Even before the crisis, Co-operatives had become the largest retail advertiser (£2.4 million out of a total retail spend) of £4.9 million), attempting to re-position themselves by emphasizing a new corporate identity (as the 'CO-OP'—a national organization distinct from the previous patchwork of societies), selective price-cutting, and an atmosphere of excitement ('It's all at the CO-OP, now!'). Promotional activity stressed price and the similarity between Co-operatives and other retailers. They aimed to recapture the average housewife (probably a C1) who would formerly have been a loyal mainstay of her local Co-op and was now shopping at somewhere like Tesco.

A major part of the old Co-operative recipe had been high dividends,

which was seen as the Co-operative differential factor and a primary inducement to trade. Dividend stamps met the need for a lower rate of dividend
which would still appeal to members. In fact, stamps had more appeal than
the sort of dividend rates being paid in the late 1960s, and their introduction
into an area was usually accompanied by a rise in turnover.

Although the aims of the Co-operative Union Regional Plan to create 250
Regional Societies (CU, 1968) were not met, society mergers were an
important mechanism of change in the Co-operative Movement. The number
of societies fell from 495 to 197 between 1968 and 1978, by which time a
revised target had been announced. As a result of mergers, societies were
able to concentrate administration and warehousing activities at the centre
(closing down peripheral operations), make better use of existing management personnel, and introduce change faster than they might otherwise have
been able to do. Specialist societies like Co-operative Retail Services (the
CRS) developed expertise in taking over unprofitable societies and turning
most of them round by a combination of cost reduction and modernization
in an average of 6 months.

By 1973 net profits were up to 4.4% of sales (compared with 2.8% in
1971). More people in total were using Co-ops—its percentage of shoppers
rose from 44% (1972) to 54% in 1974. By 1975, the *Financial Times* was
able to declare, 'The Co-op . . . does genuinely appear to be on the way up
again' (Walker, 1976) as Co-operative turnover rose by 23% in 1975
compared with multiple growth of only 21%.

The Co-operative revival proved to be short-lived. Intensified competition
in grocery started by Tesco in 1977 produced a new competitive situation,
affecting all retailers—including Tesco! New types of highly differentiated
competition (see, for example, Walters and Knee, 1985), the accelerated
trend towards larger stores, and lower gross margins harmed retailers like
the Co-operatives, whose costs were above average.

After 1980, the Co-operative position became critical, with problems in all
its main businesses. Profitability has been marginal—against sales, since 1980,
the figures are 0.8%, 0.0%, −0.1%, 0.2%, and 0.5% in 1984. Further large-
scale rationalization has occurred and a heavy fall in the number of societies
from 197 (1978) to 100 (1985). Almost one third of Co-operative trade is in
the hands of CRS and CWS Retail—the Co-operative 'ambulances'. Not
only has profitability since 1980 been either weak or negative but capital
investment and dividend payments have mainly been financed by asset sales
and drawing on reserves. Since 1980, Co-operatives have disbursed £190
million in this way. Between 1981 and 1983 Co-operatives paid out in dividend £70 million out of net profits of £4 million!

In 1985/6, however, there were signs that the Co-operatives were returning
to profitability and adopting specific re-positioning strategies.

CO-OPERATIVE PROBLEMS OF RE-POSITIONING

The key to effective re-positioning is making clear choices. Although Co-operatives cut back their uneconomic operations they did not cut costs enough to play the low-cost game with Tesco, Asda, or Sainsbury, nor did they differentiate themselves enough to protect societies from price-competition—i.e. they were stuck in the middle. There were failures both in re-positioning strategy and its implementation. Implementation was far too slow; by the time it was occurring, resources had been severely depleted, and the competitive advantage had been lost in that competitors had already progressed much further.

In fact the fall in Co-op costs was fairly small—personnel costs were down from 15.3% of sales in 1968 to 14.1% in 1978, with other costs level at 6.8%. By 1984, personnel costs were 12.5% but other costs had risen to 7.8%. Major grocery competitors based their operating costs upon the best sites, shop-size economies, integrated procurement and shop-replenishment, and high levels of operating efficiency. In none of these areas did Co-operatives seriously attempt to obtain the same advantages as multiples.

In procurement, for example, the Co-operative Movement has failed to integrate buying and physical distribution as part of its corporate needs. Although 80% of societies now draw their grocery supplies from the Co-operative Wholesale Society (CWS) Regional Distribution Centres, buying and warehousing in other areas is spread between the CWS and the individual societies rather than being an integrated part of the Movement's value chain.

The Co-operative recipe of a multi-purpose total retailer has prevented it from selling off certain individual businesses; this could have left it free to concentrate on a smaller number of activities. Thus, as before, the Movement's spread of operations runs from grocery and butchers, to department stores, footwear, and funerals. Each one of these operations is under pressure from highly professional *specialist* multiple undertakings. Diversification by each society has thus fragmented the Co-operative approach into individual businesses. Most operations, quite simply, lack the critical mass necessary to create excellence or the experience in depth to rectify problems when they occur.

Moreover, given the Co-operative size structure of shops, Co-operatives had considerable problems in achieving cost structures similar to those of the market-leaders. In spite of store closures (-76%, 1968–84) and new-store development, the gap between the average Co-operative and the average multiple grocer widened: by 1984, the average Co-operative was 3 563 ft² compared with the multiple average of 8 988 (see Table 3 for the comparative changes in the average sizes of Co-operative and multiple grocery stores).

Not only were larger multiples outspending Co-operatives in new development but they were closing almost as many shops: between 1971 and 1982, multiples closed 50.5% of their grocery outlets.

Co-operatives obviously needed to make faster progress than multiples, as their starting-point was so much lower. New stores, however, were difficult to finance, as most Co-operative societies were only marginally profitable and the largest stores were subject to long planning delays. The other option—increasing the average size of store by closing larger numbers of small stores—would also have created severe problems, for closing a high proportion of retail outlets would have cut volume sales faster than it cut costs—perversely causing percentage costs to increase. Procurement terms are also likely to have been adversely affected.

Table 3.   Change in average grocery shop size, Co-ops and multiples

Annual average sales per foodstore 1957–71 (£)

	1957	1961	1966	1971		
Co-ops	30 618	31 116	35 517	68 506		
Multiples	26 100	32 425	50 398	93 626		

Average sales area (ft²) of self-service shops and supermarkets 1967–84

	1967	1972	1977	1981	1983	1984
Co-ops	1296	1513	1998	2617	3217	3563
Multiples	1969	2835	4679	6924	8356	8988

Sources: Census of Distribution; *Survey and Directory of SS Stores and Supermarkets*, IGD.

Whilst a re-positioning change of such magnitude might have been possible some years previously, when Co-operative profitability and liquidity was stronger, under later circumstances the Co-operative strategy of cost-reduction to gain cost-leadership was simply not capable of being carried through. Hence, in practice, Co-operative societies emphasized continued store modernization, which was less risky and had a faster payback than new store development, although it could not produce the low costs typical of purpose-built large retail outlets.

Given the poor chance of success of the Co-operative Movement becoming a cost leader once again, it might, as an alternative, have attempted to differentiate itself or to focus on a market segment. This is difficult to do in food, although the experience of Safeway, Sainsbury, and Marks & Spencer shows that it is not impossible. The Co-operative Movement's attempt to differentiate itself was mainly a promotional phenomenon. It was not reflected in the actual merchandise range, and, given that Co-operatives were using the same staff and shops (albeit modernized) as before, the new positioning was not credible to the public, particularly the younger age groups. The Co-op was seen as a down-market operator; to position itself in a new market needed a carefully co-ordinated strategy that consisted of more than store modernization, some change in product range, and an increase in promotional expenditure.

Co-operative attempts at differentiation in the 1970s were based on differential pricing to meet local competition. All shops were seen as performing essentially the same task, and operating in broadly the same way with similar product ranges, even though the gross margins differed. Co-operatives now recognize that the ambiguity of their previous positioning strategies was counterproductive, and are developing new differentiated models for their stores.

The role of the managerial recipe in inhibiting strategic change amongst Co-operatives has been emphasized. In particular, as a consumer-owned organization, Co-operatives have been committed to the *form* of being a distinctive consumer-champion rather than the reality. As an example, we might cite the popularity of dividend stamps as a replacement for the dividend, which meant, as we have seen, that Co-operatives were not forced to develop a *unique* trading difference which would motivate customers and membership. Instead they continued to attempt to compete on price using a rebate system, even being prepared to dig into their reserves to fund the stamps when profits were insufficient. Similarly, the democratic format of regional Co-operatives by which members control societies is a particularly pious myth in view of the negligible participation rates. Nonetheless, to ensure 'democratic' control, the old recipe lives on in the new Regional Societies that have been created by merger. They look very much like the old multi-purpose Co-operative retailers on a larger scale. The Co-operative organization structure has carried on much as before: the failure to link mergers with the restructuring of its individual businesses as national specialist chains means that many specialist operations lack skilled management, specialist attention, and finance.

The Co-operative Movement today is very different from the Co-operatives of the 1960s. However, its inability to position itself or, more accurately, to perceive a distinctive role for itself leaves it as a 'satisficing' retailer, improving its operations steadily but not engaging the major traders either as a cost leader or as a carefully differentiated or focused trader.

WIDER IMPLICATIONS OF RE-POSITIONING

The case for re-positioning has already been made—that in an increasingly competitive market, firms must use a generic strategy to produce a *sustainable* competitive advantage.

Cost-leadership strategy

There is a danger that a firm needing to re-position will be caught in a vicious circle of decline. It may lack the management to run the new shops or to operate the business in the new manner. Low levels of efficiency mean that it cannot pay premium rents or prices for new stores, and, moreover, is not regarded as an anchor tenant for a shopping centre. Thus it may be offered only second-rate sites. Its new profile may lack credibility, and thus it loses many existing customers without gaining new ones.

This is not an untypical problem, particularly where attachment to the current managerial recipe is so strong that change does not occur unless precipitated by crisis. Many companies (the Co-operative Movement was our example) respond to change by cost reduction in the hope of gaining costs on a par with the market leaders, particularly where these are cost leaders. One has to ask, of course, whether a strategy of cost leadership is credible for a company which is seriously lagging behind the market leaders.

If the firm is seeking to achieve cost leadership it needs to link the key drivers of low costs. In grocery these would be the scale economies of larger shops, learning effects, procurement, and the use of new technology to centralize decisions, control the business, and enforce standards. Moreover, these are not separate sources of low costs—the major firms integrate them using new technology, in particular to link procurement with warehousing, physical distribution, and stock-replenishment in one total function.

Market leadership—cost or otherwise—is in many ways the pursuit of excellence at all levels through a sequential, nit-picking process of incremental change. It is difficult to see how unsuccessful firms which are neither deriving all the individual cost benefits nor integrating them fully to optimize control can vault over the industry-leaders. For reasons discussed in the context of the Co-operatives, strategies based on 'making the best' of the existing network of shops (however well modernized) staff, and sites may not be sustainable in the longer term if competitors base their low costs on new, well-sited, and carefully planned large stores. Investment in new shops by the cost-reducing company will usually be insufficient to make up for years of underinvestment and, moreover, may not be very profitable, because the cost-reducing company lacks the skills and the experience of competitors in running newer shops.

If the cost leader himself becomes resistant to change, or if the market or structure of costs changes so that the cost leader's advantages diminish, then a strategy of cost leadership could be credible. Focused cost leadership, particularly in a defined geographical area, would be possible. Generally, however, cost reduction strategies used as a means of gaining or regaining cost leadership seem doomed to failure, both because they are frequently an attempt to reinforce an outmoded recipe and because the cost-reducing firm has no real chance of overhauling the cost leaders. Hence these firms are most likely to end up 'stuck in the middle.'

Differentiation strategy

In contrast, a differentiation strategy may well be more practical for a company requiring re-positioning. In terms of shop size, for example, Hepworth's Next operation and Burton's Principles both use small stores (sales areas of 1200 and 1500 ft², respectively (EIU, 1985)) in which presentation is critical, whilst the Shoppers' Paradise discount operation represents a use for smaller Fine Fare shops. The high degree of market segmentation and the small stock range of both the 'edited retailing' and the focused discounter makes size much less important.

It is significant that Woolworth, after many years of 'making the best of it' and moving its existing shops up and down the market, is currently closing many of its large universal stores to concentrate in well-located sites on six key areas of merchandise in which the company has a clear competitive advantage. The Co-operative Movement has also decided to differentiate by developing three distinct modes of food operation—each one serving a different function. In CRS, for example, this means Superstores (cost and price appeal), 'Market Fresh' Supermarkets (fresh food supermarkets with a high percentage of high gross margin lines), and 'Stop and Shop' convenience stores (with a distinct product range to meet neighbourhood needs emphasizing either fresh foods or convenience products) (*The Grocer*, 1985a, 1985c).

Obviously this combination of cost leadership, differentiation, and focusing for specific types of shops may simply be confusing. Unless a firm strictly separates the units following different generic strategies—for example, in the way that Fine Fare does with Shoppers' Paradise—it may compromise the ability of any one of them to achieve its competitive advantage. As a further example, one could cite Tesco's decision to sell the new no-frills Victor Value discount chain (*The Grocer*, 1985b). This was justified by the need for consistency in Tesco's approach to consumers now that Tesco is adopting a softer, more up-market profile (differentiation).

Re-positioning will usually involve changing the customers' perception of the business. This means that re-positioning must be communicated: *apparent* differentiation or cost leadership can be more important than actual re-positioning of which the customer is unaware. Whether this is credible depends on the current image and on the effectiveness of what the company is doing. A company with a poor, down-market image obviously finds it difficult to establish a strong position up-market; whilst one which is already, or in the recent past has been, successfully differentiated can redifferentiate or refocus itself more easily.

A company with acute problems of customer perceptions may have to trade from completely new locations or use a new name or business style to create discontinuity with the previous business (e.g. the Next operation) if it is to be successful. Acquisition may be one way of doing this. Moreover, to be effective, differentiation as a strategy must seem relevant to buyers' needs or buyers' total costs if they are being asked to pay a premium for it.

Is differentiation costly?

Unless a firm can achieve cost leadership it is advised to differentiate. Does this mean that differentiation is costly?

Differentiation consists of trying to provide uniqueness in some relevant form. This is obviously likely to increase costs, particularly if higher service levels are being provided, high-cost locations/up-market ambience, or goods to a more exacting specification. Next, for example, according to its originator George Davies is aimed at 'women who care about fashion first and price second' (Oddy, 1984). Then there are some companies which differentiate *because* they have high costs and need to justify this in the marketplace. Thus J. W. Thornton, the vertically integrated confectionary retailer, would be unable to match Cadbury on price; but it can successfully emphasize high-quality, fresh products sold in a high-service 'old-fashioned' retail environment. Similarly, the new-style grocery/CTN convenience store adopts different opening times and distinctive product ranges at higher gross margins because it cannot match supermarket prices. If the market itself is small then scale and experience effects may also be small, thus increasing overall costs. At the extreme, high levels of differentiation or focusing *have* to be costly to impart the necessary degree of exclusivity or sophistication.

Differentiation may be costly if there are substantial scale, learning, and procurement economies in an industry. However, the differentiating firm may configure value on a large scale in ways that outdo those seeking cost leadership—as evidenced by firms such as Boots, Marks & Spencer, and Sainsbury. In the case of Marks & Spencer, differentiation is based on close linkages with suppliers, a small and standardized inventory, close understanding of customer needs, and customer loyalty. Sainsbury, which (like Marks & Spencer) is a differentiated market leader, uses large stores and emphasizes tight vertical linkages through high-value own-label lines. It has pioneered control of inventory through computer technology and the management of physical distribution. Bejam and Virgin Records are two further examples. In none of these companies is differentiation costly.

Similarly, focusing can be a low-cost approach. The cost focuser attempts to meet the needs of a market segment at lower cost than industrywide competitors. It may use locations, inventories, or operating techniques which would be unsatisfactory on an industry basis (e.g. Kwik-Save) but which enable the firm to meet the segment needs at low costs. Given the up-market, quasi-differentiated approach used in the 1980s by most large retailers, shops meeting standard needs in a practical manner (e.g. the BeWise clothing chain) or the discount shops existing in low-income areas will meet the neighbourhood's needs more precisely than national supermarkets or super-stores which may be overperforming in relation to the focuser's target segment.

Competitors' reactions

The success of re-positioning will also be affected by competitors' reactions. Obviously they are unlikely to respond to a small competitor, but the re-positioning strategies of large firms may be vitiated by competitors who engage in heavy promotional expenditure or price-competition before the new strategy can be established. A strong generic strategy which is successful will usually result in imitation—e.g. the response to Tesco's 'Operation Checkout', and the me-too strategies based on Next from Dash, Principles, Now, Look, and Surprise. In this context, focusing may be a more support-able strategy because it is less of a threat. A centralized company may find it difficult to respond to a competitor's focused strategy without jeopardizing its own industrywide approach. However, many national retail companies *can* adjust product range and prices to meet specific local conditions; and, if markets fragment, they may organize themselves increasingly to do so. If the salient characteristics of the focus strategy can be adopted by other industry-wide retailers, then the focus strategy is not supportable—an example being the wholefoods sector, which developed a market in the 1970s to see much of it taken over by conventional supermarkets in the 1980s.

CONCLUSION

In retail markets, which are, perversely, both becoming increasingly concen-trated and also segmenting and fragmenting, accurate positioning will become more important for successful retailing. Consumers increasingly demand choice and specialization where once a mass-merchandising strategy was adequate. Moreover, a policy based primarily upon price appeal may not be successful in the longer term unless the firm is also the industry's cost-leader and/or can change the managerial recipe as the nature of the business environment and consumer wants and perceptions alters. The example of the Co-operative Movement indicated the inadequacy of trading policies based mainly on incomplete cost reduction—i.e. where the organization was unable to achieve the low cost levels necessary to make the strategy successful. Without in any way minimizing the significance of price to consumer perceptions it is obviously important that retailers increasingly see their companies not as monolithic businesses with a standard appeal to that homogeneous entity 'the Public' but more as a series of separate businesses which are able to meet the needs of different market segments.

REFERENCES

Arnott, D. (1983). 'When the Co-operating faltered.' *Management Today*, October.
Bamfield, J. (1978). 'The revival of the Co-ops.' *Retail and Distributive Management*, March/April.
Churchill, D. (1979). 'International Stores—why small is not so beautiful.' *Financial Times*, 1 May.
Co-operative Union Ltd (1968). *The Regional Plan*, Manchester.
Co-operative Union Ltd (1969). *Co-operative Supermarkets*, Trade Advisory Bulletin No. 46, Manchester.
Co-operative Union Ltd (1982). *Co-operative Congress Report 1982*, Manchester.
Economist Intelligence Unit (1985). 'Review of Co-operative societies.' *Retail Business*, July.
Eliot, S. (1985). 'The Co-op's Road To Recovery.' *Retail and Distributive Management*, July/August.
Grinyer, P. H., and Spender, J.-C. (1979). *Turnaround—Managerial Recipes for Strategic Success*, London: Associated Business Press.
Grocer, The (1985a). 'CRS gives up pricefighter for market fresh fascia.' 26 January.
Grocer, The (1985b). 'Tesco gives up small store concept and sells VV to Bejam.' 8 February.
Grocer, The (1985c). 'CRS unveils plan for 460 stop and shop convenience outlets.' 6 April.
International Publishing Corporation (1973). *Survey and Directory of Self-Service Shops and Supermarkets 1972*, London: IPC Consumer Industries.
Kotler, P. (1984). *Marketing Management: Analysis, Planning and Control*, Englewood Cliffs, NJ.: Prentice-Hall International.
Norkett, P. (1985). 'A financial approach to supermarket success.' *Retail and Distributive Management*, November/December.
Ody, P. (1984). 'Fashion retailing—what next?' *Retail and Distributive Management*, September/October.
Porter, M. E. (1980). *Competitive Strategy: Techniques for Analysing Industries and Competitors*, New York: The Free Press.
Slatter, S. (1984). *Corporate Recovery, Successful Turnround Strategies and their Implementation*, Harmondsworth: Penguin.
Stacey, N. A. H., and Wilson, A. (1966). *The Changing Pattern of Distribution*, Oxford: Pergamon.
Tucker, K. A. (1975). *Economies of Scale in Food Retailing*, Farnborough, Hants: Saxon House/Lexington Books.
Walker, D. (1976). 'Co-op revival.' *Financial Times*, 30 April.
Walters, D., and Knee, D. (1985). 'Competing successfully in a dynamic world.' *Retail and Distributive Management*, March/April.

PART 3
Managing Retail Strategy

GERRY JOHNSON
Manchester Business School

The introduction to this volume included a discussion of some of the characteristics of strategy and strategic management. Strategic management was characterized as being concerned with the allocation and reallocation of organizational resources in the context of a changing and often complex environment. Strategic decisions were seen as those which might have longer rather than short-term implications and very often involve many different parts of the organization. One implication is that, as environments change, so too must strategies of organizations. Indeed, in the book so far we have seen many indications that in retailing the strategies of organizations have changed quite dramatically in the last decade or so—some authors have gone so far as to refer to the 'retail revolution'. So strategic management is to do with the management of change. How does this process of change take place, and how is it managed?

If the subject of strategic management can be said to have a tradition then it is one which associates the ideas of analysis, planning, and strategy. Indeed, some writers would happily substitute the words 'strategic planning' for 'strategic management'. A review of the literature on strategy would show that by far the greatest number of books written on the subject either assume or advocate that the management of strategy should take place through what is essentially a rationalistic process; by this is meant a process which is analytically driven, in which the manager can understand the changing environment through a process of analysis so as to establish what impact that environment has or will have on his organization. Armed with this analysis, he is then able to determine appropriate responses to such changes. He also does this by analysing the capability of the organization to make such responses through an analysis of its resource profile and the results of likely action that might be taken. Such approaches to strategic management have been very fully developed over the years as normative models through which managers can plan strategic change (see, for example, Argenti, 1974; Steiner, 1979; Lorange, 1980; Hrebiniak and Joyce, 1984).

However, a question which has been asked increasingly by those researching strategic management is whether or not such a description actually represents what managers do. In this section of the book a similar, if more specific, question is explored, which is: is it what retail managers do? The three chapters that make up the next section explore the role of planning systems in organizations, the way in which a Chief Executive involved in major strategic change actually perceived the processes at work; and, as a case study in change, the experiences of one major retailer in effecting major strategic change. However, before the specific chapters on retailing, some general comments concerned with patterns of strategic change over time will help to place them in a wider context.

There has been substantial research in many different industries which has shown that strategic management in organizations may not be as reliant on analytical approaches as the more traditional literature would have it. The findings of these researchers and the arguments that they put forward would suggest that organizations need to be thought of much more in terms of managerial action and activity than of planning and analysis. Researchers such as Henry Mintzberg in Canada and J. B. Quinn in the USA have begun to examine historically how strategic change comes about, and their findings suggest that, if we do not need to discard more traditional ideas, then we certainly need to add to them.

Strategic change in organizations is not typically in the form of major shifts in strategy. Rather, organizations seem to change their strategies gradually; the term 'incremental strategic change' has become popular. Mintzberg (1978) found that organizations may go through long periods of relative stability, other periods of step-by-step change, and only occasionally more 'global' change.

Quinn (1980) also found that incremental change was typical and has argued that managers consciously and logically use incremental forms of change in the process of strategic management. His argument is that managers recognize that the complexity and uncertainty of a business environment can best be understood and managed by continual experimentation and adjustment. They do not expect to be able to 'analyse out' the complexity and reduce ambiguity; rather, they expect and attempt to 'feel their way' through the complexity of their situations, maintain an emphasis and concentration on a core and stable business, whilst deliberately indulging in 'side-bet experimentation' in more peripheral activities as a means of sensing and testing the environment. He goes further and suggests that such a process of gradual change is much more likely to be acceptable within the organization and therefore more manageable.

This concept of incrementalism is one which has found considerable support in other areas of management studies, though with somewhat different explanations accompanying it. Whereas Quinn might argue that incrementalism is logical, other researchers have suggested that it may be managerially and politically convenient. Or that it should be thought of not as a sort of rational gradualism so much as the product of managers' inevitably limited ability to be able to comprehend in total the complexity of their situations and their reluctance to change established routines (Miller and Friesen, 1980). The argument here is that managers, faced with such complexity, must inevitably reduce it by imposing upon it their precon-ceptions of what the environment and their organizations are like. The result is that incrementalism, as an observed phenomenon, is inevitable. Managers are not changing in terms of a changing environment; rather they are changing in terms of the environment that they create for themselves, and impose on the external environment (Weick, 1979). So it is that writers such as Miles and Snow (1978) have shown that within a common organizational environment different organizations will respond to that environment differ-ently, according to the preconceptions that the managers in those organiz-ations have about their environments and the nature of their organizations. Whilst one company might be a 'prospector' seeing and wishing to see, a changing environment full of opportunities another company might be a 'defender', which sees and searches for stability within the environment so as to construct and defend strategies of minimal change. The environments might be the same objectively, but the managers impose different construc-tions upon those environments upon which they build their strategies.

Two of the chapters which follow take as their base the clothing retail industry. Certainly, if the patterns of change in that industry are examined they yield findings which are in line with at least some of the above. Figure 1 represents the strategies followed by three major UK clothing retailers over a period of twelve years. These companies—Burtons, Hepworths, and Fosters—faced a turbulent retail environment in which major changes in fashion took place, certainly impacting on each of the companies significantly. The purpose of the figure is not to describe in detail the strategic moves that the companies followed; rather it is to show that in each case certain characteristic patterns of strategic change emerge: patterns which bear a striking resemblance to those noted, for example, by Mintzberg (1978). These are as follows:

(1) Despite a turbulent environment, for most of the period under review strategic changes typically took place gradually—incrementally. One stra-tegic move evolved out of another. Indeed, if each of the decisions were to be examined in more detail their interlinking nature would be seen more clearly. In particular, over periods of years these retailers sought

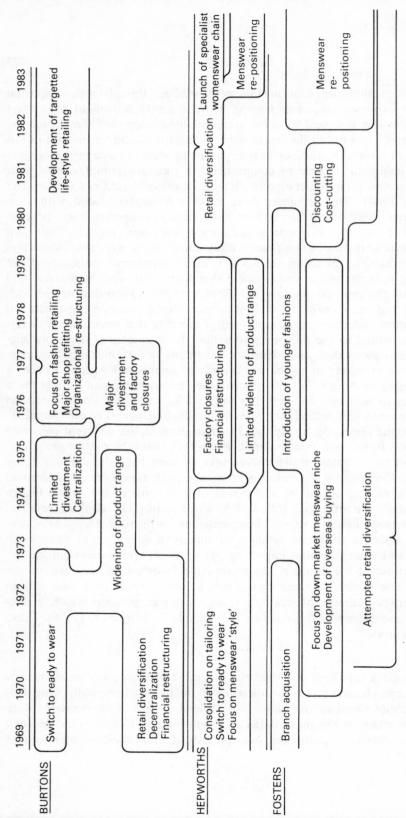

Figure 1. Patterns of strategy for Burtons, Hepworths, and Fosters, 1970–83 (Source: annual reports, financial press etc)

BURTONS

| 1969 | 1970 | 1971 | 1972 | 1973 | 1974 | 1975 | 1976 | 1977 | 1978 | 1979 | 1980 | 1981 | 1982 | 1983 |

Switch to ready to wear

Retail diversification
Decentralization
Financial restructuring

Widening of product range

Limited divestment
Centralization

Major divestment and factory closures

Focus on fashion retailing
Major shop refitting
Organizational re-structuring

Development of targetted life-style retailing

HEPWORTHS

Consolidation on tailoring
Switch to ready to wear
Focus on menswear 'style'

Factory closures
Financial restructuring

Limited widening of product range

Retail diversification

Launch of specialist womenswear chain

Menswear re-positioning

FOSTERS

Branch acquisition

Focus on down-market menswear niche
Development of overseas buying

Attempted retail diversification

Introduction of younger fashions

Discounting
Cost-cutting

Menswear re-positioning

to accommodate the changes in fashion by relatively marginal adjustments in merchandise mix.

(2) Even when such gradual change did not yield positive results of much
significance the retailers often continued to employ that method of
strategy development. For example, Hepworths had been traditionally a
menswear tailor, making made-to-measure suits in the 1950s and 1960s.
By the early 1970s not only were made-to-measure suits declining fast
but the extent to which men bought suits at all was reducing significantly.
Yet for most of the decade of the 1970s the core of Hepworths' strategy
was the retailing of suits with other merchandise gradually introduced as
'add-ons'.

(3) In each of the cases there was also reached a period at which performance
decline became so significant that changes of a more global and major
nature occurred. Such changes were typically triggered by perceived
organizational crisis, either through performance-decline or external
threat (e.g. potential take-over), or both.

(4) The periods of more global change, when quite different strategies were
more suddenly introduced, and old strategies disbanded, were typically
associated with a shakeout of previous management and their replacement by new managers external to the firm.

In the chapters in this section the idea of incrementalism in retailing is
prominent. Indeed, the argument is put forward that it may be that the
operating conditions of retailing, with relatively short time-horizons, relatively disposable assets, and a highly operational emphasis, are fertile ground
for an incremental approach. Yet we also have to understand management
processes in the context of a changing—arguably, increasingly rapidly
changing—retail environment. If strategic management in retailing is characterized by an incremental approach, then practitioners have to be wary of
the sort of internalized momentum that can give rise to an obsolescent and
drifting strategy. The chapters which follow explore the problems of
managing strategic change in retailing; they come to no prescriptive
conclusions but do offer insights into the problems of strategic management
which face retailers.

The chapters which follow

The management of strategic change in retailing is discussed in two quite
different chapters. Colin Gilligan and Clive Sutton (Chapter 11) examine the
extent to which strategic planning processes have been adopted in grocery
and DIY retailing in the UK. Their conclusion is that, whilst there are some
signs of a greater adoption of planning systems, retailing is still characterized
by the absence or low scale of formal planning. The chapter discusses why

this might be so, and concludes that there may be particular characteristics of retailing which influence this, including short time horizons in retailing relative to other industries. A different perspective on the management of strategic change is taken by Martyn Pitt and myself. Chapter 12 examines processes of strategic change as understood and described by one Chief Executive in the fashion retailing industry. The accounts of the processes as described by this manager, at the centre of substantial change in a major retailer, are mapped out and compared as between 1980 and 1983—two very different periods of time and change for his organization. The chapter also concludes that 'rationalistic'/analytical models of strategic management do not dominate the executive's perception of the strategic management processes. Rather, political and cognitive processes better describe his approach, and these seem to vary according to the context and conditions of the management situation.

Chapter 13, by Sebastian Green, takes the form of a case study of strategic change in a UK menswear retailer—John Collier. The case traces the demise of the company throughout the fashion changes of the 1970s and then concentrates on the period of the management buy-out in the 1980s. The issue which underlies Green's argument is why the historical strategy of the business was so difficult to change. In discussing this he draws on interpretative models of strategic management and argues that the powerful influence of management ideology in culture is persistent in organizations.

REFERENCES

Argenti, J. (1974). *Systematic Corporate Planning*, London: Nelson.
Hrebiniak, L. G., and Joyce, W. F. (1984). *Implementing Strategy*, New York: Macmillan/Collier Macmillan.
Lorange, P. (1980). *Corporate Planning*, Englewood Cliffs, NJ.: Prentice-Hall.
Miles, R. E., and Snow, C. C. (1978). *Organizational Strategy, Structure and Process*, New York: McGraw-Hill.
Miller, D., and Friesen, P. H. (1980). 'Momentum and revolution in organizational adaptation.' *Academy of Management Journal*, **23**, No. 4, 591–614.
Mintzberg, H. (1978). 'Patterns in Strategy Formation.' *Management Science*, May, 934–48.
Quinn, J. B. (1980). *Strategies for Change*, Homewood, Ill.: Irwin.
Steiner, E. A. (1979). *Strategic Planning: What Every Mannager Must Know*, New York: The Free Press.
Weick, K. (1979). *The Social Psychology of Organizing*, Reading, Mass.: Addison-Wesley.

CHAPTER 11
Strategic Planning in Grocery and DIY Retailing

COLIN GILLIGAN and CLIVE SUTTON
Sheffield City Polytechnic

INTRODUCTION

Senior executives in retailing have, for the most part, been slow to adopt strategic planning as a central element of their managerial style. It is, as one commentator has observed, the case that:

> Most retailers are not strategic thinkers; they are action oriented, wanting to see real results in a short time frame . . . There is no commitment by management to strategic planning. In most, but not all, retail companies, the time of top management is used inappropriately. Too often it is devoted to short-term firefighting crisis management activities (Becker, 1977).

A similar argument is pursued by Moyer (1983), who suggests that:

> . . . in retailing, strategic marketing planning is still not part of the basics. Among merchants, the emphasis is on prompt responses rather than prescient planning, in merchandising rather than marketing, and on tactical questions rather than strategic ones.

As these two comments suggest, retailers have traditionally adopted a short-term perspective in which priority is given to reacting quickly and positively in order to meet the day-to-day problems of running their businesses in a fast-moving and highly competitive environment. They tend to view themselves as being entrepreneurial and 'fast on their feet', and take pride in being so. One consequence of this is that much retail management has been reactive and dedicated more to crisis firefighting than to long-term analysis and planning. By way of explanation, retailers point to the pervasiveness of short time-horizons in the industry. A recent study of American firms, for example, found that the average long-term planning period as perceived by retailers could be as little as one quarter of the same planning period as seen by executives in manufacturing (Feinberg *et al.*, 1983).

Strategic planning does, however, require a far longer perspective than is implied by being a firefighter, and managerial qualities that make for the effective firefighter are not necessarily those of the effective strategic planner, a factor that is increasingly being recognized both by senior retail executives and by city analysts. Well-thought-out strategic plans tend to be those that are developed over a period in which time is given to a consideration of the consequences and implications of proposed courses of action, rather than those that are put together on the basis of short-term and reactive expediency—even in a rapidly changing industry such as retailing.

In this chapter we examine the nature and potential role of planning in retailing, consider the difficulties of developing a strategic perspective, and report the findings of a study of current practices and perceptions amongst some of the country's largest grocery and DIY retail organizations.

THE MANUFACTURING PROTOTYPE: IS RETAILING DIFFERENT?

It is notable that in spite of the increasingly predominant position of the service sector in developed economies, our understanding of strategic planning and strategic management is still dominated by the experience of manufacturing industry. This may reflect a tendency for analysts to concentrate on firms which have established formal systems for strategic planning: Al-Bazzaz and Grinyer (1980), for example, surveyed 48 companies with an active involvement in strategic planning, and their sample included only 12 specialist service firms. There has also been a tendency to concentrate the analysis on larger firms, and hence on more formal systems, while within the service sector it is perhaps more common to find analyses of financial services than of other areas, possibly as a by-product of the government's interest in these services (see, for example, Wood and LaForge, 1979; Robinson and Pearce, 1983).

Analyses of strategic planning in retailing are comparatively rare, although there is a common assertion that retailers do not plan but concentrate instead upon shorter-term tactical decisions. The study already quoted by Feinberg *et al.* gives some evidence for this: the planning periods used by major American retailers were significantly less than those quoted for manufacturers, even though many of these retailers claimed to be using a longer-term period in planning than they had previously. Similarly a study of the pattern of growth of a successful retail chain (Steinberg Inc. of Quebec) led Mintzberg and Waters (1982) to refer to a pattern of 'inchworm' growth, in which opportunistic ventures into attractive areas were undertaken without full consideration of the consequences, and were followed by periods during which the overall balance had to be adjusted and unforseen problems (say) in financing or staff development were overcome.

Several reasons have been suggested to explain this phenomenon, including the very rapid rate of change, the predominant influence of a small number of individualists, and a relatively unglamorous image of the industry which has, in the eyes of a number of commentators, had the effect of attracting comparatively few people with either a background in or empathy towards planning. In addition, it has been argued from within the industry that success in the past has been achieved with only limited attention having been paid to strategic planning. As a consequence, the pressures upon managers to adopt a greater degree of strategic thinking in their planning processes are correspondingly low. However, if, for the moment, the apparently low priority of formal planning in retailing is accepted as a fact then we must ask whether this observation is transitory or permanent. Can we expect retail planning to develop more formally in the future or are there some permanent barriers to long-term planning in retailing?

Comparisons with other industries may serve to focus this question but do not resolve it. For manufacturing in particular, the conventional wisdom as exemplified by Thune and House (1970), Karger and Malik (1975), and Al-Bazzaz and Grinyer (1981) might be summarized as indicating that strategic planning is more likely to have an impact in large firms which operate in a rapidly changing environment, characterized by technological change and/or fierce competition. The benefits of strategic planning in service industries were initially questioned by Rue and Fulmer (1974). However, as Hofer and Schendel (1978) pointed out, the results for service firms are inevitably coloured by their relatively late adoption of strategic planning, which left them with a shorter period over which benefits could be realized.

On the basis of these results it is tempting to conclude that the competitive pressures and rapid structural changes in retailing might increase the benefits to be obtained from formal strategic planning. However, these same factors also increase the difficulties involved in devising formal plans, and Al-Bazzaz and Grinyer (1980) reported that while the service firms in their sample could identify a wider range of contributions from corporate planning, they also found more difficulties. This poses the question of whether the difficulties and costs rise more or less rapidly than the potential benefits as the environment becomes more turbulent. In principle, the issue would seem to turn upon the extent to which the turbulence is understood and the outcomes are predictable, but this is difficult to ascertain from first principles.

There are, on the other hand, good reasons for believing that strategic planning in retailing is in a state of transition which is being prolonged by the uncertain environment of the 1980s. We argue below that it is also prolonged by the need to develop a methodology that is specific to retailing and not 'borrowed' from manufacturing. Until comparatively recently, many retailing firms lacked the organization structure needed for formal strategic planning. Many still do, but the pressures and opportunities for taking a longer view have increased as the nature and structure of retailing has begun to change in a number of fundamental ways:

> The changes that have taken place have been characterized by the growth of large multiple chains, the increasingly rapid closure of small and independent shops, a steady rise in the average store size and the widespread adoption of innovatory merchandising techniques. This shift has been most prominent amongst food-based retailers, but there is now evidence that fundamentally similar structural alterations are spreading through other retail sectors. These changes have had significant implications for the nature of the relationships that exist between manufacturers and retailers and current changes are likely to prove crucial in the general strategic planning of both groups to the end of the century. In turn, they have long-term implications for such issues as consumer welfare and government attitudes towards the regulation of competition (Davies *et al.*, 1985).

Unfortunately, the 1980s are not a good time to start strategic planning. Among others, James (1984) has observed the reaction which has occurred because strategic planning in the 1980s has failed to live up to the apparent promise of the 1970s. As partial explanations of this failure he cites a reluctance to abandon techniques which have ceased to be appropriate, a narrow focus of many planners, and an overemphasis on strategic analysis at the expense of implementation. This failure of the strategic planners to plan strategically for the future of their own activity has had predictable effects on performance and so has restricted the diffusion of the technique. An additional problem faced by retailers is the question of the extent to which strategic planning techniques that have been developed largely in the light of experience in the manufacturing sector can be applied to retailing, where the nature, structure, and, arguably more importantly, the bases of competition are very different. A broadly similar line of argument is persued by Pennington (1980), who has suggested that although many American retailers in the 1970s invested substantial amounts of time and money to develop well-conceived strategic plans for their companies, most of these endeavours failed because they focused on the trappings of strategic planning rather than its substance. The result, he suggests, was little more than an exercise in environmental scanning.

THE NATURE OF PLANNING AND THE PROBLEM OF DEFINITION

Over the past few years a great many terms have been used to describe the planning processes of business organizations. Amongst these are 'business planning', 'long-range planning', 'market planning', 'strategic planning', and 'strategic marketing planning'. However, as one might expect, precise and uniform definitions of these terms are rarely to be found. One consequence of this is that the planning processes which are referred to in one organization as 'long-range planning' may be referred to in another as 'strategic planning' or 'business planning'. Equally, in some organizations general forecasting, budgeting or even planning in functional areas such as finance, marketing, or production is often, and mistakenly, referred to as 'strategic planning'. This confusion of terms has been elaborated upon by Mintzberg (1981), who has suggested that 'We simply do not know what the word "planning" means—either in a conceptual or an operational sense'. Mintzberg's criticism of the classic use of the word 'planning', as well as that of 'organizing', 'co-ordinating', etc. is that they are too vague to be ascribed to anything in particular that managers do, that at best they describe certain vague objectives of managerial work. He goes on to suggest that the pressures of the managerial environment typically militate against the development of planning: 'The job breeds adoptive information-manipulators who prefer the live, concrete situation.' Having said this, he argues the need for a clearer understanding of what planning really means and entails, and identifies four possible definitions:

(1) Planning as future thinking;
(2) Planning as integrated decision-making;
(3) Planning as formalized procedure and articulated result;
(4) Planning as programming.

Of these four definitions, it is the final one which Mintzberg considers to be most realistic and which, in the context of our later discussion, is arguably most accurately a reflection of the situation currently prevailing in British retailing:

> A good deal of behaviour that we have studied in our research on strategy making involved no planning, yet was often highly effective. That is to say, formal procedures were not used, strategies were not formally articulated, sometimes decisions were not formally integrated. We have seen decision making—even effective decision making—that was disjointed, and we have seen strategies (which we are defining as patterns in streams of decisions)—again successful ones—that have emerged implicitly, less through conscious intention than through natural convergence over time (Mintzberg, 1981).

He illustrates this with a number of examples, including one of a supermarket chain in which the mode of strategy-making was highly entrepreneurial, with the Chief Executive having been responsible for the development of the organization from a single store to a chain of 200. This was done by a series of personally conceived and tightly integrated strategies that were never articulated formally but were instead manifested in an informal and flexible way. The need for a far more formal approach was ultimately forced upon the firm by its decision to go public to raise extra capital for further expansion. The 'plan' that emerged included a formal statement of where the organization intended to go. However, as Mintzberg comments,

> Its planning did not give the company an intended strategy. It already had one, in the head of its entrepreneur as his vision of the future . . . planning was the articulation, justification, and elaboration of the intended strategy the company already had . . . In other words, planning was programming: it was not used to conceive an intended strategy, but to elaborate the consequences of an intended strategy already conceived.

It is in the light of these comments that Abell and Hammond's (1979) use of the term 'strategic market planning' to describe the most fundamental and broad-based type of planning in which business organizations engage needs to be viewed. They define strategic market planning as 'a plan of all aspects of an organization's strategy in the marketplace'. Included within this are four distinct but related decision areas:

(1) Defining the business;
(2) Determining the mission (or role) of the business;
(3) Formulating functional strategies; and
(4) Budgeting.

What appears to happen in many cases, however—and we elaborate upon this at a later stage—is that many retail organizations still do little more than go through this process in a cursory way. As a consequence, there tends to be a *general* rather than a specific understanding and acceptance of the market segments the company is aiming at, a *generalized* set of performance-expectations, etc. It is only over the long term that this lack of precision and the absence of a detailed market understanding may be shown to be inadequate.

In making this comment we have in mind a number of major marketing failings on the part of large retail organizations in recent years, including the fact that many grocery retailers recognized the significance of the move towards larger stores, including those sited out of town, at a relatively late stage. Their subsequent and almost desperate move to sell off smaller stores and acquire out-of-town sites has been largely reactive and is reflected both in the prices that have been paid for the sites and in the shortage of appropriate managerial skills.

Similarly, one can look at the ways in which, in the clothing market, astute strategic analysis on the part of those in the Burton and Storehouse organizations has led to the identification of significant segments of the market that offer scope for expansion. The subsequent development of such chains as Next, Now, and Principles, together with the revamp of Burtons and Dorothy Perkins, has highlighted the degree of complacency in the strategic thinking of a number of the longer-established and often far larger High Street stores.

THE POTENTIAL ROLE OF PLANNING IN RETAILING

In the introduction we made the observation that, in the past, strategic planning has tended not to play a particularly important role in retailing. Many executives seem less than familiar with strategic planning techniques and have taken refuge in the argument that the sheer pace of change in many retail markets militates against its effective implementation. It is this uniqueness, they argue, compounded by the unpredictability of the changes taking place, the often fluid nature of the structure of competition, and the shortening of retail life-cycles that has major effects upon retailer revenues and costs. In turn, this level of unpredictability has significant implications for perceptions of the role and potential contribution that strategic planning can make to the development of an organization, since there is a desire on the part of many executives to maintain as high a degree of organizational flexibility as possible. It therefore follows, they argue, that strategic planning, which by its very nature is concerned with long-term commitments, has only a limited contribution to make.

The alternative view, however, is that the need for a significant degree of flexibility in order to cope with such rapid change can mean a far larger and more important role for strategic planning, since its implementation should enable executives to develop a far more effective and responsive organization. It can do this in four main ways:

(1) By generating strategic alternatives;
(2) By helping retailers to anticipate future planning scenarios;
(3) By providing a basis for built-in flexibility; and
(4) By creating an ongoing monitoring system for generating information for strategic decision-making.

The major problem for many retailers, once they have decided that they have a need for planning and are prepared to allocate resources and time to the task, is how to structure their analysis. An extension of the American 'Profit Impact of Market Strategies' (PIMS) study to cover retailing suggested that each major merchandise grouping should be treated as a separate Strategic Business Unit (SBU), with its own strategic requirements and plans. Whilst the results of the study were unable to prove in a definitive way that the results of retail strategies could be explained or predicted on the basis of general principles, its authors felt that the data indicated that:

(1) Profitability was clearly related to market share. The higher the retail business unit's share of the local market for its product classification, the greater was the level of return on investment which was likely to be earned;

(2) Profitability was positively related to the growth rate of the market in which a retailer was competing;

(3) Investment in new stores and/or store-modernization tended to depress profitability, at least in the short term; and

(4) Store locations in new planned shopping developments (such as shopping malls) tended to be considerably more profitable than other types of location (Buzzell and Drew, 1980).

In a general way these findings provide few surprises, but the risks involved in trying to implement them can vary quite markedly. Walters (1979), for example, has shown very clearly that attempts to move into new product ranges or new markets (where higher rewards can be earned) involve increasing levels of risk.

These are the most important types of strategic decisions which face retailers, but they also throw up problems of their own because of the need to analyse the changes brought about in the interrelationships between product/location sectors *within* a retail firm, rather than merely the changes *between* firms:

> As long as most retailers specialized in just one line or business, such as supermarkets or drug stores, and usually in limited geographic regions, company data provided reasonably good indications of the determinants of success or failure. But as retailers became more diversified and expanded their geographic coverage, it became increasingly difficult to analyse their performance. Even for retail executives who have access to data for individual stores, there is a need for some common approach to define meaningful business units and analyse their strategic characteristics (Buzzell and Drew, 1980).

Many retail organizations are thought to be too small to possess the climate and the resources to make this sort of long-term planning a feasible objective at the moment. Thus Kirkby (1980) has called for government-backed consultancy and advisory services specializing in the needs and requirements of the small firm. Senior retail executives have frequently been promoted from non-planning backgrounds and, because of an emphasis upon technical skills, tend to lack the strategic perspective needed. Moyer (1983) has shown that many commentators are stressing the advantages of laser-scanning equipment and the push that this will give to strategic decision-making. However, in organizations which view data-gathering as a purely technical activity, scanning could actually swamp the management because of the increased volume of unorganized data available. The pressure to react to this day-to-day data could well increase the amount of purely tactical decision-making undertaken in many firms. This would be most likely, of course, in those smaller organizations which had already failed to develop some form of strategic thinking. Thus, institutionalizing the planning function would require broad rethinking, training, and a change in the philosophical outlooks of retail executives. Planning would beget planning and satisfaction with that planning—and planning would come about most probably through the work of marketing education:

> To persuade retailers of the efficacy of marketing planning at a level above the opening of a store or the buying of a line, educators will need to show that there are practical ways of understanding retail changes and anticipating retailers' opportunities. To be useful to retail strategists, this improved capability will have to operate at a level below the theorist's conceptual models of institutional change and above the purist's theoryless projections of the fashion scene (Moyer, 1983).

THE PRESENT STATE OF PLANNING IN RETAILING

The discussion so far has suggested that strategic planning in retailing is potentially significant and is becoming more important as concentration increases and as the influence of individual retailers on the market as a whole becomes more pervasive. In effect, the largest retailers can no longer afford to be reactive but must become proactive in anticipating and seeking to influence future developments. Yet at the same time, it may still be true that the rate of change in retailing appears to deter any but the most superficial attempts at planning.

During discussions which we held with the manufacturers and processors of food and DIY products in the mid-1980s and which subsequently provided the rationale for the research findings referred to later it was apparent that many were intensely suspicious of the major retail chains. This was partly a fear of the consequences of the change which was taking place in the balance of power in distribution channels and the fear that retailers might abuse their new-found strength. However, in many cases it was supported by claims that manufacturers could see little real evidence of strategic awareness by retailers, and believed that few retailers seemed to focus upon anything other than short-term expediency.

Somewhat surprisingly, our subsequent discussions with retailers in the same market sectors often confirmed this view. Many were extremely candid. They confirmed that retailers' perceptions of strategic planning were often very narrow, and that many senior managers are still reluctant to accept the need for a long-term perspective of market and company development. In some cases there may appear to be a very clear sense of mission among the most senior executives, which becomes manifest in opportunistic responses to external changes, much in the manner of the 'inchworm' growth discussed by Mintzberg and Waters (1982) and considered briefly earlier in this chapter. It is also possible that the sense of mission does not permeate below the highest levels of such firms, and in some cases it seems that the functional managers may attempt to formulate plans for their own areas without any clear idea of how this may match the long-term needs of the organization as a whole. There appear to be several explanations for this, including the way in which many retail chains have been built up relatively quickly by entrepreneurs who, as we discussed at an earlier stage, saw—and indeed still see—little real need to explain to more than a handful of senior colleagues the direction of the organization. The continued use of this approach to management is then, in turn, fostered by a culture within the organization in which top-down approaches to planning are the accepted norm.

What is encouraging, but perhaps a little surprising in this context, is the number of retailers who at least claim to engage in some form of strategic planning. In the autumn of 1984 we approached a number of retail organizations in the grocery and DIY fields in order to assess their perceptions of strategic planning. Postal questionnaires were sent to 51 of the larger companies and replies were received from 37 (26 in grocery retailing and 11 in DIY; further details are available on request from the authors). In many cases these replies were supplemented by subsequent telephone interviews. Of the 37 respondents, 34 claimed that they used some form of strategic planning. Those who did not do so were regional rather than national chains, and while they were not among the largest organizations, each of them had more than five retail outlets. In at least two of these, subsequent telephone interviews indicated that each company was still dominated by the founding family and, as far as we could ascertain, operated with a paternalistic management style which left little room for consultation.

However, even if many retailers do now claim to be strategic planners it is clear that strategic planning in retailing is a relatively new phenomenon. Two retailers in our sample claimed to have been using strategic planning for more than 10 years, but admitted that the early applications had been extremely limited. More typically, all the DIY retailers and 80% of the grocery retailers (i.e. 19 out of 24) indicated that they have been using strategic planning for a period of less than five years. Indeed, for just over half the firms the period was less than three years. It is therefore clear that most of the respondents only adopted strategic planning in the late 1970s or early 1980s, after the significant changes in structure and competitive conduct which took place among the major multiples at the end of the 1970s. (For further details of the latter see, for example, Davies et al., 1985.) It may

therefore have occurred as a response to those changes, and to the consequent increase in the cost of making mistakes, but it cannot have had any
major influence on the development of retailing at that time.

This timing might suggest that the planning which is now practised by
retailers may be little more than an attempt to improve management information rather than a complete planning base for a corporate strategy which
co-ordinates all long-term aspects of development. The definition of strategic
planning which was suggested in our survey was the means by which an
organization produces a plan for all aspects of its strategy in the marketplace
in order to guide the further development of the business, and firms were
asked to relate their responses to this definition. A large majority responded
in the affirmative, but other considerations suggest that at a deeper level the
perceptions of what is meant by strategic planning may be far more limited.

In a survey of UK manufacturing and service firms which was reported by
Bazzaz and Grinyer (1980) the responses which related to the perceived
responsibilities of 'corporate planners' emphasized the need to analyse
systems, generate options and recommendations, evaluate results, and co-
ordinate plans for different functional areas. This requires a fairly detailed
overview of all functional areas if the planning responsibilities are to be
discharged effectively. However, in retailing, by contrast, it seems that there
is often a very limited number of inputs to the strategic planning process.
Relatively few of the firms which we contacted appear to have detailed
profiles of competitors, or to have a well-developed mechanism for collecting
competitive or market information. Within our formal survey the majority
of respondents emphasized the importance of inputs to the planning process
from the financial and merchandising areas, but a much smaller proportion
could point to the involvement of branch/store management, or of inputs
from personnel or property/estates departments. If anything, the more recent
planners in the DIY field were more likely to emphasize these less-prevalent
features than were their colleagues in grocery retailing, but the differences
in response are too small to be conclusive.

The overriding impression is that in retailing, planning is dominated by
financial forecasting and by attempts to predict the financial effects of
particular merchandising policies. Planners within our survey may attempt
to prepare targets or analyse results for individual stores, possibly grouped
by geographical area, but they were much less likely to identify product
ranges or functional areas as relevant units for analysis.

This is consistent with a view of planning which emphasizes the need to
establish targets and controls for individual stores, with a strong emphasis
on top-down planning. It is much less consistent with an alternative view,
which seeks to develop plans for future growth or change in the light of
existing strengths and weaknesses and their relation to the character of the
environment. In retailing, the latter view would surely require more emphasis

on property management and on the planning of training and development to overcome the perceived shortcomings of management. One would also anticipate more analysis of the success or failure of product lines and product ranges and of their impact on different groups of stores.

Further information from a number of respondents to our survey suggested that their limited breadth of input may be attributed to a number of factors, including:

(1) The relatively short period of time for which many organizations have been engaged in strategic planning;
(2) A relatively narrow perception of how strategic planning should be conducted;
(3) A lack of confidence in the ability of managers further down the organizational hierarchy to make a truly valid contribution; and
(4) The length of time needed to gather together views from other functional areas.

The first two points tend to confirm the view that there may still be a relatively limited concept of planning in retailing. This raises the question of whether the situation will change in the future—a topic to which we return below. However, in practice, of these four points it is the third that was mentioned most frequently, with the majority of respondents suggesting that there is currently a lack of confidence in the ability of middle management to make a worthwhile contribution to the forward-planning process. It seems, therefore, that if strategic planning is to have a greater impact on retailing in the future it may be necessary to rely heavily on consultants or external recruitment in the early stages to introduce clear programmes of management development, and perhaps to accept a higher administrative overhead in some cases than has been tolerable in the past, with its apparent emphasis on the relatively short-term cost effectiveness of merchandising policies.

For most retailers the initial introduction of strategic planning in the UK has been confined within a relatively short time-horizon. The firms in our survey were asked to indicate the average length of time covered by these strategic plans. Eleven of the 34 respondents indicated that they looked ahead for less than 2 years, while only seven firms (20%) claimed to use a planning period of more than 5 years. These results may be contrasted with the planning periods in American retailing and manufacturing organizations (Feinberg *et al.*, 1983). Although the periods quoted for American retailers were no more than a quarter or half of those quoted for manufacturers, the retailers clearly recognized a period of less than 2 years as a short period, with long-term planning periods *averaging* 5–6 years.

Some of these differences may reflect the relatively recent adoption of planning by the UK retailers, and at least half of the respondents to our survey indicated that they considered themselves to be still in the process of introducing strategic planning, and therefore expected to develop it further. In spite of the contrast with American retailers, however, and the relatively limited role which is currently assigned to planning by retailers in the UK, a number of firms are still not convinced by the potential benefits. Nine of the 34 planning respondents to our survey expected their planning activity to stay pretty much as it is now, or (in at least one case) to become less important in the future. These firms saw little likelihood, or indeed need, for their planning to be developed further, even though in many cases their experience with planning was limited—most had been using planning for 2 years or less and had found either that problems had been encountered in its implementation or, as one respondent suggested, 'the claimed benefits just haven't materialized'.

On balance, therefore, the retailers' experiences of strategic planning have been mixed. A number of benefits were claimed by the respondents to our survey, including clearer identification of goals and priorities, better performance standards, improved communication and commitment, recognition of strengths and weaknesses, and identification of resource needs. These seem to be fairly standard responses. However, without exception the respondents to our survey emphasized the very significant problems which they had encountered. Prominent among these was the difficulty of getting many of the senior managers to adopt anything other than a short-term or, at best, a medium-term perspective. Despite assertions to the contrary, it appears that in many cases the dominant managerial ethos even at the highest levels is still essentially concentrated on day-to-day problems and solutions.

The reasons which are given most frequently for attempting to avoid a long-term planning view included, as one might expect, the volatility of the markets and the changing structure of competition. A number of the respondents did suggest, however, as we have already seen, that underlying this is a general lack of strategic talent within the retailing sector. Equally, many of the respondents appeared to recognize that views of strategic planning both in grocery and DIY retailing are, with only a few exceptions, still poorly formulated. Asda and Sainsbury are generally recognized as notable exceptions, since each has demonstrated a clear understanding of strategy and an ability to identify and pursue effective courses of action, but, for the time being, they appear to remain as exceptions. For many others the development of a long-term view appears likely to be hampered by an apparent lack of perspective, the continued dominance of entrepreneurial cultures, and the sheer pace and significance of the changes which are taking place in the nature and structure of competition within the industry. This final point in particular leads many managers to believe that, faced with the possibilities of a shakeout of firms over the next few years, survival and success is more likely if a flexible profile is adopted. This flexibility, it is argued, could well be lost if formal planning techniques were adopted.

In addition to the questions of management philosophy, and hence of commitment, the main barriers to the extension and development of strategic planning in retailing are seen to be a shortage of good planning staff and the difficulty of finding a sufficiently flexible approach to cope with the volatility of retailing. The shortage of talent is a genuine problem, but, as we have suggested, with appropriate recruitment and training it should not be a permanent barrier to development. Given the talent, and hence the capacity for planning, the volatility of the sector should be less of a handicap. It is our impression that the criticisms of planning in retailing often imply that the critic is searching for a unique plan which is built upon sure and certain forecasts. However, the volatility of the sector means that this must remain a pipe-dream. Instead, it could be argued that strategic planning in retailing should concentrate on providing the flexibility which is needed if a firm is to respond effectively in a rapidly changing environment, and to some extent this may be provided by appropriate use of Multi-Scenario Analysis. This form of planning concentrates on strategic moves that would be appropriate for each perceived scenario. As a result, an appropriate plan is developed for each scenario, or for each future state of the environment, and it is less likely that the firm will be forced into harsh or ill-conceived responses. The analytical approach does not guarantee success, but it may enable retailers progressively to develop a longer-term view within their unstable environment.

REFERENCES

Abell, D. F., and Hammond, J. S. (1979). *Strategic Market Planning*, Englewood Cliffs, NJ.: Prentice-Hall.

Al-Bazzaz, S., and Grinyer, P. M. (1980). 'How planning works in practice—a survey of 48 UK companies.' *Long Range Planning*, **13**, August, 30–42.

Al-Bazzaz, S., and Grinyer, P. M. (1981). 'Corporate planning in the UK: the state of the art in the 70s.' *Strategic Management Journal*, **2**, 155–68.

Becker, A. (1977). 'Development of retail store strategies.' Paper presented to Retail Research Society, New York, 29 June.

Buzzell, R. D., and Drew, M. K. (1980). 'Strategic management helps retailers plan for the future.' *Marketing News*, 7 March, 1 and 16.

Davies, K., Gilligan, C., and Sutton, C. J. (1985). 'Structural changes in grocery retailing: the implications for competition.' *International Journal of Physical Distribution and Materials Management*, **15**(2), 3.

Feinberg, R. A., Koscica, D., and Rocobs, S. J. (1983). 'Strategic planning: what the top 100 stores say.' *Retail Control*, 9–22 October.

Hofer, C. W., and Schendel, D. (1978). *Strategy Formulation: Analytical Concepts*, Minnesota: West Publishing.

James, B. (1984). 'Strategic planning under fire.' *Sloan Management Review*, **25**(4), 57–61.

Karger, D. W., and Malik, Z. A. (1975). 'Does long range planning improve company performance?' *Management Reviews*, **64**, 26–31.

Kirby, D. A. (1980). 'Problems of small retail establishments in inner city areas.' In Gibb, A., and Webb, T. (eds), *Policy Issues in Small Business Research*, Aldershot: Saxon House.

Mintzberg, H. (1981). 'What is planning anyway?' *Strategic Management Journal*, **2**, 319–24.

Mintzberg, H., and Waters, J. A. (1982). 'Tracking strategy in an entrepreneurial firm.' *Academy of Management Journal*, **25**(3), 465–99.

Moyer, M. S. (1983). 'Market planning in retailing; making the basics work.' Paper presented to the Marketing Education Group, Cranfield, July.

Pennington, A. L. (1980). 'Do's and don'ts of retail strategic plans.' *Marketing News*, 7 March, 5 and 17.

Robinson, Jr, R. B., and Pearce II, J. A. (1983). 'The impact of formalized strategic planning on financial performance in small organizations.' *Strategic Management Journal*, **4**, 197–207.

Rue, L. W., and Fulmer, R. M. (1974). 'The practice and profitability of long range planning.' *Managerial Planning*, **22**, 1–7.

Thune, S. S., and House, R. J. (1970). 'Where long range planning pays off.' *Business Horizons*, **13**, 81–7.

Walters, D. (1979). 'Plotting retailing strategy.' Paper presented to the PTRC Summer Annual Meeting, Warwick, July.

Wood, D. R., and Laforge, R. L. (1979). 'The impact of comprehensive planning on financial performance.' *Academy of Management Journal*, **22**, 516–26.

CHAPTER 12
Managing Strategic Change: A Chief Executive's Perspective

MARTYN PITT
Aston University Management Centre
and
GERRY JOHNSON
Manchester Business School

INTRODUCTION

The long-term survival and profitable development of the business organiz-ation is the proper and, arguably, most significant task of the chief executive. However, this simple definition of strategic management gives little insight into the nature of the task, and it may be influenced by the characteristics and the outlook of the chief executive in the specific context in which the firm is operating. Research into strategic management has largely concentrated on good practice in terms of the content of strategy (what) rather than the processes of implementing it (how). Furthermore, to the knowledge of the authors, retailing as an area of business activity has received relatively little attention. Finally, even where studies exist of managing the process of change, little systematic attention has been paid to understanding these processes as the managers involved understand them.

As the rate of change in the retail business environment increases and as competitive pressures grow and the industry becomes both more concen-trated and yet, in strategic terms, more differentiated, the pressure on retailing management for strategic change becomes even more compelling. The management of strategic change is, however, problematic. Whether in manufacturing or in retailing, the evidence is that the sort of 'momentum' referred to by Mintzberg (1978) and Miller and Friesen (1980) is a powerful force which constrains managers if not to the *status quo* then to dominant and well-established strategies of the past. The problem for senior retail management is, then, not just to understand the forces at work in an increas-ingly competitive retail environment, not just to find new strategies with

194   *Business Strategy and Retailing*

which to compete effectively, but also to discover how they can actually effect strategic change within their organizations.

This chapter describes an exploratory and descriptive study of the processes of change in a major multiple clothing retailer which we will call Cooper's, as seen from the perspective of its Chief Executive (CEO), whom we call David. It attempts to relate the CEO's views about how to manage change to (1) various perspectives in the literature about how managers think and act 'strategically' and (2) strategic change in the context of the retailing environment. The work is descriptive in that we have tried to understand something of how one CEO perceives that he manages change; in this sense the chapter aims to provide an insight into the complexity of managing strategic change in retailing. We do *not* attempt to suggest or prescribe how other CEOs *should* manage change. The work is exploratory in that we attempt to investigate interpretive managerial behaviour that is very difficult to research objectively. However, making sense of strategy is precisely what CEOs are required to do every day of their working lives: it is therefore a valid and important research objective. We acknowledge the obvious danger of overgeneralizing from a single study but we note also the long tradition of rich, insightful studies of management by serious researchers and consultants, which have added greatly to our collective appreciation of managerial behaviour.

Our study concentrates on the CEO's views about managing change at two specific times: 1980, when Cooper's had completed a decade of growth in sales and profitability, and 1983, when it had experienced a dramatic performance decline and was in the middle of a major strategy reappraisal. It will be argued that in 1983 the CEO conceives of managing change quite differently from how he did in 1980. Not only have his beliefs about the substantive aspects of Cooper's strategic position changed but, we argue, he now makes sense of the *process* of strategic development differently and with a significantly altered set of managerial priorities. Some possible reasons for these changes are suggested and we argue that our findings indicate the potential value of extending this kind of study, especially in sectors of increasing economic importance such as retailing.

PERSPECTIVES ON STRATEGIC MANAGEMENT

Researchers in strategy now accept, by and large, the dominant role of managers in the processes of guiding and effecting corporate strategy. Presumably, managers in general and CEOs in particular have never doubted this aspect of their function! However, there is far from general agreement over what these processes entail. For example, during the 1950s and 1960s these management tasks came to be strongly and normatively associated with strategic planning: formulating future-oriented patterns of intended actions by means of essentially rational, formal, deliberate, anticipatory planning activities. This view remains very strong, notwithstanding increasing recognition of the importance of strategy implementation.

The concern of some researchers, ourselves included, is that this 'strategic planning' perspective simply does not acknowledge the complexity and ambiguity of managing purposeful change in the turbulent present-day conditions experienced by many businesses. In essence, it should be accepted that even the most able managers struggle to cope with anticipating an inherently unknowable, rather than statistically uncertain, future world: in these circumstances managerial insight plays a large part in strategic management. However, paradoxically there are still few empirical studies of strategic processes which start from the premise of strategic change as the product of managerial style, sense-making, and interaction as distinct from 'technical' competence and experience *per se*.

Chaffee (1985) proposes that existing models of strategic processes fall into one of three generic types. The first (model 1) portrays strategy development as a planned, sequential process with elements of search, choice, and evaluation (analysis and decision) followed by implementation (action). The second model views strategy as an evolutionary, adaptive process in which (often minor) changes occur in conjunction with the everyday business of managing and where planning, in the model 1 sense, plays little part. Model 3 treats strategic processes as interpretive managerial behaviour in which strategy is the product of individual and collective sense-making about the world of the organization and its potentialities. The major practical difference between these models lies in the way managers seek to respond to the central strategic dilemmas of complexity and future uncertainty. Model 1 adherents respond to these challenges by attempting comprehensive analytic planning and forecasting routines. Model 2 strategists put more faith in fostering responsiveness and adaptivity, using the available and largely familiar skills, routines, and programmes within the organization. Model 3 strategists do not deny the contribution of Model 1 and 2 approaches but emphasize also the part played by higher-order or interpretive human faculties of cognition, judgement, and intuition in strategic processes. These faculties can both enlighten and constrain managerial appreciation of a firm's strategic position and of the appropriate actions to be taken in the light of that appreciation. Nonetheless, for Model 3 adherents, only a full use of these faculties is likely to result in patterns of actions with which managers individually and collectively can feel comfortable.

Though the classification is not entirely original (e.g. Mintzberg, 1973) it prompts further observations. Predictably, Model 1 has received by far the most attention in the literature of strategic management, although recent studies such as Mintzberg *et al.* (1976), Horvath and McMillan (1979), Nutt (1984), Meyer (1984), and Shrivastava and Grant (1985) variously incorporate refinements to account for stepwise reiteration, political bargaining, symbolic behaviour, and learning. Model 2 also has a well-documented history, entering the policy/strategy field quite recently via Allison (1971), Steinbruner (1974), Mintzberg (1978), and Quinn (1980). So far, these Models have not proved notably helpful in developing generalized and actionable prescriptions. However, for many managers Model 2 seems to describe the *problems* they face even if it does not provide many *answers*.

Model 3 regards 'interpretive' managerial behaviour as the driving force of strategic change. Within this perspective has emerged a divergent field of study, including, for example, political processes (Pettigrew, 1977; Pfeffer, 1981a) and managerial culture (Pettigrew, 1979; Hofstede, 1980; Peters and Waterman, 1982; Schein, 1985). Chaffee (1985) argues that the three models of strategic processes stand in hierarchical relation to each other (with Model 3 the most elevated) and draws an analogy with Boulding's (1956) 'levels of system complexity'. Strategic management processes involve complex organizational systems, requiring commensurately complex explanatory models. The theoretical attraction of the interpretive model is precisely that it reflects real-world complexity.

Thus it has been argued that a full description of management processes should include various aspects of behaviour, including interpretive sense-making (Burrell and Morgan, 1979; Pettigrew, 1984). In practice this suggests the need to work with multiple models or perspectives and to combine 'objective' measurements with 'subjective' qualitative data. In this study we looked at the way one CEO involved in a fashion-retailing environment explains managing change, and we have tried to relate his ideas, as expressed in his language of explanation, to various perspectives on strategic change processes that we developed from the literature referred to.

STRATEGIC CHANGE IN FASHION RETAILING: COOPER'S RETAIL CONTEXT, 1970–83

There is a great deal of serious as well as anecdotal evidence that managing change must be understood in the industry and organizational context in which it is taking place. The business of retailing provides an external context that is characteristically different from, say, manufacturing industry. Relatively little has been written about the nature of the retailing environment, but we would argue that retailing in general, and fashion-clothes retailing in particular, is characterized by a relatively high degree of dynamism (in respect of the changing nature and level of demand, for example) but is relatively simple in respect of 'operating technology', following Duncan's (1972) terms.

Moreover, this industry is characterized by relatively low entry barriers. Thus although UK fashion retailing has seen increasing concentration during the 1970s and 1980s (fewer large retailers with multiple outlets accounting for an increasing proportion of the total sales), it would be wrong to suppose that new entrants are effectively prohibited. The industry has seen new entrants emerge and grow rapidly, notably on the back of the trend to more casual clothing. The most obvious barrier to new entrants is economy of scale, arising from volume of purchasing and distribution. Indeed our study company, Cooper's, was a prime mover in increasing entry barriers by its policy of bulk purchasing from low-cost sources in the Far East. However, it is important to note that the minimum efficient scale (the minimum volume of sales and production necessary to achieve full economy of scale), when expressed as a percentage of total market size for a particular product category, is typically quite small (under 10%). So it continues to be possible for a well-financed new entrant to overcome this barrier, provided adequate retail distribution can be achieved. For a wholesaler or manufacturer this has meant supporting the distribution of strongly branded, fashionable products, predominantly through the independent retailers (who still account for about one third of menswear clothing sales) and through the newer, smaller, but rapidly growing specialist multiples. For the existing multiples like Cooper's the trend has been towards high-volume, standardized 'fashion' products sold under the house-label.

Associated with this polarization has been the increasing separation of retailing from manufacturing (vertically de-integrating). Conventional wisdom (Porter, 1980) is that vertical integration makes sense in order to gain increased control of the total value added in the overall chain of supply (and hence control of profit potential), provided that scale economies are substantial. Conversely, integration reduces flexibility to respond to qualitative demand shifts, a notable problem in the volatile fashion sector of clothing. This factor operates to the advantage of the smaller retailers, who can respond more quickly to fashion trends and for whom a commitment to manufacturing would therefore be a liability. These factors, we argue, have served to limit concentration and integration of this retailing sector.

Cooper's main retail business had historically been men's outerwear—jackets, trousers, pullovers, etc.—within a total menswear market which, in 1971 was worth some £648 million and by the early 1980s over £2250 million per annum. To understand the context of this particular study it is important to bear in mind some significant features of this market and how it changed throughout the 1970s and early 1980s, most notably:

(1) Total expenditure on men's clothing rose roughly in line with expenditure on all clothing up to 1976. Thereafter there was a decline in expenditure on men's clothing in relation to other clothing in particular and, post-1978, in relation to most other items of household expenditure. From 1976 it was, in short, a depressed market. However, it began to show a recovery from 1983 onwards.

(2) Specialist men's retailers as a sector suffered more than other shops selling menswear (e.g. chain stores) post-1976. Marks & Spencer, in particular, made major incursions into their market.
(3) The early 1970s saw a significant change in customer preference from conservative men's suits and outerwear to more fashionable merchandise and leisure wear. This had a major effect on the traditional multiple tailors in particular, who suffered major declines in profits. However, by the 1980s most of these traditional tailors had re-positioned themselves as menswear fashion retailers selling more casual menswear. As such they were now selling what amounted to a more fashionable version of Cooper's traditional product range.

Throughout the 1970s Cooper's had kept largely to a strategy of selling what they saw as 'good-value merchandise for the working man'. This, coupled with a national network of retail outlets and a policy of commissioning merchandise to be manufactured in the Far East, yielded high margins at relatively low prices and a continuous growth in profits throughout the 1970s. As the market went into decline in the mid-1970s, Cooper's nonetheless prospered—indeed in 1979 it achieved record profits. Thus by 1980 Cooper's had experienced a decade of sales and profit growth at the time when rapid retail changes in a depressed total market were taking place. Our wider research within the company at that time showed, however, that whilst managers recognized the depressed state of the market they did not appreciate the extent to which new competitors had catered for the segment of the market they regarded as securely theirs (Johnson, 1985).

Turning to the *internal* context of strategic change we note that it has been argued that the way in which an organization is structured and managed is determined in part by the features of its *external* environment. Mintzberg (1979) and Johnson and Scholes (1984, p. 300) provide a useful analysis of these factors. The latter argue that when the external environment is dynamic but simple (as we have suggested was true of Cooper's environment during the 1970s) then one would expect the organization structure to be rather organic, allowing flexibility of response, and with central control via 'direct supervision' by the CEO as the prime co-ordinating mechanism, provided that the organization is small enough to allow the complexity of its activities to be manageable by the CEO. Conversely, when an industry has reached maturity, as evidenced for example, by a stable population of firms and overall level of demand, the well-established larger organization will, according to Mintzberg (1979), become increasingly bureaucratic. That is, job specialization, typically within a functional structure (buying, merchandising, store management, etc.) becomes commonplace. A key part of the organization then becomes the 'technostructure', those functions devoted to establishing the norms and standards which guide and constrain the normal operations of the business. In fashion retailing these functions cover standardization of buying practices, guidelines for type, style, and price levels of merchandise, store layouts, advertising, etc.

These expectations of external influences on internal structuring are to some extent borne out in Cooper's, with an important caveat. Cooper's was indeed characterized throughout the 1960s and 1970s by the dominant and personal influence of their successive chief executives—a characteristic we would associate with relatively 'simple' organizations, and one said to exist historically in many retail companies. However, the company was in the midst of a fast-changing retail environment in the late 1970s and early 1980s. If we accept the contingency notion of environmental influences we might therefore expect to see an organic approach to management, so as to cope with change. Yet Cooper's in 1980 would be rather better characterized as mechanistic (Burns and Stalker, 1961) in its style of management, with a pronounced dominance of the buying 'technostructure' (Johnson, 1985) and showing every sign of operating as if it were in a relatively stable market environment. This illustrates well the importance of understanding the distinction between objective environment 'realities' which may have little influence on strategy and structure and managerially 'enacted' environments (Weick, 1979), which most certainly do.

In any event, in 1980, 1981, and 1982 the fortunes of Cooper's deteriorated dramatically. Managerial accounts of why this occurred vary within the business, but, in the main, were seen as the result of:

(1) The extent to which the recession in the UK accelerated a decline in menswear clothing sales in total;
(2) The fact (which managers become aware of as performance declined) that the re-positioned traditional tailors (particularly Burtons) were by 1980 making major inroads into Cooper's market sector with the result that:
(3) Cooper's cut prices and therefore margins in an attempt to compete.

By 1983 David had launched a major programme of strategic change in Cooper's, had recruited a new marketing director, and had introduced an outside consultancy which took an active role in launching a new style of menswear shop for the company and in reshaping the competitive strategy of the business.

As we hinted at the beginning of this chapter, retailers generally appear to have experienced conflicting influences on their perceived need for strategic change during the last fifteen years. Cooper's illustrates this well: a decade of profitable growth with a well-tried and proved (at least, in the eyes of Cooper's management) strategy had seen the company outperform competitors. Cooper's managers presumably saw the investment in this strategy much as May (1981) describes:

> Investment in fixed assets, in inventory and in goodwill developed over time is too large simply to write off. Thus a retailer will tend to stick with his historical market segment, even when the segment appears to be weakening (p. 153).

And weakening Coopers' position was, as the market re-positioning of competing retailers, notably the Burton Group, from traditional tailors to more specific fashion segments, provided male consumers with the sort of 'sensory' shopping environment (Berry, 1982) they had not previously experienced. It was a time when the traditional, rather careful and adaptive approach of some menswear clothing retailers met speed and degrees of competitive strategic change they were ill-equipped to respond to. This, then, forms the background to our study.

THE METHODOLOGY OF THIS STUDY

Earlier we noted the three models or perspectives on strategic change processes as identified by Chaffee (1985). In this study we attempted to 'operationalize' definitions of these perspectives to provide a framework for analysing our data on how the Cooper's CEO perceives and makes sense of the change processes he observes and manages. We attempted to do this by a comprehensive literature search to establish practical and unequivocal 'rules of evidence' that could be applied to the analysis of the data. Our findings supported the notions of Models 1 and 2, but it became clear that Model 3 is best regarded as a composite of at least two subperspectives. These will now be outlined briefly.

The analytic planning perspective

In this perspective strategy is the explicit product of systematic, rational-analytic behaviour involving sequential stages of search, design, evaluation (matching resources to opportunities), and choice (decision processes) aimed at securing optimal outcomes. Action to implement the chosen strategy follows from the formulation process and outcomes are largely _intended_, that is, pre-planned.

There is seen to be, typically, a long-term orientation to strategy formulation and the process is frequently incorporated into a long-range planning process, involving substantial resources and specialist staff. Those who implement may in principle be different actors from those who formulate plans. The perspective is characterized by its systematic and comprehensive nature; for example, many objectives and expectations will be incorporated into preferred solutions while complexity and uncertainty will be contained by increasing the breadth and depth of environmental scanning and forecasting. Considerable time and effort are devoted to analysing and evaluating alternative courses of action against multiple objectives prior to reaching decisions.

Decisions reflect major strategic directions which will not normally be altered unless and until there is a thoroughgoing review of the strategy at a later date. Typically, however, the process allows for periodic reassessments, and these will adopt a 'first principles' or 'zero-base' approach in which all major assumptions will be surfaced and reappraised. The comprehensive nature of the review process ensures that decisions can be seen as the product of an essentially 'unitary' decision-maker.

The incremental perspective

Here, strategy is the product of continuing routines, procedures, and action programmes within an overall pattern or framework variously called a repertoire, recipe, or formula. Strategy is best seen as the emerging pattern of actions that results from implementing the various routines in the current repertoire. As such, strategy is essentially *realized*, though in many detailed respects it may never have been explicitly intended.

Changes in strategy arise through the periodic adjustment or re-patterning of the repertoire, by adding and deleting specific routines and amending their relative priorities. Changes are typically evolutionary, via small serial steps, based on feedback loops (learning cycles). Past experience is a major input to strategy and there is no attempt to optimize outcomes in any global sense, only to 'satisfice'. Flexibility and adaptiveness are highly valued. Systematic, comprehensive attempts to locate problems and opportunities are rare.

To the extent that explicit objectives influence incremental strategy, they do so sequentially and independently, that is, little or no attempt is made to integrate them. When options *are* considered, strategists typically consider the existing, convenient, and familiar options first. Evaluation is primarily a sequence of successive, limited comparisons. Uncertainty is handled by keeping to known practices and environments and by delaying problematic decisions for as long as possible. Major shifts in strategy are infrequent and not necessarily subject to regular processes of review.

The political perspective

Here, strategy is the product of organizational processes of influence, bargaining, and negotiation over resources and outcomes. These processes involve the exercise of authority and power (and restraint thereof) with respect to predominantly substantive, tangible issues.

Strategies (patterns of actions) are consonant with the perceived interests of the most influential and powerful actors. Decisions are essentially concerned with the allocation of scarce resources and the merits of competing claims for these; they are typically compromises designed to accommodate conflicting demands from various interest groups with differing objectives and expectations. Coalition-formation is a prime mechanism for influencing such decisions by mobilizing power around emergent interests and priorities.

The impetus for changing the strategic *status quo* is the self-interest of powerful actors. Under uncertain or turbulent conditions, perceptions of self-interest change regularly and strategies may exhibit haphazard and seemingly unpredictable shifts over time. To the extent that planning processes exist in these conditions, they are regarded by the interest groups as additional opportunities for bargaining and are treated as such. Optimizing and value-integrating behaviour is rare.

The cognitive/symbolic perspective

In a sense this is also a political perspective, but here, influencing and negotiating behaviour is focused not on substantive issues but on what might be termed 'ideological' issues. Thus strategy is the product of the ideas, attitudes, values, and beliefs of the influential actors and groups in the organization and of the prevailing signs and symbols in and around the organization which actors create and maintain in order to render implicit idea-constructs meaningful and visible. Strategy is therefore the product of competing 'worldviews' (frames) and cultural norms. The dominant cognitive framework acts to direct and filter actors' ideas and interpretations of the organizational context and potentialities. Facts not in accord with the dominant framework are ignored, de-emphasized, or relegated to ownership by dissident groups.

Strategic change is associated with challenges to the dominant framework, a painful and often traumatic process, in which deviant interpretations reassert themselves, usually at considerable risk to their proponents. Change associated with major shifts in strategic frame is said to be 'revolutionary' in nature, though frequent incremental, evolutionary shifts can also occur. Because of the implicit, taken-for-granted nature of the shared beliefs and symbols, change requires not only cognitive reorientation but also surfacing of deeply rooted assumptions and convictions, and frequently, the rejection of widely accepted legitimizing symbols. These symbols include organizational stories and myths, visual symbols, rituals, and ceremonies. Change is therefore neither systematic nor predictable; to the outsider it has an after-the-event quality that is impossible to comprehend fully without first having been exposed to the organizational culture for some considerable time.

Mindful of the exploratory nature of the study, we decided to limit our investigation to these four perspectives, that is, we divided Chaffee's (1985) Model 3 into two sets, which we chose to call Political (3a) and Cognitive/Symbolic (3b). Theoretically we can cite Pfeffer (1981b) as a justification for distinguishing the largely instrumental, resource-bargaining political aspects of managing from the concept/idea-related aspects of managing that Pfeffer calls symbolic management. In simple terms each of the four perspectives propose that 'strategy is perceived as the product of X, where X represents one or more features or mechanisms distinctive of that perspective. This particular study proceeded to explore the perceptual constructs of the Cooper's CEO as he reveals them in his attempt at making sense of and explaining his view of Cooper's strategic position in conversations with one of the researchers. It analyses the content and language of his explanations, specifically to assess (1) if any of the four perspectives on strategic management are detectable in his statements, (2) if so, which, and (3) to what degree (frequency) each is present.

It was considered appropriate therefore to work with formal rules of evidence developed from the brief outlines above. David's statements were categorized according to the support they lend, directly or indirectly, to the hypothesis that a particular perspective is present in and has influenced his thinking. The specific rules of evidence act as warrants (Toulmin, 1958; Huff and Fletcher, 1984) that legitimize the claim (such-and-such a perspective has been invoked), given the data (David's statements). In this study it is David who is the observer (in Allison's, 1971, sense) and the researchers his audience. Of course, David does not think consciously within the structure of the perspectives outlined. Rather he describes tangible acts and specific beliefs and attitudes during these interviews. The task of the researchers is to analyse these statements into discrete fragments of meaning for the CEO and to code them in the most appropriate way using the rules of evidence as guides.

The base data were a series of unstructured interviews with David which produced tape recordings on separate occasions in 1980 and 1983 covering several hours of discussions. For this study the tapes were replayed on a number of occasions to assess the general sense of the CEO's comments and to permit accurate transcription for detailed analysis. The transcripts of these two conversations were screened for the fragments of meaning (meaning units) having significance for David. Subsequently each unit was coded according to which (if any) of the four perspectives the data provided support for and to indicate whether the concept or idea expressed was a *reported* view, that is, based on historical or current facts, capable in principle of being independently corroborated, or an *espoused* view of how things could, should, or would be done in the future.

THE FINDINGS OF THE STUDY

Initially we wanted to see if the perspectives we have outlined were detectable in David's language of explanation and sense-making with regard to strategic issues. Any conclusions from a single study are only indicative in character, but, taken together, we believe our results suggest that the proposed models of strategic change were observable in David's thinking. A few examples may serve to demonstrate this general point. In 1980 many significant ideas expressed by David can be categorized as either incremental:

> The development of shopping centres was going on rapidly and we gained a lot of representation while there was a polarization of shopping habits . . . we took advantage of that situation where others did not [adaptive opportunism].
>
> We were in the casual menswear business before we realized we were. That happened without a conscious decision [no conscious search for opportunities].
>
> So the big surge forward came without any concrete plan [no real attempt to plan].
>
> I had to accept that I had to go through a period of consolidation and clearance [step-wise progression].

or political

> How do I perceive that decision having been made? I sat there and said we are going to do it [exercise of personal power/authority in decision-making].
>
> Have there been any occasions when they [other senior managers] have persuaded me not to do something? No, I don't think that has ever happened. I don't think they have [relationships influencing outcomes].
>
> Businesses only grow because the people who run them want them to grow. And they want them to grow for themselves [vested interests determining outcomes].
>
> I don't think Fred [co-director] has sufficient knowledge of the business to have a grasp of what goes on [judgements about individuals and relationships in assessing strength of personal position and effect on outcomes].

However, we do not suggest that David regards any particular way of viewing the world as correct or even a good way to produce effective outcomes, simply that he sees the world in such terms. For example:

> It would not be a good thing if the City realized quite how many of the decisions wait until I generate them [political difficulties associated with external relationships].
>
> One of the differences between retailing and, say, engineering is that you tend to take much shorter-term decisions. I am going after immediate returns [practical emphasis on incrementalism].

Given that the data supported our general proposition that the various perspectives as outlined are detectable in David's narratives, we set about analysing the two samples more comprehensively. We now state our findings in tabular form and discuss their implications in the section that follows. In a number of respects the 1983 narrative appeared to differ qualitatively from the 1980 narrative and our intention was to clarify these differences systematically. The first stage of this process was to classify each of the units of meaning according to one or other of the perspectives (or none of them) and to assess the frequency with which each perspective occurred (Table 1).

Table 1. Frequency of perspectives observed: 1980 versus 1983 (expressed in percentage terms)[a]

Perspective	1980	1983
Analytic-planning	18	21
Incremental	29	25
Political	30	9
Cognitive/symbolic	23	45
	100	100
	[a]Where $n = 117$	$n = 116$

From Table 1 it can be seen that all four perspectives are detectable in each of the two narratives but with different relative frequencies. The implications of these and other differences will be explored in the next section. We then examined the data for differences between 1980 and 1983 according to whether the statements expressed essentially normative, espoused positions or descriptive, 'reported' positions which could in principle be independently verified. Here we also found differences (Table 2), with a substantial decrease in espoused positions in 1983.

Finally we re-examined the data for quite specific references by the CEO to the nature of Cooper's external environment as he perceived it in 1980 and in 1983 and again for references to his personal involvement in strategic issues. Substantial differences were noted in the 1980 and 1983 narratives in

Table 2. Frequency of 'espoused' versus 'reported' statements: 1980 versus 1983 (%)

Category	1980	1983
Espoused	50	39
Reported	50	61
	100	100
	$n = 117$	$n = 116$

Table 3. Frequency of references to the external environment and its perceived hostility: 1980 versus 1983 (%)

References to	1980	1983
Environment	19	31
Environment hostility	3	12
	n = 117	n = 116

Table 4. Frequency of reference to CEO's own involvement in strategic processes: 1980 versus 1983 (%)

	1980	1983
All references	44	17
	n = 117	n = 116

both respects Tables 3 and 4, respectively). Specifically, David makes greater frequency of reference to the (hostile) environment in 1983 than in 1980, but, in contrast, makes less frequent mention of his own involvement in strategic management.

Thus our analysis, though straightforward, indicates certain differences across the two narrative samples. Because the samples of meaning units are relatively small ($n=117$ and 116, respectively), we cannot claim that these differences are statistically significant, but we do believe that their further analysis yields useful insights into the managerial process of managing strategic change.

DISCUSSION OF FINDINGS

It is worth reiterating the comparative position of Cooper's as the managers saw it in 1980 and 1983. In 1980 the management saw Cooper's riding the crest of a wave, with a favourable market position, record profits, and a tried and proven way of operating. Looking from the outside we might regard them as complacent, over-reliant on a dominant buying formula, and insensitive to competitive incursions into their traditional markets. By 1983, in contrast, the company had suffered a downturn in profits and the managers had all accepted the advent of Burtons as a major competitor and the reality of their own declining market share. These were clearly different circumstances for the chief executive, and we would expect to see differences in his approach to the management of strategy. When we look at the findings of our investigation what do we see?

As can be seen from Table 1, a mix of perspectives on strategic management emerges, which is in itself interesting. It was no surprise that the rationalistic approach, so common in more traditional texts on strategy, did not emerge as David's dominant perspective. What is perhaps more surprising, particularly in 1980, is that no one perspective did dominate. We might have expected, given the nature of retailing management, that explanations involving the incremental mode of strategic management would have been most marked. After all, retailing apparently provides ideal conditions for incrementalism; there is the ready possibility of small-scale experimentation with range variation and localized opportunities for trials; and fixed assets of the operation (in the form of shops and their fixtures and fittings) are rather less fixed than might be the case, for example, in a manufacturing plant. Yet the incremental perspective does not emerge as dominant. The range and hence the richness of perspectives that emerges in 1980 might also give rise to some surprise because the business itself was hardly complex and the managers saw it as being in stable conditions; we might then expect relatively 'simple' approaches to management. Instead we find that the management activity is seen by David (according to the means we used to assess it) as a complex mix.

A finding which clearly emerges, then, is that David explains managing change differently in 1983 from 1980. To illustrate this point better the data of Table 1 are re-presented in Figure 1. Although this figure contains no new data it demonstrates more clearly the nature of the shift in emphasis of David's account of managing change. At first sight the pairing of opposing perspectives might be considered arbitrary. However, we believe that it is appropriate to regard proactive analytic planning as opposed to evolutionary, reactive adaptation, a view, we argue, that is supported by Quinn's (1980) studies; and further, that this dimension can be mapped against the political dimension, by which we mean opposing the management of substantive resource allocation between competing groups, with the management of the non-substantive aspects of organization behaviour which make meanings for its managers and other staff. In making the latter distinction we take our cue from Pfeffer (1981b). The merit of the structure in Figure 1, we suggest, is simply that it offers a systematic way of mapping shifts in managerial postures over time.

Our interpretation of Figure 1 is twofold. First, there appears to be only a marginal shift in David's position on planning versus incrementalism. Though he espouses proactive planning and can point to the hiring of a marketing director, the use of outside consultants, and the installation of new planning systems his thinking still contains strong incremental overtones. Indeed his position has a lot in common with Quinn's (1980) 'logical incrementalist' position but gives little support to a more recent view (Gladstein and Quinn, 1985) that in times of major reorientation—as was going on in Cooper's in 1983—managers are likely to switch from the 'action

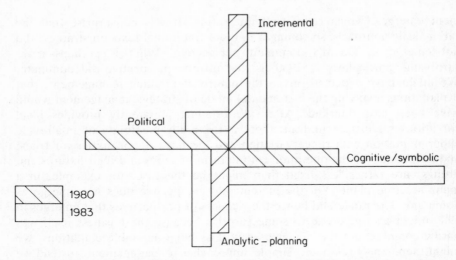

Figure 1.   Representation of apparent shifts in the CEO's perceptions about
              managing change. (See text for explanation of terms used)

rationality' of incrementalism to the 'decision rationality' of normative/
rationalistic planning.

What does emerge is support for the notion that a reformulation of strategy
requires a paradigmatic change (Sheldon, 1980) which is fundamentally cognitive in nature and which David either explicitly or implicitly seems to understand. This can be seen from Figure 1, which shows that David has apparently
become more sensitized to managing cognitive and symbolic aspects of organizational change and apparently less concerned with the substantive, political
aspects of change. In 1980 the political perspective is pronounced; we have
a situation where the chief executive is managing in a perceived steady state
and is primarily concerned with the allocation of resources between groups
of managers, themselves concerned to preserve their resources bases and
prestige. Within this arena David himself, relatively newly appointed as chief
executive, no doubt wishes to be seen as a key player. We might have
expected that in 1983, with the firm under increasing threat, the political
perspective would be at least as great. This is apparently not so, at least as
David explains it. We might conjecture that a reason for this is that he is
concerned to disassociate himself from personal responsibility for the earlier
years' difficulties and to seek to manage a collective process of change in
1983. However, a more generous interpretation is explicable in terms of
Knee and Walters (1985):

> In an environment which is increasing turbulent and in a sector of activity which
> is increasingly volatile, such as retailing, strategic thinking takes on even greater

significance; so too does the prerequisite to strategic thinking—*how business sees itself, its basic definition* [our emphasis].

Arguably, David is grappling with 'how business sees itself, its basic definition' in terms of simple, powerful and communicable images. This appeal to basic images accords with the appeal to core values noted by Peters and Waterman (1982). This may be of particular importance in a relatively disaggregated organization like a multiple retailer, as a guiding, co-ordinating, and meaning-making mechanism for store managers and others, but, of course, also for its customers. In the early 1980s Cooper's image in the minds of the buying public was both poor and poorly understood. This might not have mattered too much whilst the images of major competitors were equally poor, but 1983 Burton's revitalized image and coherent strategy served to emphasize the limitations of all of its main rivals in this respect. On the evidence of our data David is aware of these issues. He does not address them analytically: rather he searches for images that provide a conception of the kind of business he thinks can compete successfully with Burtons. In so doing, he acknowledges the paramount difficulty of sharing his images and gaining support for them in the minds of his fellow directors and his management team.

The evidence in Table 3 of a shift in the frequency of reference to the external environment and its hostility between 1980 and 1983 is less surprising. In 1980 the company was markedly insular in its views and David was apparently concerned with an inward approach to strategic management. The more hostile conditions which prevailed after 1980 have certainly given rise to a more obvious concern with environmental forces around the business.

By examining Tables 2 and 4 in the context of the shifts in perspectives we observe in Figure 1 we gain an interesting insight into David's own role in the management of the change processes. In Table 2 we see a shift from 1980, where David describes the strategic management process with equal frequency of espoused and reported positions. Then he is as likely to make statements about the future as he is about reporting the conditions of the present; as concerned with what should be as he is with what is the current situation. Given the need for future changes, we might have expected in 1983 that future-orientated (espoused) characteristics of his explanation would increase rather than decrease. In fact, there is a marked shift to reporting what is current, what is going on, rather than what should be. This goes hand in hand (as shown in Table 4) with a reduction in David's perceived personal involvement in strategic management processes. The evidence here is consistent with our earlier assertion that David sees his role in 1983 in a different light from that in 1980. In 1980 he is much involved, sees himself as central to the strategic management process, and is readily willing to espouse the future conditions and direction of the business. By 1983 he sees himself taking a much less central role and being much more concerned with the current events of change.

There are two quite different interpretations of these findings and this limited study cannot resolve the issue by itself. One interpretation is that David has withdrawn and by 1983 is primarily concerned not to associate himself personally with the changes that are occurring in the business; the withdrawal is essentially political. The other interpretation, perhaps supported by Figure 1, and discussed earlier, is that the measured shift to cognitive dimensions may reflect David's belief in achieving organizational change by means of a role as 'a cognitive support system' in fostering collective organizational change. Put differently, he perhaps realizes that in retailing, where a major resource is the people who make up the organization, strategic change must be centred on changing the views and beliefs of those in the business: and that this is the key role of the chief executive.

SOME GENERAL CONCLUSIONS ON STRATEGIC MANAGEMENT IN RETAILING

Gilligan and Sutton (Chapter 11, this volume) looked at strategic planning systems in retailing. They concluded that these planning systems are neither well established in retailing companies nor particularly well developed and that planning horizons are relatively short. The findings of our study are not based on a survey of many retailers but upon a detailed understanding of one practitioner: they are not generalizable, but they do raise some pertinent questions which can be usefully considered in the light of Gilligan and Sutton's chapter.

The 'conventional wisdom' of management theory suggests that in an increasingly competitive environment there is an increasing need for the careful analysis and considered choice which characterizes strategic planning systems. Certainly for Cooper's the early 1980s became increasingly competitive; yet Cooper's, at least as described by their chief executive, was one of those retailers who did not see the systems of strategic planning as its dominant means of salvation; and in this respect they seem to share common grounds with many other retailers. If we may be permitted to use our analysis of David's narratives as illuminating this state of affairs, what explanations emerge? An explanation which is commonly given is that the fast-moving, dynamic environments in which retailers operate is not conducive to detailed long-term planning: indeed it is the ability to sense relatively short-term market trends and respond to them that makes a successful retail formula. We accept that this view is common amongst retailers and our study suggests that this was the case in Cooper's, and certainly the view of David, its Chief Executive.

However, we believe that to see strategic management only in such terms is to miss alternative perspectives of equal, possibly greater, significance. Indeed, if proactive planning does not necessarily facilitate long-run effectiveness in retailing one is entitled to ask what can. Clearly, a high degree of adaptiveness is one answer, but one can then ask how and under what conditions that flexibility can be nurtured and then effectively channelled. It may be that senior retail executives—arguably, in common with senior executives in other industries—operate in situations of strategic change by propagating simple but powerful insights about the nature of the market environment: after all, the positioning of the organization in that environment and building constructively on its potentialities are key mechanisms for initiating and co-ordinating what would otherwise be haphazard developments. Such activities are an important part of all CEOs' roles and a necessary condition for strategic effectiveness in retailing. In saying this we do not argue that it is a sufficient condition: other 'technical' skills of marketing, merchandising, and buying remain vital as well.

To conclude, we note that the management of strategy in all industries is characterized by its complexity. In retailing it is, moreover, often characterized by short temporal horizons and relatively short cycles of change and most certainly by a high reliance on people and therefore their beliefs and values. Understanding how this complexity is managed requires of CEOs the acceptance of—and benefits to be gained from—a multiplicity of perspectives on strategic management.

REFERENCES

Allison, G. T. (1971). *The Essence of Decision*, Boston, Mass.: Little, Brown.

Berry, L. L. (1982). 'Retail positioning strategies for the 1980's.' *Business Horizons*, Nov./Dec., 45–50.

Boulding, K. E. (1956). 'General systems theory: the skeleton of a science.' *Management Science*, **2**, 197–207.

Burns, T., and Stalker, G. M. (1961). *The Management of Innovation*, London: Tavistock.

Burrell, G., and Morgan, G. (1979). *Sociological Paradigms and Organisational Analysis*, London: Heinemann.

Chaffee, E. E. (1985). 'Three models of strategy.' *Academy of Management Review*, **10**, No. 1, 89–98.

Duncan, R. (1972). 'Characteristics of organisational environments and perceived environmental uncertainty.' *Administrative Science Quarterly*, **17**, 313–27.

Gladstein, D., and Quinn, J. B. (1985). 'Making decisions and producing action: the two faces of strategy.' In Pennings, J., *Organisational Strategy and Change*, San Francisco: Jossey Bass, pp. 198–216.

Hofstede, C. W. (1980). *Culture's Consequences*, London: Sage Publications.

Horvath, D., and McMillan, C. J. (1979). *Strategic Choice and the Structure of Decision Processes*, International Studies of Management and Organisation **IX** No. 3, 87–112.

Huff, A. S., and Fletcher, K. E. (1984). 'Strategic argument mapping.' Presented at the Strategic Management Society Conference, Philadelphia, October.

Johnson, G. N. (1985). 'Strategic management in action.' In Hammond, V. (ed.), *Current Research in Management*, London: Francis Pinter.

Johnson, G. N., and Scholes, K. (1984). *Exploring Corporate Strategy*, London: Prentice-Hall International.

Knee, D., and Walters, D. (1985). *Strategy in Retailing: Theory and Application*, Oxford: Philip Allan.

May, E. G. (1981). 'Product positioning and segmentation strategy: adaptable to retail stores?' In Stampff, R. W., and Hirschman, E. C. (eds), *Theory in Retailing: Traditional and Non-traditional Sources*, New York: American Marketing Association.

Meyer, A. D. (1984). 'Mingling decision making metaphors.' *Academy of Management Review*, **9**, No. 1, 6–17.

Miller, D., and Friesen, P. (1980). 'Momentum and revolution in organisational adaptation.' *Academy of Management Journal*, **23**, No. 4, 591–614.

Mintzberg, H. (1973). 'Strategy making in three modes.' *California Management Review*, **XVI**, No. 2, Winter.

Mintzberg, H. (1978). 'Patterns in strategy formation.' *Management Science*, May, 934–48.

Mintzberg, H. (1979). *The Structuring of Organisations*, Englewood Cliffs, NJ.: Prentice-Hall.

Mintzberg, H., Raisinghani, O., and Theoret, A. (1976). 'The structure of unstructured decision processes.' *Administrative Science Quarterly*, **21**, 246–75.

Nutt, P. C. (1984). 'Types of organisational decision processes.' *Administrative Science Quarterly*, **29**, 414–50.

Peters, T. J., and Waterman Jr, R. H. (1982). *In Search of Excellence*, New York: Harper and Row.

Pettigrew, A. M. (1977). 'Strategy formulation as a political process.' *International Studies of Management and Organisation*, **VII**, No. 2, 78–87.

Pettigrew, A. M. (1979). 'On studying organisational cultures.' *Administrative Science Quarterly*, **24**, 570–81.

Pettigrew, A. M. (1985). 'Culture and politics in strategic decision making and change.' In Pennings, J. M. (ed.), *Strategic Decision Making in Complex Organisations*, San Francisco: Jossey-Bass.

Pfeffer, J. (1981a). *Power in Organisations*, London: Pitman.

Pfeffer, J. (1981b). 'Management as symbolic action: the creation and maintenance of organisational paradigms.' in Cummings L. L. and Staw B. M. (eds.) *Research in Organisational Behaviour*, **3**, 1–52. Greenwich, Connecticut: JAI Press.

Porter, M. E. (1980). *Competitive Strategy*, New York: The Free Press.

Quinn, J. B. (1980). *Strategies for Change*, Homewood, Ill.: Irwin.

Schein, E. H. (1985). *Organisational Culture and Leadership*, San Francisco: Jossey-Bass.

Sheldon, A. (1980). 'Organisational paradigms: a theory of organisational change.' *Organisational Dynamics*, **8**, No. 3, 61–71.

Shrivastava, P., and Grant, J. H. (1985). 'Empirically derived models of strategic decision-making processes.' *Strategic Management Journal*, **6**, 97–113.

Steinbruner, J. D. (1974). *The Cybernetic Theory of Decision*, Princeton, NJ: Princeton University Press.

Toulmin, S. (1958). *The Uses of Argument*, London: Cambridge University Press.
Weick, K. (1979). *The Social Psychology of Organising*, Reading, Mass.: Addison-Wesley.

CHAPTER 13
From Riches to Rags: The John Collier Story: an Interpretive Study of Strategic Change

SEBASTIAN GREEN
London Business School

INTRODUCTION

The literature on strategy is characterized by an ambivalence towards the importance of the managerial dimension. While most authors recognize that it is managers who choose or fail to choose strategies, they 'frequently postpone considering the managerial aspects of strategy formulation, preferring instead to regard strategy as an output, and its formulation an analytical process' (Bower and Doz, 1979, p. 154). Perhaps the one area where managerial aspects are accorded their rightful place is in accounts of why companies fail to make appropriate, as defined by rational analysis, strategic change.

The ability of organizations to react strategically to, or enact, fundamental changes in their external environments depends critically on managerial perceptions and interpretations. Because perceptions are subjective, there is every likelihood that, despite cultural and cognitive pressures for conformity, people will see and interpret phenomena in different ways. In our view, the most powerful way to appreciate the importance of perceptions and interpretations is by adopting an interpretive approach. The ideal would be to show how interpretations matter; how they differ; how these differences relate to cognitive, cultural, and political positions; and how outcomes are shaped by interpretations. Unfortunately, the need to rely on retrospective rather than real-time accounts, generally leads to a more modest agenda.

The story of John Collier provides an admirable setting for such an approach, although space-limitations severely constrain the depth and width of our analysis. John Collier failed to adapt to a fundamental market change: the demise of the tailored suit and the rise of casual wear. While its competitors were successfully adapting, John Collier lagged behind and was unable to differentiate itself sufficiently from them in order to ensure its survival as an independent entity. Over a decade or more events and people conspired to create a situation: the adoption of a new marketing strategy, which revealed, just how important (different) interpretations were in shaping what the company did. Before presenting the story of John Collier we identify briefly some of the ways in which social perceptions and interpretations may be expected to enter the strategic management process.

For heuristic reasons we distinguish between strategy formulation and implementation. These two processes are generally intertwined, especially when strategy emerges from managerial interaction (Mintzberg, 1978) or is intentional but the result of what Quinn (1978) terms 'logical incrementalism'. However, when a fundamental strategic shift is being actively considered within an organization, the distinction is meaningful.

STRATEGY FORMULATION

A prerequisite for any intentional change in strategic direction is that those in power come to perceive the need for change. There has to be effective problem-sensing whereby managers notice and construct meaning about environmental change so that the organization can take action (Kiesler and Sproull, 1982, p. 548). Managers notice certain phenomena and ignore others, endow some with meaning while regarding others as inconsequential, and channel solutions to perceived problems down lines which reflect these meanings. This process of sensing and constructing meanings about phenomena constitutes the interpretive process (see Daft and Weick, 1984). It is one which is reflected in the culture of the organization, for culture comprises the shared webs of meaning within which people are suspended (Geertz, 1975).

The rediscovery of the twin concepts of organizational ideology and corporate culture at the end of the 1970s focused attention on the relationship between culture and strategy, and created a bridge with cognitive psychological models of the interpretive process. In fact, the cultural approach to strategy provides a conceptual umbrella which links individual and shared managerial perceptions and refers them to the particular situational context underpinning any intentional strategic decision.

More recent writing has gravitated around three topics: culture's pre-eminence as the key strategic 'variable' determining organizational excellence (e.g. Deal and Kennedy, 1982; Peters and Waterman, 1982); culture as a constraint to strategy implementation (e.g. Schwartz and Davis, 1981; Tichy, 1982); and culture as a constraint to strategy formulation (e.g. Grinyer and Spender, 1979; Miles and Snow, 1978; Schein, 1984). The first and last of these share a common conception of the way that strategy grows from a particular seedbed culture, being more affected by this culture than by 'scientific', analytic thought.

The essential message is that culture creates blinkers, variously termed 'paradigms', 'interpretive frameworks', or 'managerial recipes', which (often reinforced by innate cognitive propensities), cause managers to define organizational environments in subjective and highly selective ways. For example, sensing and comprehending changes in the external environment is often blunted through a tendency to ignore or discount changes which go against the 'taken for granted' *status quo* or which threaten shared beliefs and assumptions about the nature of organizational and business environments. People are often unaware of their beliefs and assumptions and unshakeable in their adherence to them, even in the face of conflicting evidence (see Kuhn, 1970; Child, 1972; Miles *et al.*, 1974; Starbuck, 1983). If the rain-making ritual does not work it is because the ritual has been incorrectly carried out and not because of any intrinsic weakeness in the procedure itself. Beliefs tend to justify past actions and linger long after the circumstances in which they arose have changed (Starbuck and Nystrom, 1984).

Of course, shared beliefs do not always counter innovative action. Subcultures or the advent of new people from outside may result in challenge to received wisdoms, beliefs, and values. Alternatively, the organization culture might be one which encourages managers to actively intrude into the environment to redefine its boundaries (Miles and Snow, 1978; Daft and Weick, 1984). Nevertheless, evidence from other fields such as economic development suggests that culture tends to act as a brake rather than a spur to fundamental change.

STRATEGY IMPLEMENTATION

Once a preferred course of action has been agreed, imposed, or possibly just emerged out of an impasse, interpretations again enter onto the scene. First, managerial perceptions of strategy's multiple meanings always diverge, possibly to the extent of undermining commitment to the intended change or blocking the feedback from experience to learning.

Second, because change is frequently regarded as illegitimate, signifying discord, dirt, and even danger (Douglas, 1966) most, if not all, change-situations require legitimation in terms of a new system of meaning. Creating this legitimation is a key role for those seeking or holding power within the organization. Pettigrew (1979, p. 574) argues that entrepreneurs may be seen 'not only as creators of some of the more rational and tangible aspects of organizations such as structures and technologies but also as creators of symbols, ideologies, languages, beliefs, rituals, and myths'. Managers involved in trying to accomplish strategic change are involved in a continuous process of symbol-manipulation wherein the old symbols, meanings, and language are superseded or redefined to herald the new order.

Third, perceptions of requisite managerial resources and how to 'control' them are critical to successful implementation. For example, strategic change involves making firm and visible a particular set of judgements about the sorts of skills needed to implement the preferred strategy. Social perceptions rather than scientific analysis underpin the preferred trade-off between developing the skills internally or seeking them from outside. This is especially true when changes in relative power (Bower and Doz, 1979) are perceived to flow from a new pecking-order of appropriate skills.

Fourth, the meanings which outside stakeholders ascribe to events often interact with managerial intentions to shape outcomes in ways which escape those intentions. It is not only the perceptions of organization players which matter; those of financial backers and customers can be crucial in affording the organization sufficient headroom to undertake its preferred course of action.

In the following sections we consider how interpretations processes shaped outcomes at John Collier.

JOHN COLLIER

In September 1983, John Collier Menswear was bought out from its parent company, United Drapery Stores (which had itself been taken over two months previously by Hanson Trust) for £47.5 million. The purchasers were four of John Collier's senior management and a consortium of institutional investors. In August 1985, following boardroom disputes over marketing strategy and with trading losses likely to exceed £5.7 million in the preceding fourteen months, the institutional investors withdrew their support from the management and forced a sale to Burton.

The story of John Collier prior to the buy-out reveals a company captured by its history, organization structure, leadership, management skills, and culture which failed to change its strategic direction and adjust its marketing strategy to changes in fashion. John Collier's competitors suffered similar problems of adjustment but had greater pressure for change exerted upon them by outside interests. As a consequence of the umbrella UDS organization structure, John Collier was protected from outside pressures. It did not experience the infusion of new blood at senior management level which so transformed its competitors. After the buy-out, although freed from the clutches of its parent, John Collier was unable to make sufficiently radical strategic changes to transform its prospects (as perceived by others). A combination of cultural, political, management, and financial factors conspired to thwart the buy-out team's attempt to turn the business around within the limited time available.

Prelude to crisis

At the end of the 1960s UDS was one of the largest retailing groups in the UK. Its men's tailoring division accounted for about 35% of Group profits and just under 600 of the 1000 shops in the UDS Group. The major part of this division's turnover was sold through the John Collier and Alexandre shops: John Collier, with 340 branches, being particularly strong at the lower end of the market and Alexandre with 130 branches focusing on the higher end. They both had their own factories, thirteen in all, employing 10 000 people.

Following a change of managing director at the beginning of the 1970s a major rationalization was instigated to get rid of excess capacity and rationalize production. This coincided with similar moves by the menswear division of the Burton Group. The UDS rationalization involved bringing together the John Collier and Alexandre factories under a single management. This allowed greater specialization within factories and significant cost savings through cutbacks in duplicated areas such as buying, pattern-selection, transport, and administration. However, production and retailing were still geared overwhelmingly to tailored suits. This is not surprising, given that, in 1971, the market for formal menswear was still buoyant and the menswear division produced and sold 12% of all men's suits sold in the UK, just under half the suits sold being off the peg.

The tailoring culture

Any discussion of John Collier (or of any of the menswear specialist retailers who had their origins in bespoke tailoring) is illuminated by considering the symbolic importance of 'tailoring'. It was no mistake that the menswear division of UDS was incorporated as UDS Tailoring Ltd. Tailoring provided the conceptual underpinning for John Collier's trading strategy well into the 1970s, notwithstanding attempts to move out of manufacturing and to embrace the trend towards casual wear.

Tailoring connotes made-to-measure and customized formal clothing. Although the customer is accorded individual attention, the culture of tailoring, as with most crafts, is production-oriented: it is the skill of the tailor which is paramount and manufacturing which has pride of place in the corporate culture. The following advertisement, taken from John Collier's archives, reflects this culture:

> Hello there. This is Brian Mathews, it's Saturday night, the zippiest night of the week. It's the night when you can leave the worries of work far behind, go out on the town and live it up a little. It's for occasions like this when you want to look your very best that John Collier gives you the Saturday night suit. From the first skilful cut of the shears by a craftsman who took six years to learn how,

to the last loving stitch, you get superb styling. John Collier Saturday night suit prices start at ten pounds nineteen and six. No other tailor in the country can match John Collier at prices like this.

John Collier's culture, honed in the 1950s when made-to-measure was at its peak, was built around the key symbol of made-to-measure suits. While this accorded well with the state of demand in the 1950s and 1960s, the Carnaby Street/King's Road fashion revolution of the 1960s was to undermine this orientation. The 1970s saw a period of fundamental structural change in the menswear market, brought about through national socio-cultural and economic change and increasing import-penetration. At the beginning of the period the menswear sector was one of the strongest in the clothing industry. Although the fast growth in made-to-measure formal clothes in the latter half of the 1960s had slowed, with a well-noted shift towards casual clothes and ready to wear, the *Yorkshire Post* (22 November 1973) felt able to proclaim that:

> The multiple tailor is unique to Britain, so this could well be one field in which support for British companies will be great when we enter the Common Market.

By the end of the period, the position had changed dramatically, as Table 1 shows.

Table 1.   Value and volume of sales of men's and boys' suits in the UK and import-penetration thereof

Index 1980 = 100	*By value*		*By volume*		
	All suits index	*All suits import-penetration (%)*	*All suits index*	*Made-to-measure suits index*	*All suits import-penetration (%)*
1973					
1974	48			300	
1975	57			275	
1976	88	26	128	183	34
1977	96	31	122	150	36
1978	104	32	117	133	39
1979	110	39	117	125	47
1980	£139m	41	4.6m	1.2m	52
1981	92	48	93	83	63
1982	87	51			66
1983	99	49			64

Sources: Office; *Annual Abstract of Statistics*, 1985; Mintel, 1983; Dept of Industry.

THE MARKET

There were three major changes in the menswear market during the late 1970s. First, between 1976 and 1982 there was a steady decline in the (inflation-adjusted) sales value of men's clothing sold by specialist menswear retailers, coinciding with a 30% fall in the proportion of disposable income spent on men's clothes. This decline compared with a modest increase in the (inflation-adjusted) sales of womenswear; growth in 'real' expenditure on all items of clothing; and a growing proportion of all expenditure spent on clothing. The menswear market was generally seen as a particularly unglamorous sector of the total clothing market.

Second, there was a collapse of the market for made-to-measure suits and a steep decline in men's formal outerwear. At the beginning of the 1970s these garments formed the backbone of the menswear specialists' manufacturing and retailing operations. In just over six years the number of made-to-measure suits sold fell by two thirds, from some 3.6 million in 1974 to 1.2 million in 1980. Sales of jackets fell by almost 90% while sales of off-the-peg suits and woven trousers declined by a much more modest 12%.

Third, there was increasing import-penetration. Between 1976 and 1982 a growing proportion of suits sold in the UK were imported from abroad. Although the absolute number of imported suits fell by a little under 30% over the period, this was much less than the decline in sales volumes experienced by UK manufacturers (whose exports remained virtually constant over the period). Allied to the declining home demand, this increasing import-penetration led to severe problems of overcapacity in UK menswear manufacturing.

The reasons for the changes in fashion are complex. Certainly, the post-1974 and 1979 increases in male unemployment reduced the need, and the ability to pay, for men's clothes. This does not account, however, for the relatively greater decline of men's formal outerwear. The decline of the tailored suit in favour of casual wear traces back to the social revolution of the 1960s. This period saw the beginnings of a fundamental shift in attitudes as to what constitutes acceptable social and work wear. In addition, the emancipation of youth, concomitant to the breakdown in the nuclear family, created a vast youth market for products such as clothes which symbolize youth's independence and their initiation into a social grouping not based on ties of kinship. The social importance for men of being 'formally well dressed' diminished through default, and consumption patterns shifted into those products which signified the new social order.

Although the multiple menswear retailers were aware of these trends they did not fully appreciate the depth and significance of them. The people in charge of production, merchandising, and sales were members of the 'old order'. Many of them could not imagine that clothes which embodied values tracing back to Victorian times were fast becoming redundant. The new fashions were seen as a threat to established patterns of social interaction, and needed to be resisted rather than encouraged. A further constraint to change was that the skills, techniques, and equipment suitable for bespoke tailoring did not easily lend themselves to the manufacture and retailing of ready-to-wear, fashionable clothes. Not surprisingly, as the decline in the importance of formal menswear gathered momentum all the menswear specialist retailers suffered.

Their plight was worsened by the decision of Marks & Spencer in the early 1970s to introduce suits, targeted at the executive middle classes. Owing to its buying-power and economies of scale, Marks & Spencer could offer their product at very competitive prices. Moreover, the changing profile of customers for suits, from the working man, who could no longer afford suits, to the executive middle classes who were already Marks & Spencer customers, put the multiples at a distinct competitive disadvantage. Ironically, John Collier and some of the other multiple tailors had early on been approached by Marks & Spencer to manufacture suits for them, but had declined on the grounds that they did not want to supply a company which would eventually be a competitor. With hindsight, this was a key strategic mistake born of a failure to recognize changes in distribution channels, to understand the way in which an industry generates profits, and to perceive the distinctive competitive pressures operating at manufacturing and retailing levels.

Decline and fall

John Collier suffered more than its competitors from these changes, although at first it managed to buck the tend. At its peak in 1973/4, the John Collier chain was making trading profits of £5.0 million, derived from thirteen factories, 500 shops and over 9 000 employees. It was making 18% net on sales and looking forward very confidently to the future at a time when Burton was barely profitable on their menswear side and GUS had pulled out of multiple clothing because they could not make a go of it. From that point on, there was a slow but remorseless downhill slide.

Although Burton and Hepworth hiccoughed their way into the 1980s as reorganization and slimming-down manufacturing operations bit into profits, both benefited markedly from radical changes instigated by new leadership (Table 2). Both groups diversified away from men's clothes into the more resilient womenswear market and then applied the lessons they learned there to their menswear businesses. Operating in new markets undermined adherence to old beliefs about how best to merchandise and sell fashionable clothes.

In the latter half of the 1970s, despite the introduction of a limited range of casual wear, John Collier was slow to modernize its stores, embrace casual, fashionable clothes, and tightly segment and merchandise its markets. The reasons for John Collier's failure to adapt are various, although retrospective accounts emphasize three factors: decline (but not fall) was anticipated at

Table 2. Comparison of John Collier, Hepworth, and Burton trading performances

	1976	1977	1978	1979	1980	1981	1982	1983	1984
Net margin on menswear operations on all sales (%)									
John Collier	5.2	2.9	1.4	3.1	2.3	(9.6)	(12.6)	(6.0)	(4.0)
Burton	1.8	(0.7)	7.8	13.0	16.0	14.7	14.8	17.2	
Hepworth	9.8	10.3	12.3	12.9	9.2	5.4	4.7	8.7	12.6
Turnover (excluding VAT) on menswear retailing (£m)									
John Collier	44.1	40.1	44.0	49.2	52.2	45.2	37.3	33.6	37.7
Burton	78.1	84.6	76.9	74.4	76.9	88.5	105.7	135.0	
Hepworth	28.6	34.5	42.6	51.3	61.9	75.7	83.4	98.6	108.3
Number of menswear stores									
John Collier	400	360	360	353	352	352			
Burton	537	452	349	347	348	249			
Hepworth	345	352	349	345	506	583			
Sales per store (£000)									
John Collier	110	111	122	140	148	128			
Burton	145	187	220	214	220	249			
Hepworth	83	98	122	149	122	130			

Notes: (1) Financial year for John Collier is to January, and with Burton and Hepworth to
August.
(2) Net margin defined as pre-tax trading profit divided by turnover exclusive of VAT.
Source: Annual Reports and the Centre for Business Research at the Manchester Business
School: *UK Menswear Retailing*, October 1982.

the time; retailing was constrained by property and production strategies;
and merchandising was not up to scratch because the buyers were locked
into a subjective paradigm of what customers would buy.

According to Stuart Lyons, who was Managing Director of John Collier
before leaving to become a UDS main board director in 1975, a strategic
decision had been made by the main UDS Board that menswear was not a
good prospect for reinvestment. UDS were not prepared to match the
resources that Burton had put into their networks in order to survive. They
considered that, whereas Burton had to succeed in clothing or go under,
UDS was a retailing conglomerate with a portfolio of businesses, and there
were more attractive prospects for the limited investment funds at its disposal.
After the event, the mistake was not to have divested John Collier:

> It is a fair criticism of UDS that where John Collier was concerned, there was
> a strong belief by Bernard Lyons* that the existence of John Collier as a key
> part of UDS was given. Because of his own long involvement with the business
> which he had built up, it did not occur to him that one ought to consider closing
> it down or selling it. The intent in the 1970s was to get the business right without

*Bernard Lyons came to UDS when his company Alexandre was acquired by UDS in 1954. He
was Chairman of UDS from 1971 to 1980 and his brother Sir Jack Lyons and his two sons,
Stuart and Robert Lyons, were also on the Board.

providing additional resources but making better use of the resources already in the business (Stuart Lyons 1986).

The decision to suborn John Collier's strategic needs to those of the Group constrained marketing strategy in two ways. First, many of John Collier's shops had originally been bought in the days when 80% of the business was in made-to-measure. Consequently they were very small, as it had not been necessary to stock or display a wide range of product. Space-limitations made it impossible to reorganize the shops to meet the new market conditions and they had to be closed down. However, most of the shops were freehold, and because market conditions did not favour the sale of a large number of shops they were stuck with them.

Second, the presence of excess capacity in the manufacturing facility forced the retailing end to source internally. High overheads and dwindling production had led to high unit costs, which placed the retail outlets at a severe pricing disadvantage. The failure to rationalize manufacturing was due in part to practical difficulties (redundancy costs, supply bottlenecks, and the need to negotiate with the unions) but mainly to errors of judgement. Bernard Lyons believed that the fall-off in demand for suits had already reached its nadir. In the 1977 accounts, published in June 1978, Bernard Lyons reported that:

> Men's suit production is now in balance with requirements, our programme of factory closures now having been completed. Meanwhile we have carried out a substantial programme of shop modernization and have introduced an extended merchandise range. With the replacement demand and the effects of our own reorganization coming through we now look with confidence to an upturn in profits from our menswear chains.

Admittedly, the UDS Board's attentions were directed elsewhere at the time, owing to problems with other parts of its business which had gone wrong. Yet the extent of the decline in John Collier's core business, shown in Table 3, suggests that this is not sufficient explanation for the failure to recognize the downward trend.

Eventually, however, the Board were forced to sanction radical pruning

Table 3.   John Collier's market share of made-to-measure suits

	1974	1975	1976	1977	1978	1979	1980	1981
UK sales of made-to-measure suits	3.6	3.3	2.2	1.8	1.6	1.5	1.2	1.0
John Collier's market share (%)	15.4	14.2	13.6	14.3	13.3	11.3	11.6	9.4

Source: John Collier.

of manufacturing capacity; it was finally recognized that the halcyon days of the made-to-measure suit were gone forever. In 1980 it was announced that John Collier's Middlesbrough factory, the flagship in terms of manufacturing output though not modernity, was to be closed. This factory had a capacity of 10 000 two-piece equivalents per week (compared with a total production capacity of 26 500 units per week for all the thirteen factories in 1972). In its last year, Middlesbrough was producing less than 5 500 units per week. The closure of Middlesbrough left a single factory in Hartlepool and some minor manufacturing capacity at the Kirkstall Road complex in Leeds.

Third, merchandising continued to be a problem. The UDS Board felt that the John Collier management was targeting the wrong market segment, buying the wrong merchandise, and not being sufficiently tough on cost control. John Collier's Managing Director was felt to have failed in building up the buying skills of the business. This was essential, given the changing role of the buyer within the trade. Originally, a buyer in John Collier was responsible for selecting cloth patterns and having them made up in the company's factories. Later, the buying expertise spread to buying suits from other West Riding factories, but there was limited experience in overseas sourcing. Coupled to this was a tendency to buy staid clothes and then spend heavily on advertising and display, rather than buy the right product to be displayed:

> The key to performance, Burton style, was all about buying. Season after season the buying team would bring in new ranges, often bought in from the Far East, that they thought would be successful, and they weren't because they were too staid. They bought products that they wanted to wear, rather than products that the market wanted to wear (Stuart Lyons, 1986).

It is probable that if there had been faster and deeper rationalization of manufacturing capacity, there would have been much greater flexibility to source externally and much greater pressure to develop buying skills.

UDS eventually decided that John Collier needed a change in direction. They chose not to bring in a heavyweight retailing expert from outside (as had happened with Burton and Hepworth) but replaced John Collier's Managing Director with an internal candidate, David Hall. A new management team was created from within the company. Part of the reason was, as already indicated, that UDS did not want a radical redevelopment of the John Collier business; rather it wanted to return the company to profitability in a holding operation.

However, this message was either not communicated or not received by the new team, who set about producing a corporate plan to revitalize trading prospects. The first part stressed the need to rationalize the retail end of the menswear business (by closing 25% of the shops). The second adumbrated a new marketing strategy. UDS accepted the rationalization because it released some £30–40 million assets to reduce the Group's burgeoning overdraft. However, the plan to use £5 million of this money to implement a new marketing strategy was never realized.

There were four parts to the strategy: improve Collier's High Street image; put more value back into the product; develop contract tailoring to businesses; and seek out export opportunities. The first of these was seen as the most crucial. The company was still too dependent on suits; a uniform which was not applicable to Collier customers. Instead the company needed to enter the growth market of casual clothes, target a younger and more affluent sector of the market, and move away from the 'down-market' image created through a continuous round of raising prices to improve margins, followed by special promotions, with unsaleable stock being put away to be dusted off when trading conditions improved.

These plans met stiff resistance from the UDS Board. Bernard Lyons, in particular, felt that John Collier should sell more suits until the management could prove that they could make profits through selling other sorts of clothes. He felt that the shops were not performing well because the merchandising and the shop-presentations were wrong. He was also unwilling to sacrifice property priorities for retailing ones until the management showed that they could trade successfully.

While Lyons felt that the fault lay with the management team, the team felt that the fault lay with Lyons:

> Bernard Lyons did not want casual wear in the windows of his shops. So in order to show him the problems this was causing us, we took him to our Peterbrough shop. This was situated in the old High Street which had been overtaken by the development of the new Queen's Mead shopping centre. We took him around this centre and showed him the new shop layout of one of our competitors, explaining that this was typical of the image that successful retailers were portraying. His response was—that is all very good but we don't want to sell that trash in our shops. If we wanted to do better then we needed to put more suits and models in the window. Although the trend is to more open, less cluttered windows, his view was that space doesn't sell clothes (David Hall 1984).

There was a 'Catch 22' situation: until John Collier's management showed that they could trade successfully they could not change the fundamentals of the business; but they could not become successful unless they first made the changes. In the end the impasse was temporarily solved by a change of ownership. Following the retirement of Bernard Lyons at the age of 70, UDS was taken over by Hanson Trust in April 1983. In October 1983, David Hall and his team bought out John Collier from Hanson Trust and started to implement their chosen strategy.

After the buy-out

The buy-out team raised the finance for the deal by distancing themselves from the previous strategy and persuading the institutional backers of the merits of the new proposals. Changing the strategy had attained religious proportions. It encapsulated the team's faith in itself and became the major symbol for signifying the rebirth of the company.

At the time of the buy-out a set of accounts was drawn up for the 5-month period ended 2 July 1983. These showed a continuing loss on flat sales and, for the first time, blame was laid on existing policies rather than on external events. Particular emphasis was placed on the lack of significant change in the company's image and the freeze on investment and development of the shops. The major finding of an in-depth market research assessment, clandestinely commissioned pre-buy-out, was that a major barrier to the return to profitability was the High Street image of 'John Collier': the company was wrongly positioned in the retail clothing market, lacked a modern definitive image in both merchandise and premises, and was too concerned with price. (A number of other priorities were also established, including revamping customer-credit arrangements.)

The key to re-creating the Collier image was site-refurbishment and relocation, £7.2 million being allocated in the buy-out package for this purpose. Two shops were quickly modernized and more than doubled their weekly turnover overnight, confirmation enough for the new strategy. The plan was to refurbish the majority of the 241 shops in the portfolio within a two-year period.

The modernized shops were to be called 'Collier', given a red and black fascia, with a shop environment that was 'distinctive, attractive, and friendly, with plenty of light and space'. The target was the family man between the ages of 25 and 44 (supposedly a neglected market with the concentration on fashion and boutique shops for teenagers). Clothes were arranged by colour, so that people who came to buy a pair of trousers would hopefully buy matching shirts and even a whole wardrobe.

A few months into the buy-out, the marketing strategy was modified. The colour-co-ordinated shop designs were abandoned because 'It was a nightmare to operate and impractical for customers'. The age profile was changed: while the age range of 25–45-year-olds was still considered correct in terms of the ultimate target customer, it was too broad for merchandising the product. The buyers had interpreted the spectrum on the basis of a life-style of someone aged about 40, which was no good for attracting people at the lower end of the age range. It was decided to aim for the 30-year-old. Third, an extension of a discount chain which had a separate trading philosophy to that of Collier was planned. Although there was some disagreement among the executive directors as to the merit of these changes, the majority felt that things were going more or less according to plan, and trading results were in line with estimates produced at the time of the buy-out.

It soon became apparent however, that the expansion of sales in line with expectations, had been achieved only through lowering margins on Collier clothes and through expansion in concession sales (which contributed a lower margin). The company was facing the prospect of significant trading losses. It was beginning to look as though the original proposals had been overly optimistic in gauging the time that it would take to turn the business around.

A major factor delaying the recovery was the difficulty in finding the right merchandise to put in the shops. Part of the reason was that the buyers were not sufficiently attuned to the merchandise after the change in shop profile—hence the decision, already mentioned, to target merchandising at 30-year-olds. Delayed monitoring of sales against forecast did not help in alerting the management to what was going on in the shops. Stocks rose, partly due also to a tight spring season, which hit all the menswear retailers.

The results of the buy-out's first nine month's trading to 30 June 1984 were published in December 1984. It was admitted that the performance of the old John Collier shops had been disappointing and so the pace of modernization was to be accelerated, with a further 56 branches refitted by November 1984, in time for the peak Christmas trading period. (Fortunately for the team, prices realized for properties sold were significantly greater than had been expected, so the extra money could be used for this.) More attention was to be given to developing a discount chain, and a review of retailing activities had identified the need to close a number of small and loss-making branches. Although trading prospects for the coming year were not mentioned in the report, Collier's non-executive Chairman, John Thomson, said in a separate comment that the overall return to a trading profit might take longer than originally forecast.

The report also contained a highly significant piece of information. David Simons, the Finance Director, and one of the founding members of the buy-out, had resigned on 4 October 1984. He had been paid £46 500 in settlement of all outstanding contractual claims against the company. Although not stated, the reasons for the resignation were a clash of personalities, turf problems (finance vs. marketing), and differences over marketing strategy and prospects for the business.

Simons wanted to follow the original proposals put forward at the time of the buy-out. He thought that more radical action was needed at the retail end to bring the company back into profitability within a very short period:

> We had effectively moved away from the original designs; what happens is, you water down the ideas of the designer until eventually it doesn't reflect his design

at all. I was strongly opposed to dropping the co-ordinated colour palette. I was also unhappy about focusing on the 25- to 30-year-old.

I argued that we were not developing our original strategy but, at the behest of our new Sales Director who had come from Burton after the buy-out, we were ending up with a Burton look-alike. Because I wasn't the person at the sharp end, the only way I could argue it was by saying two things. First, it is a major change from what we have sold our buy-out on, and that needs to be a conscious decision rather than a creeping one. The second thing is that the results aren't coming through. However, it was me on one side and the rest of the Board led by the Sales Director on the other. (Simons 1985)

Simons felt that a more aggressive marketing strategy was needed in the modernized shops with more price-discounting and hard selling of credit business. He also argued that better use needed to be made of prime High Street space and concession trading should be closely examined because of its low contribution. He had become increasingly gloomy about the prospects for the business, felt that the current course of action was unacceptable, and that major changes had to be made so that the retail division could be operating at breakeven within a few months. The other members of the team were unhappy at having their retailing skills challenged by someone whose expertise lay in finance, and felt that it was unrealistic to expect that trading could be transformed overnight. They recognized that they had been overly optimistic at the time of the buy-out and should have planned on a three-year rather than two-year cycle for turning around the company. It was pointed out that the turnaround of Richards shops under Sir Terrence Conran, which had been in a similar position to that of Collier, was also taking longer than planned. Political considerations complicated the situation and forced Simons's resignation. This did nothing to bolster institutional confidence in the team's ability to turn the business around.

In March 1985 a report was issued to shareholders which showed that there had been some increase in turnover for the 30 weeks ended 26 January 1985 over the corresponding period the previous year, and that the pre-tax trading loss of £1.4 million was in line with expectations. The anticipated loss for the remainder of the trading period to the end of August 1984 was not expected to exceed £1.4 million, making a trading loss on ordinary activities for the 14 months to 31 August 1985 of some £2.6 million. This was more or less in line with budget.

However, by the second quarter of 1985 it became apparent that trading was way off target, the trading loss for this period being more than double this amount. Since Simons's departure, the institutions had been looking warily at their investment. In contrast to Collier's mediocre performance, Burton's menswear division had increased its profits by 49% in the year ending August 1984. Burton had long been keen contenders for John Collier, having tried to acquire it in 1983 from UDS and then from Hanson Trust, only to be foiled at the last moment by the buy-out. Despite strenuous efforts on the part of John Collier's executive directors to retain their independence, the institutions agreed a bid with Burton over their heads, presenting it to them as a virtual *fait accomplit*. In July 1985, in the recommended offer-document sent out to all the private investors and the remaining institutions, John Thomson stated that in the light of trading forecasts: 'Your Board has considered carefully the approaches made by the Burton Group, one of the leading multiple retailers in the UK. Your Board believes that whilst Collier has good prospects as an independent Group, the resources and skills of the Burton Group would enable these to be realized at a much earlier date.'

CONCLUSION: THE DIFFERENT INTERPRETATIONS

Our aim has been to show how strategic change is infused at every stage by managerial perceptions and interpretations. The account presented is a personal construction of other people's recollections of what they and their colleagues have been up to. We can only speculate as to the reasons why John Collier's chosen strategy was unsuccessful. It may have been the 'wrong' strategy, it may have been that virtually any strategy would have failed because the company's market position was so far behind that of its competitors that it could never catch up, or it may have been the 'right' strategy for the long run but the wrong one to please John Collier's institutional shareholders in the short term.

For our purposes, it is unimportant which of these explanations is 'objectively' correct. The merit of focusing on perceptions is that it reveals how different interpretations tripped up attempts to implement strategic change successfully: what Geertz (1975) refers to as a 'confusion of tongues'.

We can infer four distinctive interpretive schemes. First, there was Bernard Lyons, who believed that the concept of the tailored product was essentially sound. He viewed the cause of the problems that John Collier was suffering as a failure of merchandising and traditional retailing skills. In popular parlance, his view would be what Peters and Waterman (1982) call 'sticking to the knitting'.

Second, prior to the buy-out the management of John Collier believed that the cause of the problems was Bernard Lyons. They thought that the dwindling fortunes of John Collier were due to a failure to adopt a totally new trading formula. Autocratic control, a failure to invest, and an excess of tradition obstructed development of the front end of the business. Their view of what was needed comes under the rubric of 'a bias for action' and 'autonomy and leadership'.

Third, after the buy-out a conflict emerged among the executive management because the strategy was not working. The introduction of a new sales director who was not party to the original strategy formulation weakened adherence to the original articles of faith. The majority view was that the strategy needed to be modified and that expectations had to be amended. The minority view was that more should be done to implement the chosen strategy. Once again there was a conflict between a bias for action and stick to the knitting. Once again the only resolution to such opposed interpretations was the departure of one of the antagonists.

Fourth, there was the effect that these different viewpoints had on the financial backers. Their decision to pull the rug from under the management and force a sale to a third party was largely informed by the belief that no solution to the dilemma facing John Collier had been found. A confusion of beliefs cannot be expected to bolster the faith of a sceptic. The departure of the Finance Director allied to the missed forecasts shook their faith in the team's ability to turn the company around.

We said that there were four interpretive schemes but, of course, there is a fifth—our own. Like all the others, it is inherently subjective, but to fail to present it is to risk an accusation of voyeurism and sitting on the fence. Ours is an overarching interpretation of what happened but is no less biased because of this.

On the plus side there were a number of factors encouraging the change process. The effects of autocratic corporate control had been removed; the investment denied for so long had been allowed; good advice had been sought; managerial motivation to succeed was never higher; the external environment was no more hostile than usual; and the need for change had been clearly perceived.

Yet despite these good intentions and context there were also some negative ones. Managerial perceptions and interpretations of the sorts of change which were needed were, in the light of what happened, clearly at odds with consumer and institutional perceptions.

The team did not fully appreciate the difficulty of accomplishing strategic change. While the euphoria of the buy-out and the need to persuade others of the wisdom of their intentions may initially have created an excess of faith in the strategy, more important was a failure to understand the depth and complexity of John Collier's problems.

The presence of a highly visible scapegoat in the form of Bernard Lyons promoted an oversimplistic shared understanding of what was supposedly wrong with the company. Stories abounded within John Collier and the industry at large about Bernard Lyons being wedded to outmoded retailing and management concepts. Thus the simple panacea was to get rid of Bernard Lyons and implement the plans that the management had long been advocating. However, there may well have been an element of what psychologists refer to as 'illusory causation' which hampered critical evaluation of the causes of the company's decline: 'Since we observe others' behavior more readily than we do our own, others seem more causal than we ourselves do' (Kiesler and Sproull, 1982, p. 553).

Second, it must be questionable as to whether the team had the complement of skills needed either to accomplish a dramatic upturn in trading or to persuade the financial institutions that, despite initial problems, exciting changes were underway. Some responsibility for John Collier's demise prior to the buy-out must attach to its executive management. Thus a change in strategy could not have been expected, by itself, to bring the promised turnaround. The revival of Burton and Hepworth were only achieved by a radical infusion of new people who were not steeped in the ways of the old culture.

Third, although the problems facing the business could only be rectified in the long term through a fundamental adaptive change in marketing strategy, the team underestimated the need to show the financial institutions some hard evidence of recovery in trading performance. It might have been wiser to attack costs first using the immediate beneficial effect on cash flow and profits to gain time to pilot changes in marketing strategy more thoroughly. Having abandoned a cost-cutting strategy, flexibility and a toe-in-the-water approach to marketing changes were effectively denied through the need to achieve results virtually overnight. The team underestimated the need to manage the symbols which hold meaning for the financial backers of buy-outs. Given the high leverage, the large sums involved, and the untested nature of the management's ability to run their company free from the umbilical cord, there was a much greater need than usual to sustain outsiders' confidence. Insufficient attention was paid to the conflicting messages which would be given by the departure of the Finance Director.

Finally, the polarization of attitudes among the executive directors hindered their ability to adjust the strategy in line with initial outcomes. Confrontation impeded effective management decision-making. Ownership, rather than creating a shared interest, which would allow the directors to transcend sectional interests, exacerbated conflict through blurring traditional lines of authority and conventional roles. Disagreement over strategy-implementation became political and vested with personal significance. It also highlighted one of the weaknesses of buy-outs as vehicles for strategic renewal: the irksome tyranny of an overdominating parent may easily be exchanged for an equally irksome predation by a distant shareholder.

REFERENCES

Bower, J., and Doz, Y. (1979). 'Strategy formulation: a social and political process.' In Schendel, D., and Hofer, C. (eds), *Strategic Management: A New View of Business Policy*, Boston, Mass.: Little, Brown, pp. 152–65.
Child, J. (1972). 'Organizational structure, environment and performance: the role of strategic choice.' *Sociology*, **6**.

Daft, R., and Weick, K. (1984). 'Towards a model of organizations as interpretation systems.' *Academy of Management Review*, **9**, No. 2, 284–95.
Deal, T., and Kennedy, A. (1982). *Corporate Culture: The Rites and Rituals of Corporate Life*, Reading, Mass.: Addison-Wesley.
Douglas, M. (1966). *Purity and Danger: An Analysis of Concepts of Pollution and Taboo*, London: Routledge and Kegan Paul.
Geertz, C. (1975). *The Interpretation of Cultures*, London: Hutchinson.
Grinyer, P., and Spender, J.-C. (1979). 'Recipes, crises, and adaptation in mature businesses.' *International Studies of Management & Organization*, **IX**, No. 3.
Kiesler, S., and Sproull, L. (1982). 'Managerial response to changing environments: perspectives on problem sensing from social cognition.' *Administrative Science Quarterly*, **27**, 548–70.
Kuhn, T. (1970). *The Structure of Scientific Revolution*, 2nd edn, Chicago: University of Chicago Press.
Miles, R., and Snow, C. (1978). *Organizational Strategy, Structure and Process*, New York: McGraw-Hill.
Miles, R., Snow, C., and Pfeffer, J. (1974). 'Organization—environment, concepts and issues.' *Industrial Relations*, **13**.
Mintzberg, H. (1978). 'Patterns in strategy formulation.' *Management Science*, ???.
Peters, T., and Waterman, R. (1982). *In Search of Excellence: Lessons from America's best run companies*, New York: Harper & Row.
Pettigrew, A. (1979). 'On studying organizational cultures.' *Administrative Science Quarterly*, **24**.
Quinn, J. (1978). 'Strategic change: logical incrementalism.' *Sloan Management Review*, ???.
Schein, E. (1984). 'Coming to an awareness of organizational culture.' *Sloan Management Review*, Winter.
Schwartz, H., and Davis, S. (1981). 'Matching corporate culture and business strategy.' *Organizational Dynamics*, Summer.
Starbuck, W. (1983). 'Organizations as action generators.' *American Sociological Review*.
Tichy, N. (1982). 'Managing change strategically: the technical, political and cultural keys.' *Organization Dynamics*, Autumn.

PART 4
The Social Impact of Retailing Strategy

JOHN DAWSON

Shopping, from the consumer standpoint, is as much a social activity as an economic one. Sometimes in the search for higher profits or better performance the social role of shopping gets subjugated by the retailers to a position far below the economic role. It is important to remember therefore that as retailers change their operations and the organization of their industry, so they change the range of choices open to society in respect of shopping opportunities. Retailers need to be aware of the ways that they change society because, self-evidently, the consumers, and the choices they make, are the ultimate source of success or failure of retailers. If consumers are dissatisfied with the choices offered or feel themselves exploited, then they will react against a firm or type of retailing in a very simple and straightforward way. Furthermore, government may intervene in the marketplace if conflicts arise between retailers' economic aims and the consumers' social interests. A failure to appreciate the social environment and the changes in it, whether brought about by retailers or by other groups, suggests that a firm is unaware of the changes in the environment in which it operates. For a marketing-based company, as all retailers must be, this spells disaster. It is important, therefore, from a purely commercial viewpoint if nothing else, for retailers to address issues of social responsibility of the firm, both their own and their competitors'.

The social responsibility of retailers can be considered from two viewpoints. First, there are the widely discussed corporate ethical responsibilities of the firm to behave in a socially responsible way in its corporate dealings. There has been much debate on these issues, particularly on the way ethical responsibilities change as North American and European society enters a post-industrial era. A feature of the transition from pre-industrial to industrial society at the time of the Industrial Revolution was a widespread abuse of corporate power in respect of employees, consumers, other less powerful firms and the environment. There are obvious dangers in any period of rapid restructuring of an economy that narrow-targeted economic processes take precedence over social issues as firms seek competitive advantage in an uncertain environment. As the economies in Europe and North America move into a post-industrial stage, so again the pressures increase on firms to seek short-term competitive advantage to ease the transition to a new operating environment. Awareness of these pressures is important to retail companies, as they are a central element of the economic restructuring characterizing the late twentieth century.

A second type of responsibility of retailers is the sectoral responsibility to provide society with the retail facilities it requires. There are several aspects to this form of social responsibility, and they have important implications for the strategic planning of a retailer.

The retail industry as a whole is required to provide a range of types of retailing so that all groups in society have access to retail facilities. This means providing facilities for rich and poor, mobile and non-mobile, young and old, etc. as well as facilities at different types of locations. Whilst individual firms will target specific groups, nonetheless overall the sector has a responsibility to provide facilities for all groups. A failure by the industry will lead to governmental intervention to redress the balance.

It can also be argued that retailers have a duty to improve the living standards of society. Much of retail marketing is concerned with the delivery of a standard of living. This may well involve the raising of living standards by enhancing the quality and level of design of products, by providing additional information about a product, or by introducing new products, incorporating new design ideas, to the population. Whilst there may well be competitive advantage to be obtained from awareness and use in marketing of product and store design, such will not always be the case. Nonetheless, part of the retailers' role in society is to improve living standards, even if this does not always yield a hard profit.

A third example of an area where a social responsibility exists is in the area of employment. Many retailers feel that they have a responsibility to their workforce to provide jobs and working conditions which are humanizing and not dehumanizing. With the changes taking place in the job content of many retail occupations, so new challenges are placed on retailers. Making shelf-filling in a supermarket an interesting and fulfilling job is difficult, but opportunities do exist for multi-tasking in job definitions. The provision of skills training and personal development programmes are further ways of enhancing job-satisfaction and humanizing working conditions.

Thus the emergence of the new structures and processes in retailing affects not only the firms and their employees but also has much wider implications for society. The three chapters in this section address specific issues in this general area of the implication for society of changes underway in retailing. Leigh Sparks (Chapter 14) reviews the changes taking place in the structure of employment in retailing. The shift to part-time workers and the changes in the extent of subcontracting of work both point to strategic decisions being made by retailers. The strategy of retailers to reduce their labour costs has had implications for the quality of work for employees and service levels for the consumer. Career prospects for retail employees are changing as the structure of retailing evolves: some jobs are enhanced in importance and value, others are in danger of being dehumanized. The conclusion must be drawn that new approaches to staff training and development are needed in the future and that this is an important element in retailer development strategy. The chapter by Leigh Sparks is very timely in the increasingly vocal debate on the need for better training and development in the retail workforce.

Whilst Leigh Sparks addresses an issue directly within the company strategy, Gareth Shaw (Chapter 15) and Robin Ward (Chapter 16) consider broader aspects of retailers' responsibility to society. Gareth Shaw describes some of the land-use planning and social-access issues of the changes in retailing, particularly the growth of superstore retailing. Because of the extent of structural change in retailing over the last few years, the planning frameworks formerly used now have less relevance to both retailer and consumer. While the retail hierarchy has been a central tenet of British planning policy for 30 years, recently it has become an increasingly questioned concept as retailers have sought permission for new types of store which do not fit the traditional scheme. As Gareth Shaw points out, the formal planning policies were able to control and guide the initial phase of superstore development, often directing them to district centres. The second phase is proving much more difficult to control, and is causing a questioning of basic planning policy. The report of policies and the study of consumers presented in this chapter allow informed debate on this issue as well as providing retailers with insights into the rationale for retail planning. Retailers, in their strategic decision-making, have to be aware of retail planning issues, as any expansion policy based on new-store development involves a strategy for negotiating with local planning authorities.

The third chapter in this section, by Robin Ward, addresses a further aspect of the social role of retailing. With the large-scale closure of small-scale retailers there are dangers of the creation of pockets of disadvantage in which various less mobile social groups fail to get adequate access to shops. The public policy dilemma formulated in this chapter is that the implementation of competitive strategies by market-leaders can lead, particularly in the grocery sector, to higher shopping costs for low-income, disadvantaged, relatively low mobility consumers. The response can be to try to reduce access costs to the new forms of retailing, or, as is considered in

Business Strategy and Retailing

Robin Ward's chapter, to protect small retailers serving these disadvantaged groups from the full rigours of competition. The entrepreneurial activities of Asian shopkeepers particularly can be capitalized in this connection, but, as the case study of Leicester indicates, there is some (but only limited) evidence of the success of policies aimed at supporting small retailers providing essential services. It would seem, however, that the social issues highlighted here are of a magnitude unlikely to be seriously influenced by piecemeal policies for shop-front renewal. The absence of more fundamental public policies suggests a basic unwillingness of government to intervene in this type of social issue resulting from the competitive strategies of retailers. The onus therefore clearly rests with the retail sector to be willing to consider regulatory practices themselves.

The three chapters in this section illustrate the range of social issues which arise as retailers take a more strategic view of their management decisions. The change from tactical to strategic thinking for retailers is accompanied by a change in how corporate development interfaces with society in general. Given the direct, everyday contact between retailers and society in the form of shoppers, then the change in the corporate society interface is especially important in the retail sector. There are, however, few studies and minimal research in this area. The three contributions in this section are important because they begin to address some of the issues and research areas which in the next few years will become important considerations in retail strategy.

CHAPTER 14
Employment in Retailing: Trends and Issues

LEIGH SPARKS
Institute for Retail Studies, University of Stirling

INTRODUCTION

Employment in retailing has, historically, been one of the least-considered aspects of the distributive trades. For an industry currently employing more than 2 million people in the UK this omission is somewhat perplexing. However, since the onset of the economic recession in 1979, and coupled with the highly visible structural and spatial changes in retailing, the level of awareness of employment in retailing has risen substantially. This increase in awareness has taken several forms, prominent amongst which are, first, the claims of large retailers, and especially superstore retailers, to be creating employment; second, the widespread contention that service industries are the employment centres of the future, and that retailing, within the service industries, has a role to play in employment-creation; third, the realization that the statistical series on retail employment differ radically in their recording of levels of retail employment, and even in the direction of move-ment of retail employment levels; and fourth, as highlighted by the Auld Committee report, the question of whether Sunday trading will produce a net job loss or gain in retailing.

This chapter does not pretend to answer all the questions and difficulties over the assessment of retail employment change. Instead, it aims to isolate themes from an examination of changing retail employment and then to pursue these themes and issues at a variety of levels. For example, retail employment at the national level is analysed and the changes identified are considered at the company and the retail outlet levels. From the analysis of trends in retail employment at these various levels, issues for the future of employment in retailing can be extracted and considered in detail, placing emphasis on the challenges that face employers, as well as employees, in the future pattern of retailing. The aim of this chapter is therefore to examine

239

trends in retail employment, consider the present position, and then to raise issues for discussion on the likely future composition of retail employment and how employers and employees are affected by these changes.

CHANGES IN THE COMPOSITION OF RETAIL EMPLOYMENT

The level of employment in retailing, as recorded by the main official statistical series, varies according to the series consulted. The arguments why these series differ have been discussed at considerable length by Moir (1983), NEDO (1983), Reynolds (1983), Sparks (1983a), and the Distributive Trades EDC (1985a), and revolve around the methods of data collection, in particular the classification of employees and the self-employed on the introduction of Selective Employment Tax (SET). It is sufficient to note here, however, that the two main series (the Retail Inquiry and the Census of Employment) have moved at times during the period under question (1961–85) in diametrically opposed directions, and that this has understandably raised difficult issues of interpretation for the users of retail employment statistics. There are even differences within the Census of Employment series, depending on the Standard Industrial Classification (SIC) used: for example, in 1980–2 there is a much larger fall in employment under the 1968 SIC as opposed to the 1980 SIC. These recent differences may be due to the 'blurring' of the edges of retailing and distribution and the difficulty of categorizing outlets. The conclusions on retail employment statistics are well summarized by the Distributive Trades EDC (1985a) report:

> Variations in estimates make it very difficult to decide whether retailing is substantially shedding labour or maintaining it at broadly the same level. For this reason, reliable assessments of retailing's overall contribution to job creation are difficult to make (p. 35).

The overall contribution that retailing makes to job-creation may be difficult to ascertain, but it is clear that retailers employ substantial numbers of workers and have an enormous social impact through their employment policies and business strategy. Whilst there is confusion in the statistical series, certain trends within retail employment can be demonstrated (Table 1). The approach taken here is to rely upon the analysis in the Distributive Trades EDC (1985a) report, which is based mainly on the Retail Inquiry and Census of Distribution series. Whilst the absolute numbers differ therefore from other sources, broad trends are present in both series.

There has been a long-term decline in the total retail workforce, with a reduction of approximately half a million workers (including owners) between 1961 and 1984. The number of retail outlets has declined during this period from 541 000 in 1961 to a level of 350 000 in 1982. The proportionate fall in

Table 1.   The changing composition of the retail workforce, 1961–84

	(Figures in thousands)			
	1961	*1971*	*1976*	*1984 (est.)*
Total retail workforce	2 862	2 853	2 539	2 260
Working owners	591	532	422	310
Total employees	2 270	2 320	2 118	1 950
Total FTE	2 410	2 180	1 960	1 560
Number of outlets	541	471	406	n/a
Female Employees				
Total	1 396	1 511	1 408	1 290
Percentage of employees	61%	65%	66%	66%
Percentage working part-time	35%	48%	57%	69%
Percentage working <16 hours	n/a	12%	11%	29%
Part-time Employees				
Total	631	920	968	1 060
Percentage of employees	28%	40%	46%	54%
Female Part-time Employees				
Total	495	727	799	890
Percentage of employees	22%	31%	38%	46%
Percentage of part-time employees	78%	79%	83%	84%

Source: Distributive Trades EDC (1985a).

employment levels has been greater for owners working in retailing than for employees (Figure 1), although employees have fallen by over 300 000 since 1961. These figures reflect the search for labour productivity in retailing by multiple retailers, and also the effect of increased competition within retailing on the market share, and eventually, employment of the independent retailer and the self-employed shop-owner. Self-employment within retailing has declined considerably over the time period.

Second, there has been continuing feminization of the retail workforce. Since 1961, the percentage of female employees has risen from 61% to 66%, although it should be recognized that most of this change occurred between 1961 and 1971. Figure 2 shows this clearly, but also demonstrates that female employment in retailing expanded in the 'boom' years prior to the onset of recession in 1979. It is noticeable that, as the recession began to bite, female employment fell faster than male. It should also be noted that the other main statistical series (the Census of Employment) suggests an increase in employment in 1984 and 1985, associated with the continued high level of consumer spending. This is confirmed by trade surveys such as the CBI/FT Monthly Forecast. Whilst much of this recent increase is in part-time employment, reports have suggested that some full-time employment gains are now being made.

The most visible trend, however, is the rise of the part-time worker from

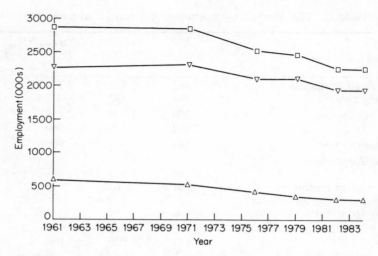

Figure 1.   Retail employment, 1961–84. ▢ Total engaged:
▽ employees; △ owners

comprising 28% of the employees in 1961 to the position in 1984, where more than half the retail employees (54%) are part-time (Figure 3). This increase in the part-time element of the retail workforce has led to a decrease in the Full-Time Equivalent (FTE) level of 35% between 1961 and 1984. The relatively small decline in total employees over the period therefore masks underlying and fundamental changes to the composition of the retail labour force, associated with changing demands for employees by retail operations.

These two trends of feminization and part-time working are, of course, linked, in that it is female workers who have occupied many of these part-time positions. It can be suggested (Figures 4 and 5) that the period 1961–71, which saw increasing employment in retailing, allowed the addition of female part-time labour to retailing, with an element of substitution of male and female full-time employees by part-time workers. Since 1971, however, the pattern is more one of substitution of female full-time employees by female part-time employees. This substitution has seen an almost doubling of the percentage of women working part-time. Female part-time employees comprised 46% of all employees in retailing in 1984. Evidence is also available suggesting that within the part-time workers category the number of hours worked is diminishing, although the extent of this is difficult to ascertain in more detail than the general figures in Table 1. This trend would be consistent with the closer matching of staff-scheduling to customer-flow.

This brief macro-level analysis demonstrates trends in the composition of retail employment quite clearly. Discussion of the reasons behind these

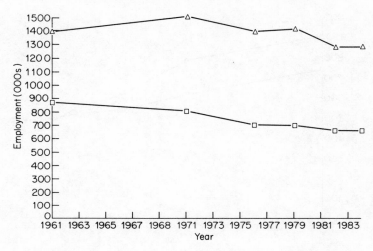

Figure 2.   Retail employment, 1961–84: employees by gender.
△ Female; □ male

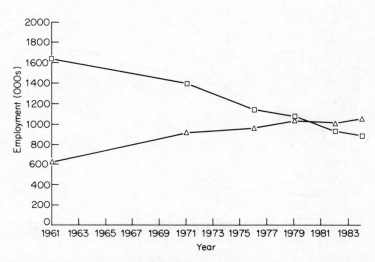

Figure 3. Retail employment, 1961–84: employees by hours worked.
△ Part-time; □ full-time

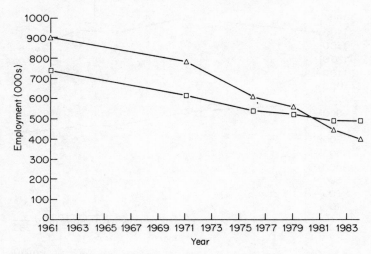

Figure 4.   Retail employment, 1961–84: full-time employees by
gender. □ Male; △ female

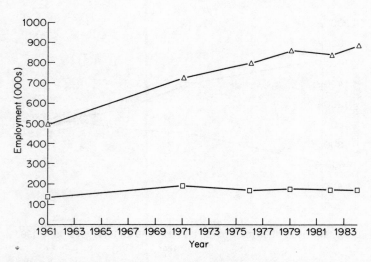

Figure 5.   Retail employment, 1961–84: part-time employees by
gender. △ Female; □ male

changes is undertaken later in this chapter once an analysis of employment at the company and outlet levels has been completed.

EMPLOYMENT WITHIN COMPANIES AND OUTLETS

In addition to the changes in the composition of the workforce outlined above, concentration in retail employment is occurring in much the same way as concentration in retailing generally (Akehurst, 1983; Davies *et al.*, 1985). Table 2 shows that the share of retail employment held by large multiple retailers (ten or more outlets) has risen from 39% in 1961 to 47% in 1982, and within this there has been a greater than proportionate increase in share of employment in companies with one hundred or more outlets, although, interestingly, the share of employees in the very large companies (i.e. with over 1000 outlets) has fallen from 1976 to 1982. Table 2 suggests a growing polarization within retailing employment between the large multiple retailers and the small firms.

Table 2. Concentration in retail employment 1961–82

	(Percentage of employment within category of company)			
	1961	1971	1976	1982
Single outlet	46	47	40	37
2–9 outlets	19	13	16	16
10–49 outlets	9	8	10	8
50–99 outlets	9	5	7	8
100–999 outlets	21	19	21	26
Over 1000 outlets	–	8	8	5

Source: Distributive Trades EDC (1985a), p. 67.

The fact that the major multiple retailers are employers of considerable numbers of workers is often ignored. For example, the grocery chains of Tesco, Sainsbury, and Asda employed 57 180, 56 300, and 35 170 people, respectively, in 1984/5. In mixed retailing Woolworth and Marks & Spencers similarly employed 53 965 and 52 667. Such figures testify to the importance of major retail companies in national employment terms. The national geographical spread of many of these companies implies that workers are employed throughout the country rather than in selected locations or regions, as with manufacturing industry.

The multiple retailers have been increasing their employment, but within this process the composition of their workforce has been changing, reflecting the macro-level changes demonstrated above. Examples of these changes are given below. Figure 6 demonstrates this change for two retail grocery companies, Sainsbury and Morrisons (a regional multiple). Within Sainsbury,

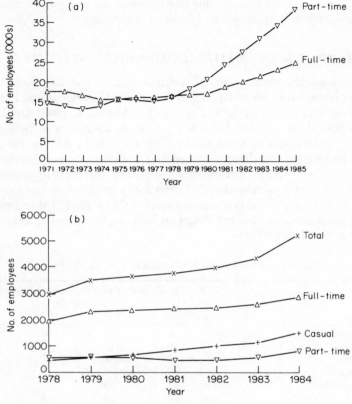

Figure 6.   (a) employment in Sainsbury, 1971–85;
            (b) employment in Morrisons, 1978–84

the growth of part-time employees is clearly seen, and is substantially greater
than full-time employees. It is noticeable also that the total employment level
rose slowly during the 1970s, with major increases occurring only in the
1980s. Total employment in Morrisons has also been increasing, but this
increase comprises mainly casual (almost all student/schoolchildren) workers.
Part-time employment is proportionately less important in Morrisons than
Sainsbury. This pattern is somewhat exceptional amongst retail companies,
but the increase in non-full-time employment is a common theme.

Part-time and casual employment has also increased in multiple retailers
outside the grocery trade, although in these cases the total level of employment may be rising less slowly, or even be static. For example, in Burtons,
Saturday-only employment has increased from 1 436 (13% of total) in 1979
to 3 541 (29%) in 1984, within an overall employment change of 1 038 (9%)

over the same period. Whilst the pattern of overall growth in employee numbers is dependent on the company and the retail sector involved, the movement to part-time employment is a common retail-employment phenomenon.

Few companies publish very detailed breakdowns of their employment structures, but one of the more detailed is presented in Table 3. W.H. Smith disaggregates its employees by hours worked and by gender, although it should be noted that the division into hours worked is not strictly comparable between the two dates in the table. Some comparison can be made, however, by assuming that the disaggregation is into full-time, part-time, and casual at each of the dates. The position in 1973 shows both a high level of casual workers and also males outnumbering females. In 1984 the casual workforce has declined considerably, and the gender balance has been reversed, with female workers comprising 63% of the total compared with 47% in 1973. In particular, the changing composition of W.H. Smith's workforce has seen enormous growth in female part-time employment at the expense of male, casual workers.

Table 3.   Employment in W.H. Smith, 1973–84

| | | No. of employees | |
	Total	Male	Female
(a) 1973			
Full-time	10 250	5 935	4 315
10–30 hours	3 866	927	2 939
< 10 hours	3 652	2 532	1 120
Total	17 768	9 394	8 374
(b) 1984			
Full-time	12 689	6 337	6 352
8–29 hours	6 386	930	5 456
< 8 hours	1 444	396	1 048
Total	20 519	7 663	12 856
(c) Percentage changes 1973–84			
Full-time	23.8	6.8	47.2
Part-time	65.2	0.3	85.6
Casual	−60.5	−84.4	− 6.4
Total	15.5	−18.4	53.5

Source: Annual Reports.

Problems can arise in examining employment in retail companies in that not all the company's employees are engaged in retail activity. This is certainly true for W.H. Smith, with its high reliance on non-retailing business, but also holds in other retail companies. For example, in Woolworth in 1984, of the company's total employees (52 667), over 3 500 were employed in administration and distribution. More extreme examples are given in Table 4, for Dixons and MFI. In Dixons, for example, only 62% of their employees are actually working in the shops. For MFI, the large increase in retail employees since 1983 (45.5%) has been matched by increases in central distribution employment (24.2%) and head-office staff (34.5%). Retail companies can therefore involve considerable employment in a variety of jobs away from serving the public in the stores.

Table 4.   Employment in Dixons and MFI

| | | No. of employees | |
	1983	1984	1985
(a) Dixons			
Retail*	2 331	2 761	2 818
Processing	572	872	1 289
Property	31	27	34
Distribution	468	475	402
Total	3 402	4 135	4 543
(b) MFI			
Retail	2 433	2 868	3 540
Central distribution	236	284	293
Head office	313	363	421
Total	2 982	3 515	4 254

Source: Annual Reports.

Other difficulties in assessing retail employment also exist. The distinction between retailing and services is becoming more blurred, especially with the introduction of High Street outlets such as business, franchised, and financial services. Many of these firms have a large proportion of their business in retailing a product to the public. In addition, many tasks at the retail outlet level are being subcontracted to outside firms (for example, cleaning of stores, maintenance of equipment, security, and distribution). The point to be noted here is that the blurring of distinctions between retailing and other services, and the changing operational aspects of retailing and retail employment, make analysis of employment in retailing much more difficult. Employment within a retail company may not be a good reflection of employment within retailing. Again, however, the trends demonstrated earlier at the national level can be seen in the examples of major retail companies given here.

The importance of part-time employment, and female employment, at the store level is demonstrated by Table 5, which reports the average employment levels by various categories in two types of store; first, the superstore, and second, the department store. The data have been obtained as part of an ESRC-sponsored research project into retail employment. The superstore data are the average figures for 175 superstores operated by three companies. This is over half of all the superstores trading in Britain. The department store figures are the mean of only nine stores operated by one company, and are thus less representative than the superstore data. Nevertheless, the data can be used here for illustrative purposes of employment types and levels in large stores.

Table 5.　Average employment levels in superstores and department stores

	(Number of employees)	
	Superstores	Department stores
Number of stores	175	9
Total employees	285	222
Total FTE	195	169
Full-time employees	108(38)	119(54)
Part-time employees	170(60)	98(44)
Casual employees	7(2)	5(2)
Male employees	80(28)	47(21)
Female employees	204(72)	175(79)
Male Employees		
Full-time	52(18)	34(15)
Part-time	27(9)	12(5)
Casual	2(1)	1(1)
Female Employees		
Full-time	56(20)	85(38)
Part-time	143(50)	86(39)
Casual	5(2)	4(2)

Note: The figures in brackets refer to the percentage of total employees within that category.

Superstore employment levels and characteristics have been detailed elsewhere (Sparks, 1983b), but the data presented in Table 5 are from a larger sample of stores than previously. The reliance on part-time and, in particular, female, part-time employees is clear. The development of superstores in Britain, and the changing structure of retail employment required by such stores, have clearly had an impact on the location and type of employee needed in both superstores and other forms of retailing. Details of department store employment are less widely available. Table 5 shows that whilst female employment is as, and if not more, marked in department stores than superstores, the reliance on part-time employees is substantially less. Thus part-time employment in department stores is less than 50% of total employment. In both types of store it is female employees who comprise the bulk of part-time employees. These figures reinforce the trends in national retail employment presented earlier.

THE REASONS FOR AND IMPLICATIONS OF THE GROWTH OF FEMALE AND PART-TIME EMPLOYMENT

The trends of feminization and increasing part-time employment can thus be demonstrated at a variety of levels. The reasons behind these trends are not difficult to identify. Within retailing, the attraction of part-time employment lies in its inherent flexibility and thus the ability to match closely staffing levels, especially at the checkout, to customer flow. This takes on added importance when the length of the trading week is almost double the normal working one, and where customer flow is heavily peaked in terms of days, weeks, and seasons. The ability to employ people to cover these various peak demands is vital to retail operational efficiency. The aim of retailers throughout this process is to increase productivity and efficiency within their outlets.

The widespread adoption of part-time employment presupposes de-skilling of many of the tasks within retail employment. Initially, this took the form of the introduction of self-service retailing, but has been extended by, for example, improved handling of goods into stores and onto shelves, and pre-processing of many products (for example, butchery products or even bakery products). Throughout the stores, and not only in food retailing, the drive has been to replace the skilled workers by the less skilled. The introduction of less-skilled workers, enabled by the routinization of tasks, allows the use of substantial numbers of part-time workers. Control and supervision of these workers is more often reserved for full-time employees. There is thus a polarization of staff within the stores between an army of day-labourers' working part-time and being low-skilled and a small number of managerial staff working full-time and being more skilled. This polarization of staff within stores may also be associated with a polarization in terms of gender. Such a position is characteristic of large stores such as superstores, but is also true of small supermarkets, large non-grocery outlets, and some specialist shops.

The development and introduction of technology has aided this process of increasing part-time employment in retailing. Management now have quicker access to more accurate information on the rate of product sales by item and customer flow. Part-time staff can thus be used in a variety of tasks, switching to the customer-serving jobs when customer flow is highest. Alternatively, part-time workers can be brought in to do specific tasks at peak times, on several days of the week. The result is that retailing offers a 'bundle' of employment opportunities, and a mix of combinations of hours with a part-time job, that appeals to many potential employees. Employees of the required quality may thus have almost 'tailor-made' hours of work. Management's ability to match staffing levels to customers in this way is a vital tool in improving retail efficiency and providing an enhanced service.

Female employment has increased in association with the change to part-time working. This can be attributed to the increasing desire of women to undertake paid employment, and the suitability of part-time employment, especially for married women wishing to return to the workforce, combining paid employment and familial responsibilities. From the employers' point of view, increasing female employment and especially part-time employment allows a flexible labour force to be deployed. Female and part-time workers may also bring cost-savings to the employer in terms of fringe benefits and possibly hourly rates of pay.

Of especial relevance to female employment in retailing has been the move to out-of-town shopping, and, in particular, is associated with the development of superstores. As has already been seen, the superstore is characterized by a large number of female and part-time employees. Given the location of many superstores on off-centre or out-of-town sites, the part-time positions are particularly important for married women living in suburban housing. There may therefore be a significant difference between the ages of the female employees in, for example, a superstore in a suburban district centre and stores in the centre of a town. This age differential of, especially, female employees may occur across the entire spectrum of retailing.

The modernization of many retail outlets and the move to purpose-built units or shopping centres has also improved the working conditions for the retail staff. The retail environment is now one that compares favourably with other employment opportunities for female workers.

ISSUES FOR THE FUTURE

Several themes emerge from the foregoing analysis and can be discussed here. The intention is not to provide definitive statements on a variety of issues but to raise these issues as being important for the future of employment in retailing.

This chapter has used the superstore as one of the examples in examining the characteristics of retail employment. The superstore is an innovative form of retailing, and, whilst demonstrating the changes occurring in retail employment, may be considered as an extreme example. The superstore is, in some ways, the 'cutting edge' of the changes in retail employment. Other spatial changes are occurring in retailing which give rise to questions of the future of the High Street. The movement of major retailers of many types and forms to off-centre and out-of-town locations has 'snowballed' recently in the UK, with announcements being made by, for example, Marks & Spencer, Halfords, and Dixons, as well as the continuation of the process established by such household goods operators as MFI, B & Q, and Harris Queensway. Foreign companies such as IKEA and Toys 'Я' Us are adding to the out-of-town pressure. Other newer, specialist, out-of-town chains are beginning to emerge. One such example is Grandstand Leisure, who aim to run a sports chain along superstore lines. The product knowledge the company requires from the staff is such that it is looking to specialist sportsmen and -women as employees.

The employment implications of such moves need careful consideration. Whilst suburban retail employment is not a recent phenomenon, the scale, type, and location of these emerging suburban centres, and thus employment, are new. Superstores are characterized by female part-time labour. 'Retail warehouses' employ fewer staff and have been more male-oriented. The development of out-of-centre retail parks or centres implies substantial employment opportunities with, if the evidence of superstores is to be believed, these employees being more likely to be female, part-time, and, quite possibly, older married women living very locally. City-centre retailing, on the other hand, may maintain a higher proportion of full-time workers, due to the need for a 'core' or 'base' level of employees, supplemented by part-timers to meet peak needs.

In the future, therefore, retailing is likely to be an industry generating high levels of part-time jobs but with a core of full-time staff in each shop unit. Any increase in shop units will increase full-time employees. The move to smaller units, such as in the subdivision of large city-centre stores, creates additional full-time jobs. Retailing will continue to be a major employer, but with a growing polarization between city-centre and suburban retailing in terms of the types of employees required. This has implications both for the type of employee liable to be employed at the store level and the quality of personnel able to be recruited by retail companies.

It should also not be forgotten that head-office employment and employment in other aspects of the company's business may have important implications. Control of the retail business may become somewhat easier due to technology, perhaps enabling more managerial decisions to be made at head office and thus reducing the content of local managerial positions. For example, Hepworth's head office controls stores in West Germany via computer links. Continued concentration in retailing may reduce the numbers and locations of these head-office and specialist jobs, perhaps restricting them to South-east England. Recent examples of such changes include the loss of jobs in Currys' computer section and the closure of Law's head office. As the activities performed by retail companies are extended, retailers are having to recruit specialists to head-office tasks. For example, retailers now require computer specialists, design specialists, and food technologists, amongst others. The requirement for skilled manpower is being reflected in extensive recruiting of graduates for jobs throughout retailing.

The issue of technology introduction into retailing has clear implications for employment. The development of EPOS systems, including laser scanning, and their links into management information systems promise great benefits for retailers. The experiment of TRADANET (computerized invoicing and ordering between retailers and suppliers) likewise holds out the possibility of improvements in efficiency. Two main implications can be seen from the introduction of technology. First, the number and type of jobs may change because of the technology's taking over previously manual functions or speeding up data transmission or transaction processing. Thus, for example, scanning systems linked to stock-control systems may obviate manual stock re-ordering and checking. Clerical jobs may be lost in retail companies through electronic data transmission. This, however, may be associated with increasing employment in computer centres. Second, the introduction of technology extends the control and supervisory powers of management, either at store level or at head office. Thus, for example, checkout operators can more closely be matched to customer flow than at present, or the store manager may lose functions due to head-office control via information systems. Technology applications also enable chains of small shops to be centrally controlled and encourage the idea of a core of full-time staff in each unit, aided by part-time employees when necessary.

An implication of technology introduction, as stated earlier, is that the traditional activities of the less-skilled workers are cancelled by technology, so the polarization within retail employment will be emphasized. Furthermore, with increasing use of new technology not only will the lower-skilled workers require training in new equipment-using techniques but also the technicians and managerial groups will require fundamental retraining in the use and maintenance of new technology, in seeing its applications, developing these applications, and then in using and interpreting the results of the applications. The need for extensive training of several types is greater now than before, but not only is training needed, awareness of the impact of new technology on work relationships, responsibilities, and types of job must also be encouraged. These points not only refer to the major multiple retailers but also to the small and medium-sized retailer where successful technology introduction may be the difference between an efficient business or closure. The work of the Distributive Trades EDC (1982, 1985b) is very important in this respect, in trying to encourage technology introduction throughout the industry.

One of the main themes to emerge from the above analysis is the importance of part-time working in retailing. It has also been noted that technology has enabled closer monitoring of operational performance and has allowed the extension of part-time working. It is suggested that this process occurs in both large and small businesses. Other operational efficiencies also allow part-time working and the likely extension of opening hours to Sundays will require companies to make decisions on a new pattern of working. The possibilities include weekend-only staff, Sunday-only staff, or other combinations of shift-working. The point to be made is that retailers now have an opportunity to employ a very flexible labour force, allowing many combinations of employees' hours. The constraints on such a process include overtime or Sunday pay rates and the extent to which businesses wish to be dependent upon part-time workers. It is possible, for example, that the further extension of part-time working in some companies may be less desirable than a higher service level generated by full-time staff. This may be especially so if 'service' becomes increasingly used as a competitive weapon.

This chapter is not the place to examine possible implications for retail employment of the extension into Sunday trading in the UK. The figures being promoted range from a net loss of 250 000 jobs to a net gain of a similar figure. Whilst such prognostications catch the headlines, they can only be meaningful if all the variables producing levels and changes in retail employment are known. This is certainly not the case. However, perhaps of greater importance in the long run is the opportunity retailers have to examine in detail their employment policies and levels and to combine the elements of employment that suit both their trading and their employees' needs.

An extension to part-time working could come about in a slightly different form. Certain tasks are already subcontracted to outside companies. For example, some retailers subcontract cleaning and maintenance, whereas department stores have run concessions or shops-in-shops for a long time. Both types reduce the staff numbers actually employed by the main retail company at the site. At the same time, some retailers, particularly in the food trade, have reduced skilled labour required in, for example, product-preparation by receiving only prepared products at the stores. Other, non-retail, companies take on the preparation role. The question can be asked as to how far these trends can continue. Is it feasible to see checkout operators being subcontracted, or perhaps shelf-fillers, such that a checkout operator may be employed full-time by a service company but work only for a few hours at any one store, or perhaps for a limited period of weeks, in a form of 'temping'? In the case of small outlets, collections of such outlets could generate considerable agglomeration economies provided that the mix of service and retail units was 'correct'. Such developments, of course, create problems in assessing retail employment levels; the problems on the revision of the SIC have already been alluded to. Although many traditional retail jobs are performed by outside retail firms, the developments occurring now and their potential in the future will make the 'true' level of retail employment almost impossible to identify.

CONCLUSIONS

Retailing employs over 2 million people in Britain. Retail companies, through their employment policies and business strategy, affect the number and type of employees recruited. They are responsible for the wage packets entering a considerable number of households. The policies of retail companies in the last twenty to thirty years have seen changes in the structure of retail employment and, in particular, increasing levels of female and part-time employment. This chapter has outlined these changes at various levels, from national to the individual outlet. The reasons behind these changes have been investigated and future changes in the employment patterns of retailing have been suggested. These range from the subcontracting of more retail functions at store-level and the possibilities and requirements of Sunday trading to the highly qualified specialists now required at head offices in support and research functions. The breadth of retail employment opportunities is immense, and retail companies are a major component of the national employment pattern.

REFERENCES

Akehurst, G. P. (1983). 'Concentration in retail distribution: measurement and significance.' *Service Industries Journal*, **3**(2), 161–79.

Davies, K., Gilligan, C., and Sutton, C. (1985). 'Structural change in grocery retailing: the implications for competition.' *International Journal of Physical Distribution and Materials Management*, **15**(2), 1–48.

Distributive Trades EDC (1982). *Technology: the Issues for the Distributive Trades*, London: NEDO.

Distributive Trades EDC (1985a). *Employment Perspectives and the Distributive Trades*, London: NEDO.

Distributive Trades EDC (1985b). *Technology and the Distributive Trades: the Experience of Small and Medium Sized Businesses*, London: NEDO.

Moir, C. (1983). *Retailing Prospects—a Discussion Paper*, London: NEDO.

NEDO (1983). *Statistics Users Conference on the Distributive Trades*, London: NEDO.

Reynolds, J. (1983). 'Retail employment change: scarce evidence in an environment of change.' *Service Industries Journal*, **3**(3), 334–62.

Sparks, L. (1983a). 'A review of retail employment since 1959 with specific focus on aspects of superstore employment.' In PTRC (eds), *Retail Planning and Development*, Proceedings of Seminar E., pp. 39–48.

Sparks, L. (1983b). 'Employment characteristics of superstore retailing.' *Service Industries Journal*, **3**(3), 334–62.

CHAPTER 15
Retail Development Strategies and the British Shopping Hierarchy

GARETH SHAW
Department of Geography, University of Exeter

INTRODUCTION

One of the most significant and consistent themes in British retail planning is that of preserving a recognizable shopping hierarchy, which is based on the traditional concepts of regional, subregional, district, and neighbourhood centres. The evolution of these ideas is deep-rooted within the planning system and have received extensive attention in the past (Burns, 1959). Furthermore, since 1968 such long-standing views have been strengthened with the introduction of both Structure and Location Plans. Important problems do, however, emerge from these local authority planning strategies that strongly impinge on the activities of retail firms and retail developers. Such difficulties are enhanced at a time when further changes in retailing methods are rendering many more of the traditional ideas about shopping centres inapplicable in the eyes of most large-scale retailers.

This chapter sets out to review some of these conflicts by examining the changing strategy of retailers towards planning controls and the reaction of local authorities to such gamesmanship. The study reviews the evolution of retail planning conflict during the last twenty-five years. Much of work focuses on the more recent attempts to promote superstores as district shopping centres, as developers try to make them more suitable and acceptable to local authorities. The arguments over such types of development turns both on the future growth policies of major retail organizations and on the perceptions of local authorities towards existing shopping hierarchies.

LOCAL AUTHORITY PLANNING AND THE SHOPPING HIERARCHY

Retail planning in Britain has witnessed some changes since the 1950s, but these have been limited to differences in approach rather than any fundamental shifts in underlying aims and ideals. During the 1950s and 1960s local authority retail planning was primarily concerned with aspects of land-use control and the matching of consumer demand to retail supply. Such development control planning as initiated by the 1947 Town and Country Planning Act was modified in the 1968 Act to encompass more than merely physical aspects of planning. This legislation introduced a two-tier system of Structure and Local Plans, and stressed the need for more forward planning in terms of economic and social aspects, as well as land use. This Act empowered local authorities to produce a series of policy statements on key planning issues. Many authorities for the first time issued specific planning policies on retail development. As Table 1 illustrates for South-west England, Structure Plan policies have been directed at a range of issues concerned with retail developments, although two main themes predominate. The first is the desire to relate retail floor-space to changes in consumer demand, as measured by population or household growth. Second, most Structure Plans contain a number of policies directed at the preservation of a clear and recognizable hierarchy of shopping centres. To some extent these policy statements also reflect the guidelines issued to local authorities by national government. In Britain these have taken the form of a series of Policy Control Notes issued by the Department of the Environment.

A detailed examination of local authority policies reveals that, despite the changed approach introduced by the 1968 Town and Country Planning Act, the philosophy behind retail planning, that of preserving a recognizable hierarchy of shopping centres, has remained remarkably constant. Within each major urban area the traditional hierarchy is based on a simple three-tier system of centres. These are first, local or neighbourhood shops and shopping centres that cater for some of the convenience-goods shopping needs of between 500 to 5 000 people, depending on the size of the city. The second level in this hierarchy are termed 'district shopping centres', which provide a wider range of retail and service facilities to a much larger catchment area (Table 2). Finally, the central retail area forms the highest level in this hierarchy, and it may operate in a wider inter-urban context as either a subregional or regional centre, once again depending on its size. In many urban areas these traditional definitions have been somewhat modified with the development of planned, purpose-built centres serving district and neighbourhood needs, and usually stimulated by local authorities (Antill, 1977, 1981).

Significantly, this hierarchy of shopping centres, and the planning philosophy that supports it, has been under considerable pressure during the last decade and is now showing signs of imminent collapse. The supporting retail policies in both Structure and Local Plans have in many parts of the country been severely undermined, and unfortunately look far less promising a future vehicle for local-authority retail planning (Shaw and Williams, 1980). These

Table 1. General policy statements affecting future retail developments

Structure plan area	Number of policy statements relating to retailing	Restrictions on development in major centres	Limitation of 'out-of-town' retailing	Controls on discount and 'cash and carry' retailing	Maintaining existing shopping hierarchy	Maintain retailing in local villages and rural areas	Improve existing retail centres	Concentrate new development in major centres
Avon	5		*	*[a]	*			*
Cornwall	0		No direct policy statements on retailing					
Devon	8	*	*	*		*	*	*
Dorset (SE)	5		*					
Dorset (rest)	3		*					
Gloucester	7[a]	*	*	*	*	*		
Somerset	5	*	*	*	*	*		
Wilts (NE)	5[a]		*			*		
Wilts (S)	4[a]		*					*
Wilts (W)	3[a]							*

[a] Size-restrictions

Figure 1. The distribution of major retail developments in Exeter

Figure 2. The use of district-centre facilities in Exeter

Business Strategy and Retailing

Table 2.   Traditional characteristics of the shopping-centre hierarchy in British towns

Type	Characteristics	Ideal catchment populations
Central retail area	Full range of shops and services, but scale depends on size of town	100 000-plus
District	Major focal points, with a range of shops and non-retail services	25 000–40 000
Neighbourhood	Serving basic needs of areas away from district centres	5 000–10 000
Local centres	Recognized in larger urban areas and vary from isolated shops to small clusters of stores	500– 5 000

difficulties have been created in three main ways, each of which are inter-related through the activities of large-scale retail organizations and developers.

The first of these problems concerns the failure of the traditional planning of the shopping hierarchy to respond to changing developments in retailing. Despite the fact that some local authorities have adopted a more flexible approach to shopping-centre definitions, many difficulties still remain. The increased importance placed on these definitions must be viewed relative to the changing types of large-scale retail developments. Indeed, as Table 1 shows, many of the retail policies contained within Structure and Local Plans were specifically designed to cope with the threat of free-standing superstores. It was the arrival of these large stores that created the initial pressures on traditional local-authority planning concepts. From the retailers' point of view such stores offered increased rates of return on investment through the ability to gain scale economies. As a further attempt to make financial savings and gain sufficient land to meet the needs of these stores, new sites were sought on the edge or outside urban areas.

A second major way in which traditional planning concepts are being undermined is due to changed economic circumstances. In particular, local authorities are being tempted into considering new, large-scale retail schemes either as a means of improving local employment or, more importantly, as an attempt to solve some of the financial problems. The former reason is perhaps more limited in its appeal, if only because of the uncertainty of the actual number of new jobs that are created (Scottish Office, 1982). However, at a time of government rate-capping and cutbacks on public spending the ability to raise extra income on property development has become more important during the last five years, bringing local authority estate depart-ments into the field of retail planning. Limited evidence from developments in Gateshead in North-east England and proposals within Devon do suggest that this factor is becoming a more potent force in the decision-making processes of both county and district local authorities.

Finally, local-authority retail planning has for some time been weakened through the exploitation of the appeal processes by developers. This takes a number of forms, particularly by developers submitting a whole series of planning applications for either the same site or closely related sites within the same area. For example, the developer may submit one plan, await the inquiry decision, modify the proposal in the light of any comments, and then submit a new plan for the same site. An alternative strategy is for developers to submit a large number of applications within the same area, causing considerable pressure on the limited resources of many local-planning departments. A more recent approach has been for developers to present superstores as district shopping centres by expanding their range of functions in an attempt to overcome the restrictions against these types of stores.

CHANGING DEVELOPMENT STRATEGIES

The discussion concerning the weakening of retail planning policy and, in particular, the undermining of the traditional shopping hierarchy highlights the changing nature of development strategies. Initially, the major pressure for a change in local authority attitudes towards retail planning came from 'out-of-town', free-standing hypermarkets and superstores, largely focusing on convenience goods. Despite the protracted debates concerning the possible impact of these new retail forms on existing centres, the threat of these · single-store type of developments were relatively easy to deal with, since they were perceived as falling outside the established shopping hierarchy and could be treated as completely new elements. If viewed in this way, many planning authorities when drawing up their Structure and Local Plans found it relatively easy to construct policies that restricted superstore developments.

Significantly, the pattern of superstore developments has changed in a number of ways, represented by an increase in the size of stores, a diversification of products, and, in particular, the rise of 'out-of-town' non-food stores in the form of DIY and household goods superstores. Many of the latter types have sought locations on edge-of-town, industrial estates, often forming small retail parks. The initial reaction of local authorities was to restrict such stores on land zoned for industry. However, during the last ten years those policies have tended to be eroded away, especially since estate developers found it increasingly difficult to let units to a declining manufacturing sector.

A more recent change in emphasis has been away from single superstores towards shopping centres. These newer developments take two main forms, either large-scale, regional shopping centres or what can be termed 'focused-centres'. Both may have the possible appeal that they appear to fit more closely into the planner's ideal of a shopping hierarchy, possibly making it more difficult to reject these developments outright on the grounds that they fail to conform with local authority policies. Obviously, this is not the main reason for such developments, as economic motives are also very powerful, especially since the rates of return on commercial schemes became far more attractive than for those from industrial properties during the early 1980s. A further reason for these changes is associated with the different character of developers, as financial institutions have moved into the construction of shopping centres. During the period 1965–82 institutions accounted for 12% of shopping-centre floor-space compared with 82% developed by traditional property companies. However, between 1982 and 1984 the proportion of floor-space accounted for by property companies had declined to 30%, whilst the share constructed by institutions rose to 29% (Hillier Parker Research, 1985). Such changes introduced more capital into retail development, thus facilitating larger schemes.

The emphasis given to shopping centres by developers also represents a natural progression in the construction of new retail forms in 'out-of-town' locations. The move away from mainly single-stores towards shopping centres allows greater flexibility for retailers to secure inroads into new-product areas in the hope of attracting more consumers.

With the early exception of Brent Cross in north London, the development of 'out-of-town' regional shopping centres are as yet very limited, although the pressure for such schemes is gaining in momentum. Two major projects have made some progress during the mid-1980s. The most advanced is the Metro Centre at Gateshead in Tyneside, which occupies a site in an enterprise zone, giving the developers financial advantages in terms of capital allowances together a rate-free period for tenants up to 1991. Extra government funding for the provision of infrastructure, improving the site, roads, and services is also available. The centre provides about 1.5 million ft^2 of floor-space, comprising seven major stores and some 200 smaller shop units. The major food component is a Carrefour superstore of 110 000 ft^2, together with a number of major department stores. Despite the fact that the centre will have a major impact on central Newcastle and Washington, the local authority did not oppose the scheme because of the employment it would generate, together with its location within an enterprise zone. A second development is that of Centre 21, south of Leicester at the junction of the M1 and M69. This proposal has been termed a supra-regional centre due to both its proposed size·(approximately 1.25 million ft^2) and its potential catchment of 4 million consumers (Askham, 1985). Despite an initial public enquiry, the development of Centre 21 is still very much in the balance.

The significance of these schemes is that a major change in retail development strategies appears to be underway with, as Askham argues, very little concern being expressed by the local authorities. In the case of the Centre 21 proposal, during its initial stages very few people took it seriously, and even by the time of the public enquiry the arguments voiced against the proposal by local authorities were not always that convincing. Proposals for similar centres in other areas seem to be increasing as developers attempt to introduce a new dimension in shopping centres. For example, the retail development firm Capital and Counties have a scheme for a regional centre of about 1 million ft² at Thurrock; whilst in Devon two different and competing proposals have recently been submitted to develop 'out-of-town' regional centres along the lines of the Metro Centre.

A second major change in retail development strategies has been concerned with the construction of so-called 'focused-centres' to act as district shopping centres. These schemes are often characterized by a superstore together with a grouping of a few smaller shops; one of many recent examples is that of the Estover centre, on the outskirts of Plymouth in Devon. This is slightly smaller than some recent proposals, being only 60 000 ft² of floor-space, but it is typical in its structure, with the whole development centred around an Asda superstore. One point that should be stressed is that most of these schemes differ from those purpose-built district centres constructed in conjunction with local authorities (Antill, 1977).

From the developer's point of view it could be argued that these new centres are designed to by-pass existing planning restrictions on superstore development. This type of strategy is made easier due to the problems of defining district centres, a fact that is often well exploited at planning enquiries. The difficulties of identifying what constitutes a district shopping centre are not new, since, as early as 1971, the Distributive Trades Council attempted to tackle this problem (National Economic Development Office, 1971). They argued that district centres should have a complete range of convenience goods, a choice of outlets for these products, together with easy accessibility from all parts of the centre's catchment area.

These points have been re-emphasized by the Department of Environment in Policy Note 13 (1978), which provides a series of guidelines for local planning authorities. This document also states that district centres should be of sufficient size to provide competition with larger stores, and as such have a wide variety of facilities, including non-retail services conveniently located within or close to the centre. It is these general ideas that have been loosely incorporated into local planning and they lie behind many of the Structure and Local planning policies on retailing. These issues have there-fore formed the basis of discussions between developers and local authorities, from which it is possible to identify two main types of district centre. One type is characterized by centres which have evolved over a long period and usually are based around a series of traditional shopping streets, located primarily on main radial roads. In contrast, the second category is represented by the more modern, purpose-built centres, which often contain a relatively large anchor store, supporting retail units and community facilities. Significantly, it seems that developers are now attempting to create a third type, which are based around large superstores and contain only limited support facilities of the type normally associated with district centres.

Unfortunately, little attempt has been made by local authorities to examine the merits of these new shopping-centre proposals and consequently they are not fully covered by existing planning policies. Indeed, the research that does attempt to re-work the traditional ideas concerning shopping centres 'ias largely emerged from the work of geographers and has yet to be incorporated into the planning literature (Dawson, 1983; Davies, 1984). The problems raised by this neglect affect both developers and local authorities, each of which are attempting to achieve quite different aims and often using very different definitions of shopping centres. For example, neither groups are using the same definition of a district shopping centre, a fact that becomes clear at many planning enquiries. In the case of this problem, establishing the precise role of superstore-based, focused centres relative to the functions of traditional district centres may go some way toward producing a more workable classification. It may also serve to highlight some of the fundamental problems between development strategies and the demand from local authorities to preserve a traditional shopping hierarchy. The remainder of this chapter draws attention to these problems through examining a specific case study.

THE ROLE OF FOCUSED CENTRES IN THE SHOPPING HIERARCHY: A CASE STUDY OF EXETER

One major issue concerning the development of 'focused centres' based around a superstore is whether they can perform an effective role within the established shopping hierarchy as district centres. Surprisingly, little empirical work has been directed at this question, and the handful of studies that do exist relate to those planned centres initiated by local authorities (Finney and Robinson, 1976). The Exeter case study from which much of the material in this chapter is drawn was directed specifically at this problem. The work was originally funded by the local authority and formed part of a project aimed at examining shopping provision and community needs in the face of increased pressure for edge-of-town retail developments.

Exeter, like many other parts of South-west England, was relatively late in being developed by large superstore organizations. As a consequence the region has come under considerable pressure in the last 5 years from retail developers eager to exploit a new market. Furthermore, because of the recent nature of such interests the developments reflect the latest strategies of retailers, such as superstore-based centres. The combination of these forces has produced considerable pressure on an often unprepared local authority planning system. The Exeter area has received much of this recent attention, and during the time of this project in 1984 a number of planning applications had been submitted by developers (Figure 1).

Much of this study focuses on the Tesco application to develop a so-called 'district centre'. The application by Asda for a similar centre was not considered in the same detail as this was subsequently withdrawn before the planning enquiry (Figure 1). The major aim of the research was to compare the consumer utilization of a superstore-based centre with two more recognizable district shopping centres within Exeter.

The concern over such developments within the city has shifted from the usual impact arguments to focus on a wider set of issues and, in particular, the role of superstores within the local shopping hierarchy. The local planning authority has therefore called into question the adequacy of superstores to act as district centres.

To fully understand the changing nature of this debate it is necessary to examine planning attitudes at both national and local levels. As was shown in the early part of this chapter, national retail policy regarding district centres is confined to some rather general guidelines. However, at a local level the development of superstores would only be acceptable if they met the specific criteria given in Table 3. Such policies have helped to widen the discussion on superstore development, but at the same time provided new opportunities for developers to exploit the Local Plan and the inadequate definition of district centres. The Tesco proposal was an attempt to overcome district and county retail planning policies by presenting their superstore as a district shopping centre. The proposed development was for a food store of 52 000 ft², a number of small shops covering in total approximately 10 000 ft², and some community facilities. The precise nature of the non-retail facilities were never fully given in the application, but would have included a doctor's surgery.

Table 3.   Planning issues in Exeter's local retail policies regarding superstores

---

(1) That they can serve as district shopping centres within a subregional centre such as Exeter
(2) That they are well related to residential areas
(3) That they will not undermine the functions of existing shopping centres

---

The study set out to compare the use of district centres and existing superstores, a task not without problems. First, it was not entirely possible to find a superstore in Exeter that exactly characterized the one proposed by Tesco. There did exist, however, a smaller Leo's store (17 500 ft²), which had in close proximity a group of neighbourhood shopping facilities and occupied a site within the residential area of the city (Figure 1). It was this store that was used as a surrogate of the Tesco proposal. It is important

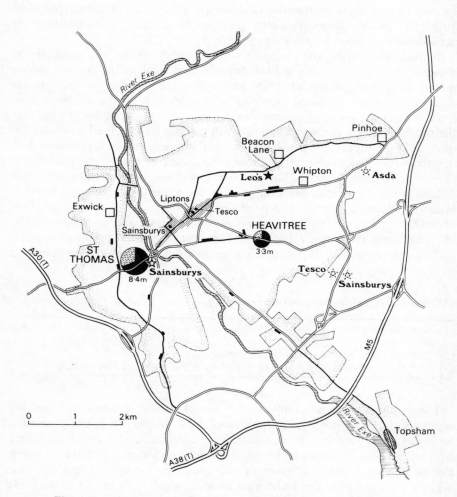

Figure 1.   The distribution of major retail developments in Exeter

therefore to modify any results from this comparison in the light of differences between the size and character of the two superstores.

The two district centres used in the analysis represented both a traditional unplanned development within the Heavitree area and a centre at St Thomas in the west of the city that was a mixture of older shops and a newer shopping precinct (Figure 1). The Heavitree centre has a total floor-space of 45 000 ft^2, with 46 shops and service establishments, 26% of which are food retailers accounting for 43% of turnover in 1980. The St Thomas centre has a total of 104 commercial premises with a total floor-space of 95 000 ft^2. Food retailers accounted for 31% of all establishments and 69% of the total turnover. In both these centres Gateway supermarkets are the main food outlets. Furthermore, health service facilities and schools are located in close proximity to the shopping areas of both district centres.

Table 4.   Consumer profiles of district centres and a superstore in Exeter

| | Consumer groups | | | | | |
	1	2	3	4	5	6
Leos	4.9	4.9	27.2	59.3	1.2	0.0
St Thomas	12.5	12.5	25.0	37.5	0.0	12.5
Heavitree	7.5	3.0	16.4	67.2	0.0	4.5

1: Retired.
2: Unemployed.
3: Professional/managerial.
4: Skilled/semi-skilled/unskilled.
5: Students.
6: Others, including self-employed.

Table 5.   Methods of consumer travel for main-food shopping in Exeter   .

| | | | Percentage travelling by | | |
Locations	Car	Bus	Walking	Cycle	Others
Leos	86.3	2.5	11.2	0.0	0.0
Heavitree	36.4	13.6	50.0	0.0	0.0
St Thomas	35.7	21.4	42.9	0.0	0.0

Measurements were made of the way shoppers used the district centres and the superstore for their main food-shopping trips. As Table 4 shows, there were only small differences in the types of consumers using the different facilities. More significant variations are shown in Table 5, which stresses the importance of car-based trips to the superstore. This may appear an obvious difference, given the characteristics of superstores, yet it should be stressed that the store in question was not an 'out-of-town' development but located within a residential area. At this simple level of analysis, superstores such as the one proposed by Tesco are used in a very different way by consumers compared with traditional district centres. Such differences are reflected in the extent of trade areas, with the two district centres having limited catchments for main food-shopping that ranged between 1 and 2 miles. In contrast, the trade area of the superstore was considerably larger, drawing consumers from all parts of the city, over 86% of whom travelled by car (Table 5). Obviously, one problem arising from such differences is that increased car traffic penetrates into residential areas, placing greater pressure on suburban roads.

A second major dimension to the question of district-centre development involves the provision of non-retail facilities. The integration of community facilities into district centres is more than just a planning ideal, and has in the past received support from both retailers and developers (Duerden, 1977). For example, the provision of clinics, health centres, libraries, and dentists have been seen as important elements in the structure of most modern district centres. Indeed, in many local authorities such policies have been formalized and given further importance within their Local Plans.

An ideal hierarchy in the provision of these facilities is obviously extremely difficult to achieve unless the environment is dominated by planned district centres. In most urban areas the situation is complicated by having a mixture of different types of centres, with a large number that have evolved over a considerable time period without the aid of any overall plan. Under these circumstances, many district centres do not contain an entire range of community facilities but rather a few of the more basic ones. In the Exeter example the two district centres contained a limited number of non-retail services, ranging from doctors, post offices, solicitors, and banks.

Unfortunately, little empirical work has been undertaken into the use of these non-retail facilities both at a local level and more especially in relation to the overall role of district centres. In the Exeter survey, data were collected at two levels; first, in terms of the use of all local non-retail services, and second, with reference to those located within district centres. Given the emphasis of this chapter, attention will be directed mainly to the use of district-centre facilities. However, because of the range of services examined in this survey it is obvious that general patterns of use will vary considerably. In this context Table 6 shows that comparatively fewer people use local dentists compared with, say, chemists and post offices. This is because most dentists are geographically concentrated in certain parts of Exeter, especially in the central area. It should also be pointed out that in this part of the survey people's ideas of the term 'local' did vary and the figures tend to slightly over estimate the use of local facilities.

Figure 2 shows the use of different non-retail functions in the two district centres as measured by the proportions of residents in each ward who use a particular district facility. From these data it can be seen that the use of such services varies with residential location, although the Heavitree centre has a

Table 6.   The use of local non-retail facilities in Exeter

Facility	Percentage of sample using facility in local area
Doctor	75.4
Dentist	47.8
Chemist	61.5
Library	38.3
Bank	43.3
Post office	80.8

wider geographical catchment than that of St Thomas. In terms of the latter centre the heaviest use, apart from by residents in the St Thomas ward itself, comes from the Cowick and Exwick areas. With regard to specific facilities, the use of doctors is more geographically diffuse than that for other services, primarily because when people move house from one area to another they sometimes retain the same doctor (Phillips, 1981). The use of chemist shops in St Thomas is also relatively widespread among people from a number of adjoining wards. In contrast, the use of post offices is relatively concentrated, and very few people living outside the St Thomas ward use the St Thomas district centre, the reason being quite simply that this facility is also very often available in neighbourhood-level centres. Generally, in the case of both district centres, as one moves from doctors through to post offices the patterns of use become more spatially concentrated. This is due to the fact the facilities are either available lower down the retail-service centre hierarchy or are provided only in the central shopping area.

It is nevertheless clear that, even in a small city like Exeter (100 000 population, 1981), district centres play an important role in the provision of service facilities, some of which are used extensively by the community. However, the importance of having such facilities available in district shopping centres remain difficult to measure directly. One method of tackling this problem of measurement is to compare the patterns of use of those residents living in areas with district-centre facilities, with those of people located in areas of poor provision.

In Exeter an area of low retail and service provision had already been identified in the Local Plan, consisting of the Wonford ward in the east of the city (Figure 2). The plight of residents in this area was all the more difficult, given the very low levels of car-availability (almost 59% of households had no access to a car). A comparison was therefore made between residents of the Wonford ward with people living in the St Thomas and Heavitree wards. As Table 7 shows, for two key facilities the people of Wonford were forced to make far more use of doctors and chemists located in the central area compared with the residents of St Thomas and Heavitree. Such findings must be considered within the context of the proposed Tesco

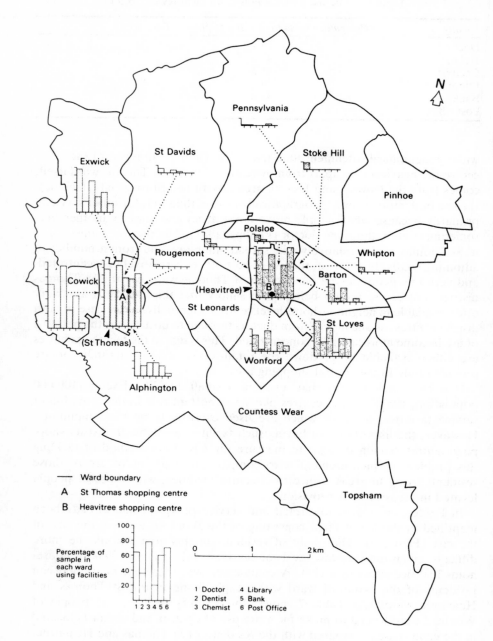

N

Ward boundary
A   St Thomas shopping centre
B   Heavitree shopping centre

Percentage of
sample in
each ward
using facilities

100
80
60
40
20

0   1   2 km

1 Doctor   4 Library
2 Dentist   5 Bank
3 Chemist   6 Post Office

Figure 2.   The use of district-centre facilities in Exeter

'district'/focused-centre in east Exeter. It could be argued that the disadvan-taged consumers living in areas such as Wonford would have little to gain from the proposed new centre, especially as it would be peripheral to their area, be orientated towards car-based shopping trips, and only have a limited range of service facilities.

Table 7.   A comparison of three residential areas by their use of service facilities

Facility	Location	Percentage in each ward		
		Wonford	St Thomas	Heavitree
Doctor	Central	21.9	15.0	14.3
	Local[a]	3.1	77.8	65.1
Chemist	Central	40.6	7.4	23.8
	Local[a]	3.1	83.3	58.7

[a]Local means, in this instance, facilities located within the same ward.

When viewed within the context of shopping centres providing a service to the wider needs of a community the whole debate becomes far more important than mere attempts to preserve any ideal of a shopping hierarchy. The issues shift towards the role that shopping-centre developers should play in meeting the retail and service requirements of consumers. It may also be argued that these two issues, of shopping hierarchies and community needs, when explored in detail are closely interlinked, especially in the minds of local authority planners.

RETHINKING RETAIL PLANNING STRATEGIES

This chapter has attempted to highlight the difficulties that both county and district planning departments have in defending traditional shopping hierarchies. At a regional level the proposals for large out-of-town develop-ments such as the Metro Centre and Centre 21 are, for the first time, exposing the lack of any broad-scale planning strategies. The demise of Structure Plans and the all-too-often failure of adjoining county planning authorities to provide common, rather than competing, policies for retail development add further to such difficulties. The urgent need at this level is for a regional approach to retail growth, since both Structure Plans and the present system of planning enquiries fail to tackle the problems of large new shopping centres. No-one, for example, has seriously considered the role that the Metro Centre can play within the North-east, or indeed how its development will impact on existing centres. In many of the new proposals for similar regional centres developers are stressing the complementary nature that these schemes can have relative to existing shopping areas. However, none of these developers explain how such centres may be integrated into the existing shopping hierarchy, neither is such information available from national or local government. All the existing planning literature focuses on the problems of accommodating or restricting superstores, and in this sense is lagging behind the development strategies of major retailers.

At a more local level the evidence provided from Exeter suggests that a rethinking of the traditional concepts of district shopping centres is urgently required. The promotion of superstores as district centres may have been an initial ploy on the part of developers to undermine local plans, but, in doing so, these actions have raised serious doubts about the validity of some shopping policies. In the light of this evidence local authorities need to either adjust their attitudes towards what comprises a district centre or, alternatively, attempt to utilize the concepts of focused centres. Recent trends in local authority expenditure cuts suggest that the latter strategy is the most likely course of action. Indeed, fewer local authorities will be in a position to initiate district-centre developments with their own funds, and a greater emphasis is being placed on private capital for shopping centres. These changed economic circumstances make the problems all the more difficult and solutions that much more important.

In the past, planners have been relatively successful in limiting the size of major superstores in all types of environments. However, the second generation of such developments are far more difficult to deal with in that they represent an upgrading of the single-superstore idea rather than a downgrading of traditional district-centre ideas, as the early phases of such developments tended to be. The way ahead would appear to lie in local authorities broadening the policies on urban shopping hierarchies and examining what role the newer types of focused-centres can play. Conversely, retailers need to show a greater appreciation of local shopping needs as often expressed in the Local Plans, rather than attempting to impose uniform developments which may be out of step with community requirements. In the absence of any national guidelines or advice it seems likely that the progress of policy change may be slow and fragmented for some years to come.

REFERENCES

Antill, L. (1977). 'District shopping centre development.' In *District Shopping Centres*, Reading: Unit for Retailing Planning Information. See also URPI (1979). *Service Outlets in Shopping Centres*, Reading.
Antill, L. (1981). 'Changes in district centres.' *Chartered Surveyor*, **113**(7), 494–6.
Askham, P. (1985). 'Supra-regional shopping centres.' *Estates Gazette*, **275**, 869–70.
Burns, W. (1959). *British Shopping Centres*, London.
Davies, R. (1964). *Retail and Commercial Planning*, London.
Dawson, J. (1983). *Shopping Centre Development*, Chapter 3, London.
Department of Environment (1978). *Large New Stores, Development Control Policy Note 13*, London.
Duerden, B. (1976). 'Community facilities and District Centres.' In *District Shopping Centres*, Reading: URPI.

Finney, J., and Robinson, J. (1976). 'District shopping centres: some case studies.' *PTRC Proceedings* of retailing seminar, London.

Hillier Parker Research (1985). *British Shopping Developments, 1984 Supplement.*

National Economic Development Office (1971). *The Future Pattern of Shopping*, London.

Phillips, D. R. (1981). *Contemporary Issues in the Geography of Health Care*, Chapter 5, Norwich: Geobooks.

Ridgway, J. D. (1976). 'The future of district shopping centres—a retailer's view.' *PTRC Proceedings* of retailing seminar, London.

Scottish Office Central Research Unit (1982). *Retail Employment Change in Scotland.*

Shaw, G., and Williams, A. (1982). 'Structure plans and retail developments.' *Estates Gazette*, **264**, October, 25–7.

Tesco Stores Ltd Planning Appeal, Department of Environment, July 1984.

URPI (1979). *Service Outlets in Shopping Centres*, Reading.

CHAPTER 16
Small Retailers in Inner Urban Areas

ROBIN WARD

Department of Business and Management Studies, Trent Polytechnic

Changes in consumer demand and in competitive strategy have, in recent years, had a marked impact on the urban retailing system. Nowhere have the effects been more severe than in small, independent retailing in inner urban areas. In 1950 there were 450 000 independent retail shops in Britain; thirty years later the total was 220 000, less than half the earlier figure (Dawson, 1983, p. 19).

Multiple retailers have grown steadily stronger over this period, with their share of the retail groceries market, for example, increasing from 47% to 76% between 1961 and 1981 (GLC, 1985, p. 151). Economies of scale, of particular importance in retail sectors such as grocers selling largely standardized goods, have also been won through the search for ever-larger sites, mostly located on the fringes of urban areas. Here they are conveniently situated for the suburban middle class, who account for a large and increasing proportion of disposable income.

Superstore shopping has a strong appeal to the car-owning public: it provides an attractive environment for 'leisure shopping', offers a wider choice and more economical prices, and in many cases allows easier access and parking. However, the success of the suburban superstore has had a dramatic impact on the independent outlets which form the backbone of retailing in inner urban areas. By 1980 a mere 45 000 grocery stores had survived, compared with 117 000 thirty years before, leading Dawson (1983) to speak of 'independent retailing becoming a marginal economic enterprise in post-industrial Britain' (p. 19).

Economic trends which have maintained the level of purchasing power among the increasingly dominant middle class have at the same time sharply reduced the disposable income on which retailers in inner areas can depend. The effects of the switch to a low-income population in many inner areas formerly occupied by the middle class were masked in the 1950s and 1960s by the increasing population density and the high level of employment. Since then, occupancy levels have declined sharply, especially among Asian and Afro-Caribbean households, and employment more so.

The typical consequences for inner-city retailing have been a sharp reduction in demand, the withdrawal of multiples, high vacancy and turnover rates, and a general deterioration in both the fabric of the premises and the general appearance of the shops (Davies, 1984).

As a result, the implementation of competitive strategy by the retail giants, taking advantage of changes in consumer demand, has led to higher shopping costs for the low-income, disadvantaged, less-mobile consumers dispro- portionately concentrated in inner areas and has thereby created a dilemma for public policy. How can the social impact of retail strategy be cushioned by measures to protect the competitive position of surviving inner-area stores?

PUBLIC POLICY RESPONSE

The public response to the dilemma sketched above, contained in structure plans and other strategy and policy documents, has taken various forms:

(1) The basic need is to ensure that the physical fabric of existing inner area shops is given sufficient attention to protect them from demolition. Some local authorities have used Urban Programme funds to improve shops in the main inner-area shopping parades. This has been done in the West Midlands, for example, by adapting the system of block-renewal of substandard housing known as 'enveloping', which affords significant economies of scale, to the rehabilitation of complete blocks of shops.

(2) A second objective has been to make shops more attractive to local customers by improving the general appearance of the shopping centre through environmental improvements (sometimes linked to rehabilitation of retail premises). Attempts to give shops more appeal by improving store layout and image and concentrating on the level of customer service complement attention to the wider shopping environment.

(3) A further emphasis has been on identifying opportunities for attracting more shoppers into the area by differentiating the goods and services provided so as to create a stronger external image. Davies (1984) has written of the possibilities of creating 'retail theme centres' in such areas as DIY, home and garden, and motor-related trades. A successful adap- tation of a local shopping parade to such purposes would help to preserve its viability, but at the probable cost of losing the essential convenience- based retail outlets on which local residents depend.

(4) There is also some scope for using public policy to make inner residential areas more attractive to higher-income households, whose extra spending power could help to preserve local stores. 'Gentrification' of areas in inner London in the 1960s gave rise to public concern on the grounds

that it could only succeed by depriving low-income tenants of the only housing available in a very tight housing market. In the different circumstances of the 1980s, with far more inner-area houses being owned by their occupiers and occupancy levels much lower, planning for a greater social and economic mix in residential development in inner areas is less threatening to existing residents. An example of such a move would be negotiating the transfer of a block of hard-to-let council flats to a private developer for conversion to owner-occupation.

(5) Despite the sharp contraction in the numbers of surviving inner-area shops the drop in aggregate local purchasing power may be even greater. Thus in some localities overcompetition may continue to be a problem which stands in the way of local retailers maintaining a reasonable level of sales. Selective demolition, therefore, and the withholding of planning permission for shops in residential streets may be quite compatible with providing a stable retail sector in the local area.

(6) Finally, there is a wide range of possibilities for helping local retailers to remain competitive by reducing costs. There is much to be learnt from the strategy for support of small retail businesses adopted in Japan (Kirby, 1984). This is designed to avoid overdependence on government and to encourage survival through more cost-effective operations within a system in which the value of small stores to economic wellbeing is recognized in a co-ordinated government programme of support for the distributive sector. As a result, whereas small shops are in decline in most industrial societies, in Japan the numbers seem to be increasing (Kirby, 1984, p. 44). Areas of intervention under consideration in Britain include more effective training in shop management and arrangements to use local authority influence, services, and purchasing power to obtain the benefits of economies of scale for small retailers in such functions as purchasing, use of retail technology, and distribution (GLC, 1985).

THE IMPACT OF ASIAN RETAILING

While local authority strategy and policy documents show an increasing concern with the need to maintain the viability of inner-area retailing, the discussion in the previous section suggests that, at a time when public expenditure has been coming under increasing pressure, the prospects for effective interventions may be rather small. Even if shop premises are rehabilitated through government subsidy, differentials between inner-city and suburban stores in the demand for low-order, convenience goods such as groceries are unlikely to diminish. A great deal depends, therefore, on the ability of shopkeepers to survive through minimizing costs and so keeping prices as competitive as possible.

This raises as a central issue for consideration the impact of Asian shopkeepers, who have been moving into inner-area shopping centres in large numbers, on retailing patterns. How far have local residents come to depend on Asian-owned stores for the purchase of convenience goods? Are Asian shopkeepers more able to resist the increasing domination of retail giants? (In London, for example, two firms, Sainsbury and Tesco, accounted for 55% of the packaged grocery trade in 1985 (GLC, 1985, p. 151).) How does their increasing presence in inner-area shopping centres affect the prospects for the public policy objectives outlined above being achieved?

The presence of Asian retailers in inner areas

A detailed consideration of the impact of Asian retailing and its implications for the continued viability of inner-area shopping centres presupposes a sufficient quantity of Asian shopkeepers to have a significant effect on outcomes. Unfortunately, accurate aggregate data on the proportion of Asian retailers in inner-city centres is not available. However, an approximate figure can be estimated which will be sufficient for the argument being advanced. About 60% of Asian firms in Britain are in retail distribution (Smith, 1976, p. 220; Brown, 1984, p. 210). Applied to a figure of 45 000 for the estimated size of the Asian business population (Ward, 1987), this gives some 27 000 Asian firms in retail distribution. The total size of the independent retail sector in Britain in 1980 was given as 220 000 (Dawson, 1983, p. 19). Thus an estimated 12% (i.e. one in eight) of all independent retail outlets in Britain are Asian-owned. However, Asian shopkeepers are very unevenly spread between urban areas, within urban areas, and between retail trades. Ward (1985) has shown, for example, that the move of Asians into small firms has varied greatly, depending on what other economic opportunities are available. Aldrich *et al.* (1981) have concluded that Asian retailing is closely associated with areas in which Asians have settled, and a variety of local studies have shown the concentration in particular retail trades, notably grocery stores, confectioners, tobacconists, and newsagents ('CTNs') and chemists (Lambeth, 1982; Wilson, 1983; Wilson and Stanworth, 1985; Islam, 1985). Even if it is assumed that the probability of Asian shopkeepers being located in inner areas (where almost all Asian residential concentrations are based) was only double that for whites, and the same probability was applied to the proportion of Asians among those running convenience shops on which local residents in inner areas depend (principally grocery stores, but also CTNs, greengrocers, etc.), the combined effect of applying these two corrections to the overall figure of one in eight independent retail stores being Asian-owned would produce a working estimate of half of the convenience stores in inner urban areas being in the hands of Asian proprietors.

Indeed, this may well be a substantial underestimate. For example, Krčmář (1984), in a comparison of Asian and white grocery stores in inner Glasgow (a city without a numerically large Asian population), had great difficulty in finding fifty white-owned independent grocery stores in inner areas to form a control sample. Thus even allowing for a substantial margin of error, the estimated figure of half of all inner-city convenience stores being Asian-owned shows that local residents in inner urban areas in Britain are extensively (and, it may be assumed, increasingly) dependent on Asian shopkeepers. If recent trends continue, they will constitute the majority of retailers to whom local authorities must look to maintain the viability of key sections of inner-area retailing.

Asian retailing in inner Leicester

No study is available which deals with all the questions raised above. However, research on shopping undertaken in inner districts of Leicester by Ward and Johnson in 1984 sheds a good deal of light (Ward and Johnson, 1987). The selection of Leicester as a case study allows an examination of the effects of settlement by two contrasting Asian communities. Of the city's population of 280 000, some 60 000 are of South Asian origin. They include roughly equal numbers who have come direct from India, many of them from rural areas and non-English-speaking, and Asians of Indian origin from East Africa, more anglicized and with extensive experience of business, especially in retailing. (The same contrast is seen in the settlement of different South-East Asian communities in the Los Angeles area, for example, or Latin communities in New York City.)

A total of 620 interviews were undertaken with shoppers: 349 at four sampling points in Highfields (a long-established area of low-status immigrant settlement from Eastern Europe, the Caribbean, and India), 185 at two sampling points in Belgrave, a centre of settlement for East African Asians since the 1960s which received many of the refugees from Uganda in 1972, and 76 in Narborough Road (an inner area of still mainly white residential settlement) (further details of research design and methodology are contained in Ward and Johnson, 1987). Table 1 sets out details of respondents by interviewing point and ethnic origin.

The analysis in this chapter is concerned with comparing retailing in the low-status area of Highfields and the more up-market Belgrave to see how far the strategy implemented by Asian shopkeepers is consonant with the objectives of public policy outlined above. The contrast in the status of the shopping centres is seen in the proportion of convenience stores in each area (Table 2).

Table 1.   Respondents by interviewing point and ethnic origin

Shopping parade	White	Asian	Afro-Caribbean	Other	Total
Highfields:					
Sparkenhoe Street	21	4	15	0	40
Melbourne Road	38	34	15	0	87
Evington Road	52	21	27	4	104
Green Lane Road	57	52	15	4	128
Belgrave:					
Belgrave Road	29	41	18	0	88
Melton Road	72	25	0	0	97
Other:					
Narborough Road	73	2	1	0	76
Total	342	179	91	8	620

Table 2.   Proportion of convenience-goods shops and of Asian proprietors (all shops) (%)

	Convenience-goods shops as proportion of all shops		Asian proprietors as proportion of all proprietors
	White-owned	Asian-owned	
Melbourne Road/ Sparkenhoe Street	33	58	76
Green Lane Road	26	32	57
Evington Road	25	38	45
Narborough Road	23	30	21
Melton Road	18	23	44
Belgrave Road	13	24	90

Among both Asian and white proprietors a much higher percentage of shops in Highfields sold convenience goods of low value (and so would attract an essentially local population). This suggests that shopkeepers in Highfields would be less able, and conceivably have less incentive, to make the changes outlined above designed to protect the future of the business.

Table 3.   Proportion of shops carrying out improvements in the past five years (%)

	Ethnicity/religious community of proprietor			
	White	Hindu	Muslim	Sikh
Belgrave Road	78	86	100	86
Melton Road	50	58	100	100
Narborough Road	50	67	50	40
Green Lane Road	30	71	78	40
Evington Road	45	50	50	6
Melbourne Road/ Sparkenhoe Street	50	0	31	0

This is confirmed when we examine the figures in Table 3 relating to the first policy goal noted above, i.e. the extent to which shopkeepers had been carrying out improvements to their premises—in all areas a large majority of shops (up to 100%) were built before 1919. It is in the areas with a higher proportion of comparison shops that retailers are more likely to have been undertaking improvements over the previous five years. This holds true for whites and for all three Asian religious communities. However, whereas in Belgrave Asian shopkeepers were more active in investing in the future by paying for improvements to their premises, in Highfields the picture is much more mixed. In Green Lane Road, on the fringe of Highfields, Asians are again more active in improvements. In Melbourne Road/Sparkenhoe Street, in the heart of Highfields, the reverse is true. Thus, in so far as the future of inner-area retailing depends on the maintenance of the physical fabric of shops, in most inner areas in Leicester Asian shopkeepers were outperforming their white counterparts, although in the centre with the highest proportion of convenience stores Asian shopkeepers had been less active than whites.

A similar pattern recurs when we examine a measure of how far shopkeepers were giving their shops an attractive appearance. Shops were scored for the quality of their frontage image and shop display (Table 4). In general shopping centres with a higher proportion of comparison shops were more likely to be presenting an attractive appearance, though the low score for white retailers in the premier centre on Belgrave Road is an exception. There is little consistency in the pattern of scores achieved by white and Asian shopkeepers in different centres. At the extremes, however, Asian shops were much better presented in the best centre in Belgrave Road and much worse presented in the lowest-status centres within Highfields.

A third public policy objective was to attract outside shoppers into the area to raise the purchasing power available to inner-area retailers. How far

Table 4.   Mean score for frontage image and shop display

| | Ethnicity/religious community of proprietor | | | |
	White	Hindu	Muslim	Sikh
Belgrave Road	3.0	2.6	2.0	2.4
Melton Road	2.6	2.9	3.0	2.5
Narborough Road	2.9	2.7	3.0	3.0
Green Lane Road	3.0	2.5	3.1	2.6
Evington Road	2.9	2.8	3.2	3.2
Melbourne Road/ Sparkenhoe Street	2.8	3.2	3.5	3.0

Note: The quality of frontage image and shop display were assessed on a four-point scale (1—excellent; 2—good; 3—average; 4—poor).
Source: Yeo (1984).

local consumer demand was supplemented by outsiders in Belgrave and Highfields is seen in Table 5. Results were obtained by comparing place of residence with place of interview. 'Local' means living within a block of nine grid squares, each 1 000 × 1 000 m. In practice this means that the great majority of addresses defined as 'local' are within 1500 m of the shopping centre at which the interview took place, i.e. within about 15 minutes walk. Leicester 'outskirts' refers to districts outside but within a few miles of the city.

Table 5.   Proportion of comparison shops and distance travelled by shoppers

	Place of residence of those passing by shops				*(n)*
	Local	*Rest of Leicester*	*Leicester outskirts*	*Elsewhere*	
(1) Belgrave Road					
White	65.5	31.0	3.4	–	29
Asian	60.0	12.5	–	27.5	40
Caribbean	60.0	20.0	20.0	–	15
(2) Melton Road					
White	41.8	46.3	10.4	1.5	67
Asian	76.0	12.0	8.0	4.0	24
(3) Narborough Road					
White	48.5	47.0	3.0	1.5	66
(4) Green Lane Road					
White	78.6	10.7	3.6	7.1	56
Asian	86.5	11.5	1.9	–	52
Caribbean	80.0	20.0	–	–	15
(5) Evington Road					
White	89.4	8.5	2.1	–	52
Asian	94.7	5.3	–	–	27
(6) Melbourne Road/ Sparkenhoe Street					
White	93.0	7.0	–	–	59
Asian	94.0	3.0	3.0	–	38
Caribbean	89.7	10.3	–	–	29

Note: Respondents whose place of residence could not be identified have been excluded. Shopping areas are listed in decreasing order by proportion of comparison-goods shops.

It can be seen that the shopping centres with the higher proportions of comparison goods shops were far more likely to draw in shoppers from further afield. At one extreme, 27.5% of Asian shoppers in Belgrave Road were from outside the Leicester area—they had come from other parts of the East Midlands, the West Midlands, the North, and the South. Yeo (1984) refers to a regular bus service bringing shoppers from North London and to Asians from the Continent doing their shopping in Belgrave. Clearly, Belgrave Road, despite its inner-city location, has attracted a great deal of custom from outside the city. By contrast, the white shoppers in Belgrave

Road come from within the city, one third of them from outside the local area. Thus Belgrave's chief appeal is as a regional up-market comparison-goods centre for Asians, specializing in high-value ethnic items such as saris and jewellery. However, it is not a centre which appeals exclusively to Asian customers, despite more than three quarters of the shops there being in Asian hands. In addition to the remaining white customers, Belgrave Road is the only centre which attracts a significant proportion (20%) of Afro-Caribbean shoppers from outside the city.

At the other extreme, 90% or more of shoppers of all ethnic origins in the Melbourne Road/Sparkenhoe Street parades of convenience stores in the heart of Highfields, as well as Evington Road on the edge of the district, live within a few minutes walk of the shops. In most areas there was little difference between ethnic groups in the proportion of local residents among shoppers; Asian shoppers are in general slightly more likely to be living in the immediate area, except in Belgrave Road, with its attraction to shoppers from other parts of the country. In all areas there is a close match between the distance travelled by Asian and Afro-Caribbean shoppers.

Thus it is the shopping parades oriented towards comparison goods that draw in more outsiders, Belgrave Road in particular becoming an ethnic 'theme centre', while those providing a convenience-goods function serve an almost exclusively local population. This is further supported by evidence that in Belgrave Road almost half (46%) of Asian shoppers came in by car, whereas in Highfields over two thirds (69%) walked to the shops (Ward and Johnson, 1987, p. 22).

The relationship between Asian retailing patterns and the other objectives of public policy noted above cannot be directly evaluated by using data from the Leicester shopping survey. However, there is less direct evidence which bears on the remaining points. Possibilities were identified for attracting higher-income residents into inner areas as a way of preserving local retailing. Data are not available on household income among respondents in the shopping survey, but there are various indications that in Belgrave the value of sales had been increasing: bank managers spoke of the spiralling sale prices achieved when shops came on the market, and the residential estates near Belgrave, judging from the spread of house prices asked for, were attracting a much higher income population than in Highfields. While residents with higher incomes would assist in maintaining the level of trading in the local shopping centre, the quality of local shops would, in turn, increase the attractions of residence to more affluent households. This would not apply in the essentially convenience-oriented shopping parades in Highfields. Both in Belgrave and in Highfields, however, Asian and Afro-Caribbean households were spending more than whites on a wide range of food and non-food items (mostly of a convenience nature) covered in the survey. In the two parades in Belgrave, Asian and Afro-Caribbean households spent about 25% more per week, while in Highfields average spending was about 12% more (calculated from Ward and Johnson, 1987, p. 40). Thus while the expenditure of present Asian and Afro-Caribbean residents cannot be compared with that of former white residents, in terms of the existing population segments it was the Asian and black households whose disposable income was making a larger contribution to shopkeepers' receipts (and thus helping to preserve viable trading).

Finally, respondents were asked where they usually bought a variety of comparison goods. In the case of furniture and carpets Asians were slightly more likely to buy locally than whites in Belgrave and only in the middle of Highfields was there more local purchasing by whites. Asians were substantially more likely to buy electrical goods locally than whites in both Belgrave and Highfields. In the case of clothes and footwear, Asians were more than twice as likely to buy locally. Finally, with jewellery, the probability of Asians buying in the local shopping centre was even greater; figures for Asians ranged from 27% to 79%, for whites from 6% to 18%. In most cases Afro-Caribbean spending approximated to that of Asians. Thus there were no comparison goods where Asians and blacks were less likely to buy locally, and in most cases, particularly with ethnically distinctive items such as jewellery, Asians in particular (but also blacks) were very much more likely to be patronizing local stores.

A further possible objective of public policy designed to maintain local retailing was selective demolition or restriction of planning permission in the interests of reducing overcompetition. The spiralling of commercial property values in Belgrave suggests that this was not a problem. In Highfields the pattern is more mixed; the work of Aldrich and his colleagues implies that too many Asian retailers were chasing too little local trade to be able to face the future with any confidence (Aldrich *et al.*, 1984; McEvoy and Aldrich, 1986).

Finally, the possibility was considered of maintaining competitiveness in an increasingly difficult trading environment by reducing the cost of operations. As with other policy aims, forms of public intervention to achieve this result have been receiving increasing attention (GLC, 1985). It is still highly pertinent to consider, however, in the light of the increasingly dominant Asian involvement in inner-area shopping centres, how far their business strategy results in reducing costs.

There is a growing literature on Asian retailing in inner areas (see, for example, Aldrich *et al.*, 1984, McEvoy and Aldrich, 1986, and the literature cited therein, Krčmář, 1984, Wilson, 1983, Wilson and Stanworth, 1985, Islam, 1985). While a detailed financial analysis of the pattern of Asian retailing has not yet been undertaken, it is quite clear that Asian shopkeepers do, in practice, compete by lowering the financial barriers to entry and to survival in business. Their very presence, at a time when small, white-owned shops have been disappearing in vast numbers through an inability to survive in the face of competition from the market leaders, itself suggests a more favourable cost structure. There is a high rate of turnover in Asian as well as white-owned shops; but there are more Asian shopkeepers willing to set up shops in inner areas and there is a higher survival rate for Asian-owned than white-owned shops in such areas. McEvoy and Aldrich (1986) showed that 39% of white-run stores in inner Bradford, Leicester, and Ealing in 1978 were still in existence in 1984; the equivalent figure for Asians was 52% —indeed, the contrast would have been greater but for the effect of demolition of Asian-owned shops in inner Bradford during the period as a result of urban renewal.

It is also becoming clear, though it has not yet been fully documented, that Asian shopkeepers succeed in part by their superior access to a labour supply, including family members, which is cheap, flexible, and trustworthy, a combination of qualities ideal for effective management of a 'buying and selling' business open long hours and selling standard items (cf. Ward, 1986a). This is of great assistance in enabling Asian corner-shops to reduce the extent to which they are in direct competition with the large multiples by concentrating on providing a complementary service, offering longer opening hours and a wider range of services, as well as supplying the specialized needs of local ethnic communities where relevant. Privileged access to labour helps to keep down the cost of these supplementary services (Wilson and Stanworth, 1986).

CONCLUSION

We have shown that, in general, Asian shopkeepers are coping more effectively with the problems of surviving in inner-city retailing. Thus, in Belgrave they have gone beyond white retailers in making improvements to their premises, in presenting an attractive frontage image and shop display and in bringing outside shoppers into the area. Asian households were also spending more on convenience goods and using local shops more frequently to buy higher-value, durable comparison goods of various kinds. Given the pressure on available sites, there are few dangers of overcompetition—indeed, the concentration of outlets in key areas of ethnic comparison shopping helps to attract so many outsiders to the shopping centre. The use of ethnic resources such as labour to best advantage gives a further competitive edge. However, it has to be recognized that this has been achieved at some cost to the survival of the local convenience stores, whose ability to service immobile local residents lies at the heart of public policy concerns. Even in Belgrave, however, one in four Asian-owned shops was oriented to convenience goods (a much higher figure than among remaining white proprietors). The transition of centres such as Belgrave Road and Melton Road, therefore, from white to Asian ownership can be seen as a significant contribution to public policy goals for inner-area retailing.

However, there appear to be very few inner-city shopping centres as successful as Belgrave. Current research on the impact of improvement schemes on a wide variety of inner-area shopping centres in the West Midlands, for example, has shown none with as good a record for attracting outside custom (Ward, 1986b). Areas such as Highfields are far more typical, and here the position is much less clearcut. First, there are significant differences between the shopping parades in the heart of Highfields and those on the fringe. In the former, Asian shopkeepers are doing less than whites to protect local shopping, in the latter the reverse is true. While those on the fringe bring in a small proportion of outside shoppers, those in the middle of Highfields depend entirely on local custom. The level of expenditure on convenience goods is higher among Asian households throughout Highfields and for most comparison goods, too, Asians were more likely to buy in the local area. It is here, most of all, that overcompetition is likely, with large numbers of shopkeepers struggling to survive in an increasingly difficult trading environment. Most of the local white-owned shops have already gone. All the resources of the ethnic community are needed to maintain a bare survival. Measures to reduce competition may be much more important here.

Overall, then, Asian retailers have been making an important and positive contribution to public policy goals of protecting disadvantaged, inner-area residents from the impact of competitive strategy among the largest retail multiples. However, the transition in progress in areas such as Belgrave, while preserving the retailing function, threatens the viability of low-order, convenience-goods shops which public policy seeks to preserve. Meanwhile, in areas such as Highfields the sheer survival of local retailing depends increasingly on Asian proprietors whose low returns make their future somewhat insecure. In the short term, therefore, Asian business has come to the aid of the public purse. In the long run, however, assuming that present policy objectives are maintained, authorities seem likely to have to find more of the full economic cost of supporting inner-city retailing.

REFERENCES

Aldrich, H., Cater, J., Jones, T., and McEvoy, D. (1981). 'Business development and self-segregation: Asian enterprise in three British cities.' In Peach, C., Robinson, V., and Smith, S. (eds), *Ethnic Segregation in Cities*, London: Croom Helm.

Aldrich, H., Jones, T., and McEvoy, D. (1984). 'Ethnic advantage and minority business development.' In Ward, R., and Jenkins, R. (eds), *Communities in Business*, Cambridge: Cambridge University Press.

Brown, C. (1984). *Black and White Britain*, London: Heinemann, PEP.

Davies, R. (1984). *Changes within Shopping Centres within Metropolitan Areas*, Birmingham: Public Sector Management Research Unit, Aston University Management Centre.

Dawson, J. A. (1983). 'Planning for local shops.' *The Planner*, Jan./Feb., 18–19.

Department of the Environment (1979). *National Dwelling and Housing Survey*, London.

Greater London Council (1985). *The London Industrial Strategy*, London.

Islam, R. (1985). *The Structure of Asian Businesses in Glasgow and their Problems and Needs*, Glasgow: The Queen's College.

Kirby, D. (1984). 'Government policies towards the small retail business in Japan.' *International Small Business Journal*, **2**, 4, 44–58.

Krčmář, K. (1984). *Asian Retailing in Glasgow*, MBA project report, Glasgow: Strathclyde University.

Lambeth, London Borough of (1982). *Black Businesses in Lambeth: Report of Survey*, RM20, London.

McEvoy, D., and Aldrich, H. (1986). 'Survival rates of Asian and white retailers.' *International Small Business Journal*, **4**, 3, 28–37.

Smith, D. (1976). *The Facts of Racial Disadvantage: A National Survey*, London: PEP.

Ward, R. (1985). 'Minority settlement and the local economy.' In Roberts, B., Finnegan, R., and Gallie, D. (eds), *New Approaches to Economic Life*, Manchester: ESRC and Manchester University Press.

Ward, R. (1986a). 'Ethnic business and economic change: an overview.' *International Small Business Journal*, **4**, 3, 10–12.

Ward, R. (1986b). *Evaluation of Shopping Centre Improvements Funded under the Urban Programme in the West Midlands: the Ethnic Dimension*, Working Paper No. 8, Public Sector Management Research Unit, Aston University Management Centre.

Ward, R. (1987). 'Ethnic entrepreneurs in Britain and Europe.' In Scase, R., and Goffee, R. (eds), *Small Business in Europe*, London: Croom Helm.

Ward, R., and Johnson, M. (1987). *Ethnic Minorities and Retail Behaviour in an Inner City*, Coventry: Centre for Research in Ethnic Relations, Warwick University.

Wilson, P. (1983). *Black Business Enterprise in Britain: A Survey of Afro-Caribbean and Asian Small Business in Brent*, London: Runnymede Trust.

Wilson, P., and Stanworth, J. (1985). *Black Business in Brent*, London: Small Business Research Trust.

Wilson, P., and Stanworth, J. (1986). 'Growth and change in black minority enterprise in London.' *International Small Business Journal*, **4**, 3, 13–28.

Yeo, S. (1984). 'Patterns of Asian Retailing in Inner Leicester', MBA project report, Birmingham: Aston University Management Centre.

Index